Forging the Nation: 1763–1828

The Structure of American History

DAVIS R. B. ROSS, ALDEN T. VAUGHAN, AND JOHN B. DUFF, EDITORS

VOLUME I
Colonial America: 1607–1763

VOLUME II
Forging the Nation: 1763–1828

VOLUME III
The Nation in Crisis: 1828–1865

VOLUME IV
The Emergence of Modern America: 1865–1900

VOLUME V
Progress, War, and Reaction: 1900–1933

VOLUME VI
Recent America: 1933 to the Present

Forging the Nation: 1763–1828

edited by Davis R. B. Ross
COLUMBIA UNIVERSITY
Alden T. Vaughan
COLUMBIA UNIVERSITY
John B. Duff
SETON HALL UNIVERSITY

THOMAS Y. CROWELL COMPANY
NEW YORK · ESTABLISHED 1834

L. C. Card 78–101951

Series design by Barbara Kohn Isaac

Manufactured in the United States of America

Preface

The Structure of American History is designed to introduce undergraduate students of United States history and interested general readers to the variety and richness of our historical literature. The six volumes in the series offer selections from the writings of major historians whose books have stood the test of time or whose work, though recent, has met with unusual acclaim. Some of the selections deal with political history, some with diplomatic, some with economic, and others with social; all however offer thoughtful and provocative interpretations of the American past.

The volumes, with seven substantial selections in each, cover the following chronological periods:

- I. Colonial America: 1607–1763
- II. Forging the Nation: 1763–1828
- III. The Nation in Crisis: 1828–1865
- IV. The Emergence of Modern America: 1865–1900
- V. Progress, War, and Reaction: 1900–1933
- VI. Recent America: 1933 to the Present

Each volume opens with a general introduction to the period as a whole, in which we have suggested major themes that give coherence to the era and have outlined briefly the direction of past and recent scholarship. An editors' introduction precedes each selection; in these we have not sought to tell the reader what he is about to encounter but rather to identify the selection's author, establish its historical setting, and provide its historiographical context. Finally, a short bibliographical essay follows each selection, in which the reader is introduced to a wide range of related literature.

Several criteria guided us in our choice of readings: the distinction of the author, the significance of his interpretation, the high literary quality of his style. Because we conceived of the series as a supplement to, rather than a substitute for, the reading usually assigned in college-level survey courses, we have tried to avoid material that merely expands in detail the coverage offered in the traditional textbooks; we have sought, instead, selections from works that shed new light and raise new questions, or at the very least provide a kind of reading experience not customarily encountered in traditional assignments. For at bottom, *The Structure of American History* stems from the editors' conviction that the great works of historical writing should not be reserved for the graduate student or the professional scholar but should be made available to those readers who can perhaps best benefit from an early encounter with Francis Parkman, Samuel Eliot Morison, Allan Nevins, Oscar Handlin, and their peers. We want college students to know from the outset that the stuff of history is neither the textbook nor the latest article in a scholarly journal. What has often inspired us, as teachers and writers of history, and what we hope will inspire students and lay readers, is history written by the great practitioners of the art: men who have written with vigor and grace the results of their own meticulous research and meditation.

In order to make our selections as extensive as possible, we have, with reluctance, omitted all footnotes. We urge readers to remember that the authority of each historian rests largely on the documentation he offers in support of his statements, and that readers who wish to investigate the evidence on which a historian has based his argument should refer to the original published version—cited on the first page of each selection. Readers are also reminded that many of the books recommended in the bibliographical notes appended to each selection are obtainable in paperback editions. We have refrained from indicating which volumes are currently in paper for the list of paperbacks grows too rapidly. We refer those interested to R. R. Bowker Company, *Paperbound Books in Print,* available at the counter of most bookstores.

D. R. B. R.
A. T. V.
J. B. D.

Contents

Introduction

The period from 1763 to 1828 marks the forging of thirteen colonies into the strong alloy called the American republic. It marks too the emergence of a generation of heroes, the creation of the Constitution, the shift of the nation's early Federalist course to a Republican tack, and the establishment of a distinctly American foreign policy.

The historical writing about this period runs a wide gamut, for it has not been an easy task to retain perspective when viewing such momentous times. A popular folklore, for example, has grown out of the American Revolution. As perhaps the single most important event in early American history it has lent itself readily to mythmaking. The Revolutionary tableau is indeed rich: Paul Revere riding through the night on the eve of Lexington and Concord; Betsy Ross creating that durable national symbol, the flag; Thomas Jefferson penning the Declaration of Independence; George Washington outfoxing the British at Trenton and sharing his soldiers' winter distress at Valley Forge, and Benjamin Franklin exploiting republican simplicity to win a favorable peace treaty.

Professional historians, however, have been able to tell the Revolutionary story with less and less reliance on mythology. From an early emphasis on military events, historians have turned more to examining the political and intellectual aspects of the War for Independence. Not surprisingly, considerable controversy has arisen over the very nature of the Revolution. Was it merely a stroke to sever the ties that bound the colonies to the mother country? Or did the revolutionists desire to achieve changes in local government, society, and economy as well? Even more contentious has been the debate among historians as to the motives behind the adoption of the Constitution at the close of the Articles of Confederation period. Some consider the Constitution as the final act in the drama of the Revolution, the fulfillment of goals set three decades before; others, however, see the great charter as a Thermidorean reaction to the democratic and radical excesses of the so-called "critical period."

Other facets of the history of the early republic have been receiving attention in recent years. Prominent among these have been studies of the rise of political parties, of the changes in democratic institutions prior to the so-called Jacksonian Revolution, of the new nation's economic development, and of the causes of the War of 1812. Despite many distinguished efforts—including those presented in this volume—historians have not been particularly successful in writing syntheses of the period as a whole.

Although comprehensive perspectives are absent, one binding theme can be suggested. In general terms the Revolution can be viewed as a broad movement toward independence that manifested itself, not by a single convulsive effort at arms, but as a half-century-long process. The selections in this volume deal with key moments in that process: the initial impetus given to the movement toward independence by British attempts to modernize the empire after 1763; the acknowledgment of American independence by a vanquished mother country; the writing and adoption of the Constitution in 1787 to 1789; the bitter internecine warfare of the Hamiltonians and the Jeffersonians in the early 1790's; the spirit of the new nation in 1800; the struggle for stability in the aftermath of the panic of 1819; and the portentous achievement of international prestige—fancied if not real—with the promulgation of the Monroe Doctrine in 1823.

By hindsight, of course, the era from 1763 to 1828 blends

at either end with movements and events from which it can never be extracted. The thrust toward independence had roots in the colonial period, and the survival of the new nation had to face its greatest challenge in the 1860's. Yet to the extent that any large period of American history can be viewed as an entity with a consistent theme and mystique, that from the end of the French and Indian War to the election of Andrew Jackson stands forth as the birth time of the American nation.

Turmoil over the Stamp Act

Edmund S. and Helen Morgan

*I*n 1760 the French fortress of Quebec fell to the English; three years later at Paris the two nations signed the peace treaty that formalized the exclusion of France from the North American continent. Thus the Seven Years' War, whose American portion is dubbed the French and Indian War, had ended. England had achieved hegemony over a huge geographic expanse, extending from Hudson's Bay in the north to the Florida keys in the south. London ruled the eastern third of the continent, with only Spain on the west bank of the Mississippi and scattered Indian tribes barring expansion westward. Neither of these two obstacles seemed insurmountable. With more than two million presumably loyal English subjects inhabiting the thirteen original colonies alone, the imperial future looked promising.

To be sure, there were some clouds on the horizon. The North American colonists had exhibited certain disturbing tendencies during the late war. For example, some had carried on illicit trade with the French West Indies, and the Molasses Act, passed in 1733, had been

Source: Edmund S. and Helen Morgan, *The Stamp Act Crisis: Prologue to Revolution* (Chapel Hill, N.C.: The University of North Carolina Press, 1953), pp. 119–142. Reprinted by permission of the University of North Carolina Press and the Institute of Early American History and Culture.

ignored. Few of the colonies had responded to the capital requisitions asked of them by the mother country, hard-pressed for war funds. To colonial officials in London it appeared that reorganization and greater exertion of imperial controls would be needed. Now, with larger territorial responsibilities and a formidable war debt, was the time for England to end the long period of "salutary neglect." Americans should assume their financial share of the imperial burden; they should begin to obey the Navigation Acts that were designed to benefit all.

But what seemed a natural and rational conclusion on the one side of the Atlantic appeared unnatural and unreasonable on the other. The colonists, after all, had fought bravely and well, despite the English regulars' reluctance to admit it. Furthermore, the colonists resented bitterly the "modernizing" of the empire. Instead of desirable reforms, they saw greater tax burdens, widening of the juryless Admiralty Court's powers, an increase of arbitrary customs' authority, and possible establishment of ecclesiastical courts and an episcopal hierarchy. All these, they claimed, violated their constitutional rights as British subjects. Not reform, but tyranny was in the air. The 1763 road signs that in London pointed to the greater glory of the English empire, pointed to Runnymede in America. Looking backward we can see that in 1763 the colonists began their trip down the road to revolution.

Many American and British historians have chronicled that journey. Some of them have fought the old battles anew. Seemingly, all facets have been examined from every conceivable angle. Sometimes the views have followed political lines. English historians of the Whig persuasion, for example, have added their scholarly voices to an amplified chorus that chanted "if only George III and his ministers had heeded the wise counsel of Edmund Burke and Charles James Fox." American historians, sharing the same Whig asumptions and often prodded by their own patriotism, have over many generations enshrined James Otis, Samuel Adams, John Hancock, and Patrick Henry in a grand pantheon of native heroes.

Yet whether Whig, filiopietist, or Tory, historians, until recent times at least, have concentrated on the events of the early 1770's, especially the dramatic episodes of 1773–1775. Thus, the period from 1763 to 1773, although not ignored, was usually foreshortened. This approach had merit. Indubitably, the pace of events leading to the Concord and Lexington greens had quickened its tempo in the years immediately preceding 1775. Yet this narrow focus tended to obscure the significance of earlier events. An understanding of the events of the late 1750's and 1760's was in fact necessary for an appreciation of the growing revolutionary movement.

Alert to this need, Edmund S. Morgan and his wife, Helen, turned their attention to that early period. Their book, *The Stamp Act Crisis* (1953), has contributed significantly to the scholarly literature on the coming of the Revolution, for in their hands the Stamp Act of 1765 and American colonial reaction to it took on greater meaning. As a result of meticulous research, the Morgans concluded that, contrary to traditional belief (endorsed by no less an authority than the late Carl Becker), the colonists did not distinguish between the right of Parliament to levy "internal" and "external" taxes. The colonists denied that Parliament could do either. Instead, they granted to Parliament the right to legislate matters of imperial concern, so long as that legislation conformed to their conception of English constitutional rights. Thus, as early as 1765, according to the Morgans, the colonists had enunciated a principle that they would follow consistently over the next decade. Although some scholars, like Lawrence Henry Gipson, still adhere to the traditional view, the Morgans have produced considerable evidence for their interpretation.

The Morgans' stand on the "internal versus external tax" controversy, although of great historical importance, does not represent their book's sole claim to enduring value. Their lively account of the actual form of colonial reaction is equally important. Colonial resistance had both noble and ignoble sides: peaceful remonstrance went hand in hand with more violent reaction. The patriots that move across the Morgans' pages are not all animated by virtuous political principles; local politics and economic interest play important roles as well. Colonial nabobs manipulate mobs as instruments of protest, and sometimes the creatures master the creators. Nor are the officers of the Crown and other loyal colonial subjects cast in the devil's image as some filiopietists have done. The Morgans, in brief, treat their historical characters with an even hand.

The selection that follows from *The Stamp Act Crisis* demonstrates the Morgans' style. No dreary recitation of facts greets the reader; events in Boston come alive again A rapid pace, wit, and an eye for colorful detail typify their approach. The result is a thoughtful and provocative account of a crucial phase in the development of the American Revolution. The Morgans have shown that the short two-year span of time between the establishment of the Stamp Act itself, the appointment of collectors, the colonial reaction, final repeal and the subsequent Declaratory Act in 1766, was perhaps as important as any other in the Revolutionary story. For that period indeed was the "prologue to Revolution."

The resolutions which the clerks of colonial and intercolonial assemblies were recording in the summer and fall of 1765 were outspoken denials of Parliament's right to tax the colonies. But only in Rhode Island did the Assembly approve outright resistance. It was one thing to define a right and another to fight for it, particularly if you must fight against a body which you had hitherto accepted as supreme and to which you still acknowledged "all due subordination." Nevertheless, while men like James Otis blew hot and cold, now for colonial rights and now for Parliamentary supremacy, and while others followed Daniel Dulany in affirming colonial rights but wishing only passive resistance, a substantial number of men in every colony recognized that the time had come when more than talk was needed. They had been convinced by Dulany and Otis and by the Virginia Resolves and the declarations of the Stamp Act Congress that Parliament had no right to tax them. They also knew that there was no branch of government higher than Parliament to prevent Parliament's doing what it had no right to do. The burden therefore was left to those whose rights were endangered: they must resist Parliament to preserve their rights, and if that meant an end to Parliamentary supremacy, then that was what it meant.

It would be too much to say that these men wished to throw off the authority of Parliament altogether. Perhaps some of them did, but there is no reason to suppose that they were not content with the constitutional position which their representatives had defined, denying Parliament's right to tax but allowing its right to regulate trade and to pass other general legislation affecting the empire at large. The only point at which they went a step further than the resolutions was in their determination to prevent the supreme legislature from doing what it had no right to do. In this determination they ignored the distinction which Dulany had drawn between propriety and power. But if anyone had told them that in spite of the impropriety of its action, Parliament's power was supreme, they might have answered that supremacy in power cannot be determined by argumentation or declaration. If Parliament lacked the authority to tax America, then its power to do so would have to be tested in American fields and streets. And this was precisely where they proposed to test it.

Although the Virginians had been first to suggest resistance, it was not in Williamsburg but in Boston that argument first gave way to action. The Massachusetts radicals saw that if the colonists were to defeat Parliament's attempt to tax them, they could not rely on their representative assemblies to do the job. The assemblies might resolve, as that of Rhode Island did, that officers of government should carry on business as usual, as though the Act had never been passed. But what if the officers of government who had to use the stamps lay beyond the immediate control of the assemblies? Most of the documents which would require stamps after November first were papers used in legal proceedings. In some colonies the assemblies might withhold the salaries of the judges as a means of bringing them into line, but in others the judges of the superior courts were not appointed by the assemblies, and in all the colonies the independence of the judiciary was regarded as a principle of the British constitution which could be tampered with only at the peril of civil liberty. The assemblies were also powerless to control the royally appointed customs officers who must issue clearances for all ships leaving American harbors. According to the Stamp Act, clearance papers issued after November first would have to bear a stamp. If the customs officers chose to comply with the law, and as royal officials they doubtless would comply, what could the assemblies do about it? The duties of customs officers did not fall within their jurisdiction, and royal governors would certainly have vetoed any orders from the assemblies which attempted to regulate matters beyond their authority.

Obviously the radicals who had determined to turn from words to deeds could expect little more than words from their assemblies. For action they must look elsewhere, and where was not hard to guess. In Boston particularly the answer was clear, for in the past the good people of that city had frequently turned from the niceties of theological controversy to achieve some necessary social reform in their own way. Perhaps a few inhabitants could recollect with some amusement how they had laid out a street through Jonathan Loring's barn near Love Street some thirty years before. The selectmen had surveyed the proposed street and found Loring's barn square in the way. There was some doubt whether they had a right to seize the barn, but a gathering of the townspeople resolved the question without argument. Under cover of night and with blackened faces, a technique they had already learned and would employ again in 1773, they levelled the building, and the road went through. In 1747 Boston had demonstrated that even the British Navy must watch its step in Massachusetts. Commodore Knowles in that year anchored his fleet off Nantasket and sent press gangs ashore to fill gaps in his crews. When the Governor and Council would not, as they could not, prevent him, a mob arose in Boston which ruled the city until Commodore Knowles released the men he had seized.

Bostonians sometimes seemed to love violence for its own sake. Over the years there had developed a rivalry between the South End and the North End of the city. On Pope's Day, November 5, when parades were held to celebrate the defeat of Guy Fawkes' famous gunpowder plot, the rivalry between the two sections generally broke out into a free-for-all with stones and barrel staves the principal weapons. The two sides even developed a semi-military organization with recognized leaders, and of late the fighting had become increasingly bloody. In 1764 a child was run over and killed by a wagon bearing an effigy of the pope, but even this had not stopped the battle. Despite the efforts of the militia, the two sides had battered and bruised each other until the South End finally carried the day.

When Boston had to face the problem of nullifying the Stamp Act, it was obvious that men who fought so energetically over the effigy of a pope might be employed in a more worthy cause. The problem was to make them see the threat to their liberties that the Stamp Act presented and to direct their energies accordingly. Sometime in the early summer of 1765 a group of men got together in Boston to prepare for the day when the Stamp Act was supposed to go into effect, November first. An organization was formed which first called itself The Loyal Nine and later, when its ranks had expanded, the Sons of Liberty. The Nine were John Avery, Thomas

Crafts, John Smith, Henry Welles, Thomas Chase, Stephen Cleverly, Henry Bass, Benjamin Edes, and George Trott. They were not the most prominent citizens of Boston, nor were they the men who did most of the talking against the Stamp Act. In general they were artisans and shopkeepers, and they shunned publicity. The names of James Otis and Samuel Adams were conspicuously missing from the list. So was that of John Adams. Perhaps this division of labor was deliberate, in order to keep the radical leaders of the Assembly, who were always conspicuously in the public eye, from bringing too much attention to the group. Or perhaps the effectiveness of the radical leaders in the Assembly might have been impaired if they were openly associated with an organization engaged in the treasonable activities which the Loyal Nine envisaged. Whatever the reason, no conclusive alliance can be proved between the leaders of the Assembly and the organizers of the popular demonstrations, but it is probable that the Nine maintained close communications with both Otis and Samuel Adams, and on one occasion at least, John Adams spent an evening with them at their headquarters in Chase and Speakman's distillery on Hanover Square.

Only two members of the Loyal Nine enjoyed any local distinction: John Avery, a Harvard graduate, was a distiller and merchant; Benjamin Edes was the printer, along with John Gill, of the *Gazette,* Boston's most enterprising newspaper. Avery's membership lent respectability to the group; Edes's gave it a mouthpiece. Of the two, Edes's contribution was doubtless the more valuable, for his paper published a continuous stream of articles to stir up feeling against the Stamp Act.

By August 14 the Nine felt that Boston was ready for action. They were confident that the well-to-do stood behind the moves which they were contemplating, and that the propaganda published in the *Gazette* had aroused the mass of the people. More important, they had enlisted the services of the man who had led the South End mob to victory over the North

Enders the preceding November. Ebenezer McIntosh, a South End shoemaker, was soon to become notorious as a man who could control his two thousand followers with the precision of a general. The Nine had persuaded him that he might do his country a real service by forgetting local quarrels and directing his strength against that hated Act which was designed to rob Americans of their constitutional rights.

On the morning of August 14 the signal for impending action was given by the hanging of an effigy on a tree near Deacon Elliot's house on Newbury Street. It represented Andrew Oliver, the man who, according to reports from England, had been appointed Distributor of Stamps for Massachusetts; alongside hung a piece of symbolism designed to connect Oliver and the Stamp Act with the most hated man in England. It was a large boot (a pun on the Earl of Bute), with the devil crawling out of it. When Governor Bernard heard of the event he took it seriously. Some members of his council assured him that it was only a boyish prank, not worthy the notice of the government, but in view of the incendiary pieces appearing in the newspapers Bernard thought otherwise. So did Lieutenant-Governor Hutchinson. Hutchinson, as Chief Justice of the Colony, ordered the Sheriff to cut the image down; Bernard took an easier way out: he summoned the Council and turned the problem over to them. Before the Council could gather together in the afternoon, the Sheriff returned with the breathless news that his men could not take down the image without endangering their lives.

Governor Bernard urged upon the Council the seriousness of the situation, but for various reasons they preferred to do nothing about it. Some thought it a trifling matter which would subside by itself if no notice were taken of it. Others admitted its seriousness, but felt that the government was not strong enough to force the issue and had better not risk the attempt. Unwilling, however, to have it go on record that they had done nothing, they passed the problem on to the Sheriff, advising that he be instructed to summon the peace officers. They could scarcely have expected the peace officers to have any effect on the crowd that was gathering about the tree where the image hung, but some gesture must be made in order to save face. Even as they sat in the Council Chamber the gentlemen could hear the rising voices outside, for the effigy had been cut down from the tree, and taking it with them the mob marched ominously to the Town House, gave three huzzas to let the Council know who was running the town of Boston, and then passed on.

Andrew Oliver had recently constructed a building at his dock on Kilby Street, intending to divide it into shops and rent them. Under the circumstances it was plausible enough to suggest that this was the office where he intended to distribute the stamps. From the Town House then, with McIntosh in the lead, the mob moved on to Kilby Street, and in five minutes Oliver's venture in real estate had gone the way of Jonathan Loring's barn. The next stop was Oliver's house, in the nearby street which bore the family name. Standing in the street the leaders presented those inside with a bit of pantomime, in which Oliver's effigy was beheaded, while the rest of the crowd showered stones through the windows. From here Fort Hill was only a step, and taking what was left of the effigy the mob moved on to the summit where they ceremoniously "stamped" on the figure and burned it in a bonfire, made appropriately of wood which they had carried from the building on Kilby Street.

For the more genteel members of the mob, disguised in the trousers and jackets which marked a workingman, this seems to have been the last stop on the evening's excursion. But McIntosh had not yet completed his work. With his followers he now returned to Oliver's house. Both Oliver and his family had meanwhile retired to a friendly neighbor's, leaving the house in charge of a few trusted friends, who barricaded the doors. Finding the entrance blocked, the mob proceeded to demolish the garden fence and then systematically beat in the doors and windows and entered the house, swearing loudly that they would catch Oliver and kill him. The trusted friends quickly departed, and the mob were preparing to search the neighboring houses when a gentleman informed them that Oliver had gone to Castle William and thus saved his life.

It was possible to take revenge on his house, and this they did, destroying the furniture, including "a looking glass said to be the largest in North-America," and a large part of the wainscoting. Governor Bernard meanwhile had sent a message to the Colonel of the Militia ordering him to beat an alarm. The Colonel, a realistic man, replied that any drummer sent out would be knocked down and his drum broken before he could strike it—and besides the drummers were probably all up at Oliver's house engaged in what they would consider more worthwhile activities. With this, having made his gesture, Governor Bernard retired to Castle William, safely isolated from mobs by the waters of Boston harbor.

Lieutenant-Governor Hutchinson was more foolhardy. About eleven o'clock, when the tumult seemed to be subsiding, he took the Sheriff with him and went to Oliver's house to persuade the mob to disperse. He had no sooner opened his mouth than one of the ringleaders, perhaps McIntosh, recognized him. "The Governor and the Sheriff!" went the cry, "to your Arms my boys," and a rain of stones descended on the two men as they hurried off into the darkness. The mob was thus left to have its way and continued to make sport of the Stamp Distributor's house until about midnight, when McIntosh evidently decided to call it an evening.

Thus ended the opening move in the program to defeat the Stamp Act. Everyone agreed that it was the most violent riot the town had ever seen. The next day a number of gentlemen called on Andrew Oliver and persuaded him that what had occurred was only the beginning and suggested that he immediately resign his office. Oliver, like other stamp distributors who later followed his example, must have been somewhat confused by the fact that he had not received his commission and thus really had nothing to resign. He promised, however, to write home for leave to resign and in the meantime to do nothing toward executing the Act. This satisfied the Loyal Nine, but their followers could not understand this devious language. In the evening they built another fire on Fort Hill—Governor Bernard, watching from Castle William, knew that the mob was out again—but the leaders who had produced the previous evening's entertainment were able to dissuade their followers from turning the site of Oliver's house into a vacant lot. Instead the mob diverted themselves by surrounding the house of the Lieutenant-Governor. Hutchinson listened to them beating on the doors and shouting for him to come out, until finally a neighbor convinced them that he had fled, and they gradually drifted away.

During the next ten days McIntosh proved his worth by keeping his followers quiet, and the Loyal Nine could rejoice in a job well done. They had obtained the resignation of the Stamp Distributor a good two and a half months before the Act was scheduled to take effect. Moreover they had made plain what would happen to anyone who dared take Oliver's place. When one gentleman let it be known that he would not have been intimidated had he been the stamp master, they gave him a chance to see how Oliver had felt by fixing the date when his house should be pulled down. The gentleman quickly recovered from his courage and retracted his statement. Few people could be found in Boston who would condemn the proceedings of the fourteenth. Even some of the ministers gave their blessing, and the Loyal Nine, feeling their oats, began to think of other grievances that needed redressing. The officers of the customs and of the admiralty court were obvious targets, and during these days there was much talk of the malicious reports they had sent home about the Boston merchants. Then there was Thomas Hutchinson, a man to reckon with.

The conduct of the Lieutenant-Governor, in ordering the images cut down and in attempting to stop the pillage at Oliver's house, marked him as a friend of the Stamp Act and an enemy of colonial rights. It was insinuated that his letters home had encouraged passage of the Act. Still, the Loyal Nine may not have intended to give Hutchinson the treatment they had handed Oliver. On the evening of the twenty-sixth, Hutchinson himself heard the rumor that the mob was to be out that night, and that the officers of the customs and of the admiralty court were to suffer, but that nothing was contemplated against him. On the other hand, Ebenezer Parkman, the minister of Westborough, thirty-five miles from Boston, heard on the twenty-sixth that Governor Bernard, Lieutenant-Governor Hutchinson, and Mr. Story, the Deputy Register of the Admiralty Court would be attacked. The information came in a letter from a friend in Boston, dated the twenty-fourth.

Neither Hutchinson's nor Parkman's information proved entirely correct. On the evening of the twenty-sixth the mob rallied around a bonfire on King Street and then proceeded in two separate bodies. One went to William Story's, and in spite of the fact that Story had published an advertisement in that day's papers denying that he had written home ill reports of the Boston merchants, they destroyed a great part of his public and private papers and damaged his house, office, and furniture. The other group went after the Comptroller of Customs, Benjamin Hallowell. His house was acknowledged to be one of the finest in town—before they got there. Afterwards the windows, sashes, shutters, and doors were gone, the furniture broken, the wainscoting ripped off, the books and papers carried away, and the wine cellar all but empty.

It is possible that the men who originated the program for this evening had intended that it should go no further, but the letter which Parkman received shows that someone at least had planned what now occurred. McIntosh, who was still master of ceremonies, after the work at Story's and Hallowell's was completed, united his two companies and led them to the Lieutenant-Governor's. Whether he did this on his own initiative or at the request of the Loyal Nine or at the request of some other group will probably never be known. In later years William Gordon, who came to Boston in 1768 and knew most of the persons who were active in the revolutionary movement there, stated that ". . . the mob was led on to the house, by a secret influence, with a view to the destruction of certain papers, known to be there, and which, it is thought, would have proved, that the grant to the New Plymouth Company on Kennebec River, was different from what was contended for by some claimants. The connection between the New Plymouth Company and the riot remains a secret. It may be that McIntosh saw no harm in killing two birds with one mob. He may have attacked the customs and admiralty officers for the Loyal Nine and Hutchinson for someone else.

Certainly in leading the attack on Hutchinson he had an enthusiastic following. Hutchinson was a cool and haughty man, about whom it was easy to believe any evil. McIntosh and company went about the work of wrecking his house with a zeal that far surpassed their previous height of August 14. They destroyed windows, doors, furniture, wainscoting, and paintings, and stole £900 in cash, as well as clothing and silverware. They cut down all the trees in the garden, beat down the partitions in the house and had even begun to remove the slate from the roof when daylight stopped them.

The fury of the attack on Hutchinson alarmed the best people in town. It looked as though the mob had got out of control and was bent upon transforming a commendable hostility to the Stamp Act into a levelling revolution. Rich men began to send their most valuable possessions to the homes of poorer neighbors where they might be safer. The town of Boston held a meeting and disavowed the attack on Hutchinson, though many of the participants in the pillaging must have been present at the meeting. Hutchinson himself concluded that "The encouragers of the first mob never intended matters should go this length, and the people in general express the utmost detestation of this unparalleled outrage." Three companies of militia and a company of cadets were called out to patrol the town and thereafter for many weeks the streets of Boston echoed with the steps of marching men. Even the children were caught up in the excitement. As one harassed parent complained, "the hussa's of the mobbs, the rattleing of drums, the clamour of the soldiers—who comes there—we are all well—and the continual hubub takes up all their attention. . . . As for James, wee cannot keep him from amongst the hurly burly without I would chain him. Thers no getting them kept to their sett times of schooling, eating, goeing to bed, riseing in morning in the midst of this disorder and confusion."

Governor Bernard meanwhile could think of no better way to meet the crisis than by calling a meeting of the Council. Here it came out that McIntosh had led the assault on Hutchinson, and the Council ordered a warrant issued for his arrest. Sheriff Greenleaf found him on King Street and took him up without resistance. McIntosh was evidently so sure of himself that he felt no need to resist. It had already been rumored that the custom-house would be pulled down. Those who felt that the riots had gone far enough were ready to prevent this by use of the militia, but they were not ready to see McIntosh, who could name the instigators of both riots, tried in court. The word accordingly went around that unless McIntosh was released, not a man would appear to defend the custom-house. At this the officers of the customs went to the Sheriff and asked him to release his prisoner. Sheriff Greenleaf agreed and went to the Town House to tell the Governor and Council what he had done. "And did you discharge him?" asked Hutchinson.

"Yes," said Greenleaf.

"Then you have not done your duty."

"And this," Hutchinson wrote later, "was all the notice taken of the discharge."

McIntosh thus went free, and no one was ever punished

for the destruction of Hutchinson's property. But from this time forward the persons directing the mob were careful to keep matters more firmly under control, an accomplishment made possible by the willingness of the militia and of McIntosh to cooperate. Further demonstrations of violence were in fact unnecessary, for the Loyal Nine had made it plain that they were not afraid to bring out the mob against anyone who dared oppose them. Governor Bernard, retired in the safety of Castle William, was ready to admit that he did not have the command of ten men and was governor only in name.

By the end of August, then, Boston was ready for the Stamp Act. With both the Stamp Distributor and the mob under control nothing remained to be done until the first of November, when it would be necessary to adopt a more vigilant watch to see that the Act should not be obeyed in any instance. A minor crisis occurred toward the end of September when the stamped papers arrived on a Boston merchantman. Governor Bernard was prepared for this and had announced earlier that he would lodge them in Castle William for safekeeping, since Oliver had disclaimed any responsibility. Fearing that Bernard would make an attempt to distribute them from the Castle, the Loyal Nine hinted that the people would storm the Castle the moment the papers were landed there and destroy them; but the Governor promptly stated in the newspapers that he was not authorized to distribute them and would make no attempt to do so. With this assurance the Loyal Nine were apparently satisfied, and when the papers arrived they were landed safely at the Castle under cover of two men-of-war in the harbor.

In the ensuing weeks Boston waited uneasily for November first. Governor Bernard, brooding in Castle William over his grand scheme for reorganizing the empire, felt bitter about the mess which George Grenville had made of things. Although he had written to Richard Jackson on August 24, "to send hither Ordinances for Execution which the People have publickly protested against as illegal and not binding upon them, without first providing a power to enforce Obedience, is tempting them to revolt," yet he could not quite believe that the people of Massachusetts would be so foolish as to prevent the execution of the Act. At first he told himself that the rest of the province would disavow the hotheaded proceedings of the Bostonians. There had always been a split between the coast and the country, and the country had always been more moderate. Bernard had hopes of getting some backing for law and order from the farmers of the interior when the General Assembly should meet. "I depend upon the Assembly to set these Matters to right," he wrote to his friend John Pownall after the first riot, "as I really believe that there is not one out of twenty throughout the Province but what will disapprove the Proceedings of Boston."

When the Assembly came together on September 25, he pointed out to them that the doctrines of the *Boston Gazette,* however appealing in Boston, would never find acceptance in Westminster. Though Parliament may have made a mistake in passing the Stamp Act, it was still an act of Parliament and the General Court of Massachusetts ought to see to its enforcement. When his speech was over, it appeared that the radicals had won over a majority of the farmers in the Assembly, and so, as they prepared to draw up an answer to the speech, Bernard adjourned them. Eventually he had to confess that the country people were even more violent in their opposition to the Stamp Act than the Bostonians: "They talk of revolting from Great Britain in the most familiar Manner, and declare that tho' the British Forces should possess themselves of the Coast and Maritime Towns, they never will subdue the inland."

When he became disillusioned about the interior sometime in September, Bernard still clung to the idea that economic necessity would force the people of Massachusetts to accept the Act. He understood well the dependence of Massachusetts on trade. After November first, no ships would be cleared until the Stamp Act was accepted. Then Massachusetts would repent of her folly:

> If the Ports and the Courts of Justice are shut up on the first of November, terrible will be the Anarchy and Confusion which will ensue; Necessity will soon oblige and justify an Insurrection of the Poor against the rich, those that want the necessaries of Life against those that have them; But this is not all, it is possible that, when all the Provisions in the Province are divided amongst the People without regard to Property, they may be insufficient to carry them through the Winter, by cutting off the Resources from Pennsylvania and Maryland, upon which this Province has great dependance, a Famine may ensue. Less obvious causes, but very lately, were so near producing one, even with the help of the usual importations, that many perished for want: And who can say that the present internal stock of the Province, is sufficient, without importations to support the Inhabitants through the Winter only?

Bernard was shrewd enough to see that the men directing the opposition to the Stamp Act wanted no insurrection of the poor against the rich. What he did not see was that these men would be able to turn the hatred of the poor against the British government instead of against the rich. It was true that if the ports were closed, famine would be the result in Boston, but before the poor should rise against the rich their fury would be aimed against the men who had closed the ports. In the face of that fury the ports would not stay closed, and neither would the clearances be on stamped paper. Bernard knew how to analyze the difficulties in the British imperial system, but not the immediate political situation. His opponents had taken his measure correctly in the last weeks of August, and they knew that when the crisis came, he would give them little trouble.

As the first of November approached, and word spread that there would be a grand parade and pageant that day, Governor

Bernard performed his usual gesture. He called the Council and pointed out the danger that such a parade would end in more violence. To make matters worse, November 5 (Pope's Day) would follow hard after and give fresh occasion for riot. In order to forestall both these outbreaks, Bernard and the Council decided that several companies of militia should guard the town from October 31 to November 6. On the thirty-first the officers of the militia came to the Council Chamber and, as might have been expected, announced that the militia could not be raised. The first drummer sent out had had his drum broken, and the others were bought off. If Bernard had chosen, he could have had 100 regulars on hand. On September 10, General Gage had sent his aide-de-camp to offer that many troops for the maintenance of order. Bernard refused them, because, as he said, things had quieted down then, and because he was afraid that so small a number would only irritate the people without providing adequate protection to the government. When November first came, then, Bernard was helpless. He was assured that his image would not be paraded, but nevertheless he retired to Castle William —not that he was afraid, he hastened to assure his correspondents, but he did not wish to be present when insults should be offered to His Majesty's government.

As if to demonstrate how well they had the situation in hand, the Loyal Nine—or the Sons of Liberty, as they now began to call themselves—maintained perfect order in Boston on November first. The day was ushered in by the mournful tolling of church bells. The images of George Grenville and John Huske (whom the Bostonians took to be an instigator of the Stamp Act) were hung on the tree which had held those of Oliver and Bute on August 14. The tree had since been named the Liberty Tree, and a copper plaque commemorating August 14 (but not August 26) hung around the trunk. At two o'clock in the afternoon the images were cut down, and a procession of "innumerable people from the Country as well as the Town," marching in exact order, carried them through the streets to the gallows, hung them again, and then cut them to pieces. On November 5, there was a similar orderly demonstration, in which the union of the South End and the North End was celebrated with all the decorum of a church supper.

No one in Boston supposed for a minute that these polite celebrations were the end of the Stamp Act troubles. The Sons of Liberty had begun to plan for the next step on their program as soon as they had forced Oliver to resign. On August 26, the day when Hutchinson's house was attacked, Benjamin Edes's paper had carried this item:

> Since the Resignation of the Stamp Officer, a Question has been thrown out—How shall we carry on Trade without the Stamp'd Papers?—Carry on no Trade at all, say some, for who would desire to increase his Property, at the Expence of Liberty.—Others say, that in Case there shall be no Officer to distribute the Stampt Papers after the first of November, a regular Protest will justify any of his Majesty's Subjects, in any Court of Justice, who shall carry on Business *without* them?

Governor Bernard naively supposed that the colonists would attempt to defeat the Stamp Act by ceasing all activities which required the use of stamps, but the Sons of Liberty had the second alternative in view—to proceed as though the Stamp Act had never been passed. Before attempting to achieve this by direct action, they tried to persuade the Assembly to effect it by law, as the Rhode Island Assembly had done when they resolved to indemnify officials who suffered by disregarding the Act. When the Massachusetts Assembly convened again on October 23, a committee of both houses was appointed to consider a resolution declaring that since the Stamp Distributor had resigned, whereby the people were prevented from obtaining stamps, it should be lawful to do business without stamps, the Act of Parliament to the contrary notwithstanding. Governor Bernard, still underestimating the boldness of the people with whom he was dealing, supposed that this was simply another means of harassing him. "It is true," he wrote to John Pownall, "that they who bring in this Bill know that I cannot and shall not pass it: But what of that? it will answer their purpose; which is to bring upon me all the odium of the inconveniences, losses and miseries which will follow the non-usage of Stamps. The People will be told that all these are owing to me, who refused passing an Act which would have prevented them, and no notice will be taken of my incapacity to pass such an Act: so that I shall be made to appear to bring on these Evils, which I have taken so much pains to prevent."

To Bernard's surprise the resolve did not pass the House, but the reasons for its failure were not calculated to reduce his uneasiness. The representatives rejected it, because they felt that it implied a right in Parliament to levy the tax. If the reason for ignoring the Act was simply that the stamp officer had resigned, the legality of the Act was admitted. If the resolution were adopted and a new Stamp Distributor should be appointed, it would be morally incumbent upon the Assembly to support him. These complex considerations could be avoided only by an open defiance of the Act, and this was more than the Assembly wished to put on its records. The matter was left, therefore, for the Sons of Liberty to resolve in their own way.

The most pressing problem would be the opening of the ports so that the trade which was Boston's lifeblood might go on. By putting every possible vessel to sea before November first the merchants gained a little time in which to consider the risks of ignoring an act of Parliament. The risks seemed to diminish in importance as ships returned from voyages to lie idle, accumulating wharf-charges instead of profits; and the conviction that the Stamp Act must be ignored grew stronger.

While the Sons of Liberty waited for public pressure to

rise, the customs officers, the Attorney General, and the Governor engaged in an elaborate rigmarole, in which the question of clearing vessels without stamps was tossed from one to the other and back again with graceful and disgraceful gestures, each person trying to shift the unpleasant decision from himself. The whole procedure is only to be understood in the light of the personal feud which had been going on for over a year between the Governor and John Temple, Surveyor General of the Customs. Temple's headquarters were in Boston, but he supervised the collection of the customs in the entire Northern District from Nova Scotia to Connecticut. Bernard was jealous of Temple's power and did all he could to subordinate it to his own inside Massachusetts. Temple, on the other hand, regarded Bernard as a corrupt and grasping politician who had sabotaged the collection of the King's revenue (one example was the slowness with which he had moved to the support of John Robinson when Robinson had been put in the Taunton jail at the suit of Job Smith). Knowing that sooner or later either he or Bernard might have to take responsibility for clearing ships without stamps, Temple was anxious, if possible, to put the onus of the decision on Bernard.

The whole situation was further complicated by the fact that the only knowledge of the Stamp Act in Boston was hearsay. Two copies of the Act had come in private letters and from one of these the Act was printed in the newspapers, but Governor Bernard had received no official copy. From the newspapers he discovered that he was obliged by the terms of the Act to take an oath to support it, and accordingly he did so, but he naturally felt somewhat less responsible than he might have, had he known for certain what he was supposed to support. The same was true of Temple, and to a less degree of Oliver himself. Oliver received a notice of his appointment from the Secretary of the Stamp Office in England, but by November first he had not received his official commission as distributor. He surmised that this might be in the packet of stamped papers which was stored in Castle William, but neither he nor anyone else cared to break open the packet and find out.

Although everyone concerned with enforcing the Stamp Act could thus plead ignorance on November first, no one seriously doubted that the Act which had been printed in the newspapers was genuine, and it was plain that the customs officers whose duty it was to grant clearances would have to decide in the near future what course they should take. Accordingly on October 29 Benjamin Hallowell, Comptroller, who had already tasted the fury of the mob, and William Sheaffe, Collector, asked John Temple what they should do. On October 30 he replied that "as I have nothing in Charge from my Superiors concerning the Stamp Act, I can give you no other Advice or direction, for your Conduct than that of strictly observing all Acts of Parliament that have any Relation to the Duty of your Office, and wherein you may be at a loss for the true meaning of any Act of Parliament, I recommend you to the Advocate and Attorney General for their Advice." No help there.

The next day, October 31, Sheaffe and Hallowell went through the formality of asking Oliver for the stamped papers needed in their office. Oliver replied the same day that he had no commission as distributor and even if he did would not be able to handle the stamps. The next step was to ask Governor Bernard what should be done. He replied as quickly as Oliver that he had no authority to appoint a distributor or to distribute them himself. Sheaffe and Hallowell accordingly sent copies of their correspondence with Bernard and Oliver to the Attorney General, Edmund Trowbridge, and to the Advocate General of the Admiralty Court, Robert Auchmuty, and asked for their advice—all this by the evening of October 31.

On November first, while Boston was diverting itself with the effigies of Grenville and Huske, Trowbridge sent his answer: ask Mr. Temple, the Surveyor General. As Auchmuty did not choose to make any reply at this point, the Collector and Comptroller were now back where they had started from, and here a disturbing thought occurred to them. Suppose they should refuse to grant clearances on the ground that they had no stamped paper. To grant clearances was their job, and no one else could do it. If they refused would they not be liable to suits for damages from every individual who applied for a clearance and was refused? On the other hand, suppose they granted a clearance on unstamped paper, and suppose further that the ship proceeding under this clearance were seized by the British Navy and condemned for proceeding under improper clearance papers. Would they not be liable in such a case to a suit for the value of the ship? Whatever they did were they not thus liable to innumerable suits? And were not the New England merchants notoriously quick to sue customs officers whenever they could?

Hastily they put their questions to the Surveyor General. Without hesitation he replied, "With regard to the Queries you have put to me, as they are mere points of Law, I must refer you to the Advocate and Attorney General." To the Advocate and the Attorney General they went, and this time obtained a reluctant opinion, that the Comptroller and Collector would not be liable to damages if they cleared ships on unstamped paper, provided they certified that no stamped paper was available. Having received this opinion, which of course was only an opinion and not a guarantee, Sheaffe and Hallowell still hesitated to proceed without some authorization from either the Surveyor General or the Governor. Accordingly they told Temple of the legal advice they had received, and he of course referred them again to the Governor. The Governor gave them the same answer that Temple had previously: "It is the Business of the Attorney General and the Advocate General to advise you in matters of Law and not mine."

It was now the nineteenth of November, and the merchants were becoming restless. Temple still refused to take responsibility. On his advice Sheaffe and Hallowell approached Bernard again on November 22, saying that they were afraid he might not have read Auchmuty's opinion at the time when he told them to go to the Attorney General and Advocate General for advice. Bernard was not to be caught in this trap: "I must again repeat to you that it is not my business to advise you in matter of Law. . . . I have perused the opinion of the Attorney General and Advocate General but desire to be excused giving my opinion upon the case myself."

Sheaffe and Hallowell next pressed the Attorney and Advocate for more explicit instructions, about how the clearances should be drawn up, and whether bonds as well as clearances might be unstamped. The only result was that Trowbridge got cold feet and withdrew his former advice. On November 30 he wrote, "I do not look upon myself as the Proper Person by whose advise You (in an affair of such importance, and which seems to be at present a matter rather of prudence than of Law) are to govern yourselves and therefore must be excused advising you either to grant Cockets or Clearances upon unstamped Papers or to refuse to do it."

On this same day, November 30, Andrew Oliver's commission finally arrived. Sheaffe and Hallowell again hopefully applied for stamps, but Oliver replied quickly enough that though he had received his commission it was still impossible for him to exercise it. Sheaffe and Hallowell therefore went back to plying Auchmuty and Trowbridge with questions. This time Trowbridge folded up completely. They received an answer written by a friend of Trowbridge's who was directed "to inform you that last Monday night he was seized with the Rheumatism in his right Arm and Shoulder to such a degree, as that he hath not ever since been able, either to write as much as his Name or attend to any business, wherefore he must be excused considering or answering those Questions."

By now the pressure was acute, and the Sons of Liberty were almost ready to take action. On December 11 Sheaffe informed the Surveyor General "that the Town was in an uproar and that there was a meeting of the Merchants and that the Mob intended at night to storm the Customhouse." Temple promptly sent the news to Bernard, with the additional intelligence that there was over six thousand pounds sterling of the King's money in the custom-house. As it grew dark, and the King's customs officers listened for the approaching rumble of the mob, Bernard penned his answer: "I will call a Council tomorrow."

But December 17, not December 11, was the day which the Sons of Liberty had scheduled for opening the custom-house, and the night of December 11 passed calmly. On December 13 Sheaffe and Hallowell made one more nervous attempt to get the stamps out of Oliver or to put the blame more squarely upon him. This time they got a categorical response: "In answer to your Letter of this date demanding my determinate and absolute answer to this question, whether I will or will not deliver you any stamp'd papers after having answered it twice already: I say No."

This was plain enough as far as Sheaffe and Hallowell were concerned, but the Sons of Liberty wanted a public statement. Before they put the final pressure on Sheaffe and Hallowell, they wanted to be certain that there would be no stamped papers available. On December 16, therefore, Benjamin Edes published an anonymous letter in the *Gazette,* asking whether Oliver intended to execute the commission he had lately received. Before publishing the letter Edes secured an answer from Oliver, which he also published, stating "that altho' he had now received a Deputation to act as Distributor of the Stamps for the Province of the *Massachusetts,* He had taken no Measures to qualify himself for the Office, nor had he any Thoughts of doing it."

To the Sons of Liberty this did not appear to be a satisfactory answer. They met in their headquarters at the distillery on Hanover Square and wrote another letter to Oliver:

Hanover Square Dec. 16, 1765

Sir,

The respectable Inhabitants of the Town of Boston, observe your Answer to an anonymous Letter published in Messi'rs Edes and Gill's News-Paper of Today, which we don't think satisfactory; therefore desire that you would, To-morrow, appear under Liberty Tree, at 12 o'Clock, to make a public Resignation. Your Non compliance, Sir, will incur the Displeasure of *The True-born Sons of Liberty*. N.B. Provided you comply with the above, you shall be treated with the greatest Politeness and Humanity. If not . . . . !

When a messenger knocked at Oliver's door and handed his servant this letter, it was too late in the evening and the weather too dirty for Oliver to consult the Governor. The next morning, the weather still stormy, notices were found posted up all over town, reading:

St-p! St-p! St-p! No.

Tuesday Morning, Dec. 17th, 1765

The true-born SONS of LIBERTY are desired to meet under Liberty Tree at XII o'Clock This Day, to hear the Public Resignation, under Oath, of Andrew Oliver, Esq; Distributor of Stamps for the Province of the *Massachusetts-Bay* . . .

A Resignation? Yes.

Oliver realized that he had no way out. He sent for his friend John Avery, who was one of the Loyal Nine and would be able to act as an intermediary between himself and the Sons of Liberty. Avery came to him at nine o'clock and told him that effigies were already prepared as a signal for a riot in case he failed to appear at the Liberty Tree. In a last-minute attempt to save his dignity Oliver offered to make his resignation at the courthouse. This was not acceptable, and so at 12 o'clock noon, escorted by the redoubtable McIntosh himself, Oliver marched through the streets, the rain beating down tempestuously, and read his resignation from an upper window of the house which stood next to the Liberty Tree. In spite of the rain two thousand people had assembled, and when he was finished they gave three huzzas. Oliver replied with a polite, if somewhat bitter, statement that "I shall always think myself very happy when it shall be in my power to serve this people," upon which there were more cheers, and the crowd departed.

Meanwhile messengers had been hurrying back and forth through the rain from Sheaffe and Hallowell to Temple, Trowbridge, Auchmuty, and Bernard. Auchmuty alone seems to have had the courage to advise flatly that the clearances be issued without stamps. Trowbridge still had the rheumatism, and Temple and Bernard refused to offer any advice. Sheaffe and Hallowell were still afraid to take the responsibility themselves. But when two thousand people could assemble on a rainy day to watch Oliver resign for a second time, present danger loomed larger than future damage suits. On the afternoon of the seventeenth the custom-house opened for business, and in the evening the Sons of Liberty sat down in their headquarters to a dinner of celebration, to which they invited their good friend Samuel Adams and spent the evening drinking healths.

With the ports open, the Sons of Liberty wasted no time in arranging for the opening of the courts. On the morning of the eighteenth the town of Boston, by petition of "a number of Inhabitants," held a special meeting in Faneuil Hall, at which a memorial to the Governor was drawn up. The memorial stated that "Law is the great rule of Right, the Security of our Lives and Propertys, and the best Birth right of Englishmen." With the courts closed, the rule of law must cease; therefore the Governor was requested to order the opening of the courts. Since the memorial was addressed to the Governor in Council, Bernard seized upon his customary method of avoiding unpleasant decisions and appointed the next morning, December 19, for a Council meeting. When the

Council met, Bernard informed them that he would leave the matter entirely to them. Since most of the members present were no more anxious to face the question than Bernard himself, and since many were absent, the meeting broke up with a decision to call in all the Councillors who lived within twenty miles of Boston for another meeting the following afternoon. As the gentlemen descended from their chamber in the upper story of the Town House, they could find a hint of what was expected of them in a paper hung up in the room below:

> Open your Courts and let Justice prevail
> Open your Offices and let not Trade fail
> For if these men in power will not act,
> We'll get some that will, is actual Fact.

When the Councillors assembled the next day, the lawyers of the town of Boston presented them with a long harangue on the necessity of opening the courts. The arguments were by now familiar. John Adams told them that the Stamp Act was "utterly void, and of no binding Force upon us; for it is against our Rights as Men, and our Priviledges as Englishmen." Parliament, he said, could err, and when it did, need not be obeyed. "A Parliament of Great Britain can have no more Right to tax the Colonies than a Parliament of Paris." James Otis, moved to tears by his own eloquence, argued that "The shutting up of the Courts is an Abdication, a total Dissolution of Government," and he too affirmed, as a principle well known to lawyers, "that there are Limits, beyond which if Parliaments go, their Acts bind not."

Listening to these arguments, Governor Bernard perceived that the lawyers had given him another loophole. What they had said, he told them, "would be very pertinent to induce the Judges of the Superior Court to think the Act of no Validity, and that therefore they should pay no Regard to it; . . ." The question at issue was a matter of law, and it would not do for the executive branch of the government to determine a matter of law. In short the judges must decide the question. The Council welcomed this solution, and adopted a resolution to the effect that the memorial presented to them was none of their business. In order to appease, as they hoped, the wrath of Boston, they added a recommendation that the judges of the several courts determine the question as soon as possible. When the answer was delivered to the town meeting, on Saturday afternoon, December 21, the meeting considered the extraordinary question of whether the Council's reply was satisfactory, and came to the unanimous conclusion that it was not.

The Superior Court of the province was not scheduled to meet until March, so that there was no immediate necessity for the justices of this court to make a decision, but the Inferior Court of Common Pleas for Suffolk County was to meet in Boston during the second week in January, and the session of the Probate Court of Suffolk County was already overdue. In the Probate Court the obstinate figure of Thomas Hutchinson again appeared in the path of the Sons of Liberty. Hutchinson as Chief Justice of the Colony could postpone acting until March. Hutchinson as Judge of the Suffolk County Probate Court would have to take his stand at once. His friends told him he must choose between four things: "to do business without stamps, to quit the country, to resign my office, or—" Here one may assume the friends supplied a significant gesture.

Hutchinson was not an easy man to scare, but his friends assured him that he had no time to deliberate. His brother, Foster Hutchinson, did not share his unwillingness to do business without stamps. Governor Bernard suggested therefore that Hutchinson deputize his brother to act for him, but Hutchinson could find no precedent for such a proceeding. The Governor then offered to appoint Foster Hutchinson as Judge of the Probate Court for one year only. Such a limited appointment, Governor Bernard persuaded himself, could be made without stamped paper. Hutchinson complied with this arrangement, and so the Probate Court opened.

Meanwhile the Boston town meeting had made inquiries—one suspects that the questions were heavily weighted—and discovered that the judges of the Inferior Court of Common Pleas in Suffolk County were ready to proceed without stamps. When the next town meeting was held on January sixteenth, both the Probate and the Inferior Courts in Suffolk County were open for business as usual, but the courts in the other counties of the province were still closed. Since the only way in which the Bostonians could bring pressure upon these courts was through the General Assembly, the town meeting instructed their representatives in the Assembly to use their influence "that Measures may be taken that Justice be also duly Administered in all the County's throughout the Province and that enquiry may be made into the Reasons why the course of Justice in the Province has been in any Measure obstructed."

The House of Representatives was by this time so thoroughly in accord with the town of Boston that on January 24, 1766, a resolution was passed by a vote of 81 to 5, stating that the courts of justice in the colony, and particularly the Superior Court, ought to be opened. When the resolution reached the Council, there again stood Thomas Hutchinson, prepared to block it. He wished the Council to reject it at once, but the other members postponed consideration until January 30. The *Boston Gazette* immediately went to work on Hutchinson with a highly colored story to the effect that he had said that the resolution was "Impertinent and beneath the Notice of the honorable Board, or to that effect." The *Gazette* had attained such a degree of power by this time that the Council thought it necessary to answer the charge. Governor Bernard, recognizing his old enemy Otis as the author, wanted the Council to have him arrested, but the Council was no more ready than Bernard himself to assume responsibility for so dangerous a move, and contented themselves with passing resolutions in which they denied that Hutchinson had ever said anything derogatory to the House of Representatives.

At the same time the Council thought proper to inquire of the judges of the Superior Court whether they would proceed with business when the next scheduled meeting should come up on March 11. The judges were as reluctant as everyone else to take a stand on the question but delivered their opinion that if the "Circumstances" of the colony remained in March what they were in January, and the lawyers should wish to proceed, they would be obliged to do so.

This report from the judges was published without any mention of the provision that made opening contingent upon the wishes of the lawyers. Actually the judges were shifting the responsibility back to the lawyers who had pleaded so eloquently before the Council for the opening of the courts. When March 11 rolled around, rumors of the repeal of the Stamp Act had already begun to arrive, and the revolutionary tension had relaxed to the point where the lawyers were dubious about risking their interests in an irregular procedure when a regular one might be obtained by waiting. Hutchinson, the Chief Justice, manufactured an excuse to be absent from the March session—much to the annoyance of John Adams, who found himself as a lawyer in the dilemma which Hutchinson had escaped as a judge. When the judges, perhaps perceiving the hesitation of the lawyers, declared themselves ready to proceed, even James Otis, who had led the movement to force the opening, was unwilling to plead. Finally a case was dug up which had been continued from the previous session, and after disposing of this, the Court postponed other civil business until April and from then successively until June. The newspapers announced that "all the courts of Justice in this Province are now to all Intents and Purposes open." With this token victory, which everyone could hope was the prelude to a real victory in Parliament, the agitation for opening the courts subsided, and Massachusetts waited for the news of repeal.

For Further Reading

So vast is the literature and so varied the interpretations on the causes of the American Revolution that the subject is perhaps best approached through anthologies of the major works. Four excellent collections that offer thoughtful introductions as well as representative extracts from earlier writings are Edmund S. Morgan, ed., *The American Revolution: Two Centuries of Interpretation* (1965), Esmond Wright, ed., *Causes and Consequences of the American Revolution* (1966), and two by Jack P. Greene, *The Ambiguity of the American Revolution* (1968), and *The Reinterpretation of the American Revolution, 1763–1789* (1968).

The most extensive modern analysis of the decades before the Revolution is Lawrence Henry Gipson's monumental history, *The British Empire Before the American Revolution* (15 vols., 1936–1969). Shorter but very detailed histories of the 1760's and 1770's are John C. Miller, *Origins of the American Revolution* (1959), and Merrill Jensen, *The Founding of a Nation* (1968); and Gipson has provided a condensed version of his interpretation in *The Coming of the Revolution* (1954). On the Revolutionary implications of pre-1763 colonial history, much can be gained from Charles M. Andrews, *The Colonial Background of American History* (rev. ed. 1921), and Arthur M. Schlesinger, *The Birth of the Nation* (1968). For the British background of the story, see Sir Lewis Namier, *England in the Age of the American Revolution* (2nd ed. 1963), and J. Steven Watson, *The Reign of George III* (1962).

Among the most important treatments of special topics are Oliver M. Dickerson, *The Navigation Acts and the American*

Revolution (1951); Philip Davidson, *Propaganda and the American Revolution* (1941); Michael Kammen, *A Rope of Sand: The Colonial Agents, British Politics, and the American Revolution* (1968); Bernard Knollenberg, *Origin of the American Revolution, 1759–1766* (rev. ed. 1961); John Shy, *Toward Lexington: The Role of the British Army in the Coming of the American Revolution* (1965); Arthur M. Schlesinger, *The Colonial Merchant and the American Revolution* (1918); Benjamin W. Labaree, *The Boston Tea Party* (1964); Charles R. Ritcheson, *British Politics and the American Revolution* (1954); Carl Ubbeholde, *Vice Admiralty Courts and the American Revolution* (1960); Carl Bridenbaugh, *Mitre and Sceptre: Transatlantic Faith, Ideas, Personalities, and Politics, 1689–1775* (1962); and Bernard Bailyn, *The Ideological Origins of the American Revolution* (1967).

Some useful collections of source materials on the coming of the Revolution are Samuel Eliot Morison, *Sources and Documents Illustrating the American Revolution* (1929); Edmund S. Morgan, *Prologue to Revolution: Sources and Documents on the Stamp Act Crisis* (1959); and Alden T. Vaughan, ed., *Chronicles of the American Revolution* (1965).

The Diplomacy of Independence

Richard B. Morris

Many legends have emerged about events and personalities of the American Revolution. This is especially true of military topics. Revolutionary tales have become part of American folklore; patriots have been enshrined in a pantheon of national heroes. Monuments, obelisks, and road signs dot the American countryside memorializing battles and men: Lexington and Concord, Bunker Hill, Trenton, Valley Forge, Saratoga, Yorktown; and Washington, Lafayette, Knox, Gates, Greene, and Steuben. The collections of some local historical societies contain little other than prized Revolutionary relics. Grown men still clad themselves in Revolutionary garb and reenact some bygone skirmish. Symbolically, over one-third of the U.S. Post Office's commemorative stamp issues during the sesquicentennial period 1925–1933 were devoted to the Revolution; philatelists look forward to a similar outpouring during the bicentennial.

But mythmaking has not stopped with stories of Washington's crossing of the Delaware. The course of diplomacy during the Revolution has its share of legends. A

Source: Richard B. Morris, *The Peacemakers* (New York: Harper & Row, 1965), pp. 411–437.

persistent version of Franco-American relations from 1776 to 1783, for example, stresses a rather romantic theme: American patriots, led by a simply clad yet canny Benjamin Franklin, persuaded the French to support their cause by appealing both to Gallic reason and to a commonly held philosophic tradition. French military aid flowed from this happy alliance, secretly at first, then later more triumphantly manifested in the combined Franco-American investment of the British troops under Cornwallis at Yorktown. America was deeply in debt to France. So deeply, in fact, that almost a century and a half later Americans would disembark in France proclaiming "Lafayette, we are here!"

That this story distorts the reality should have been obvious from the start. Nations rarely, if ever, act with disinterestedness; national interest dictates foreign policy. A French monarchy would support republican revolutionists only if the gains at the expense of an ancient foe, Great Britain, seemed large and certain. Once granting support, France hardly would consistently press for American interests without properly considering its own. Alliance did not mean undeviating friendship. So France proved when at one point during the Revolution its envoys actually informed England that American access to the Grand Banks fishing grounds would not be viewed favorably by the French Foreign Office.

Shearing away romantic notions about diplomacy during the Revolution, however, does not lessen the interest of the real story. In fact, it would be difficult to improve upon the complicated networks of spies and informers that made late-eighteenth-century diplomacy as exciting as the latter-day "007" agent escapades. Dr. Edward Bancroft, for one, served both the Americans and the British as a double agent. The thrill of the chase livens the diplomatic narrative as well. Henry Laurens, South Carolinian and former presiding officer in Congress, had been sent to Holland to negotiate a loan in 1779. On the high seas, the brigantine that bore him was overtaken by a British vessel after a day's run. Laurens, concerned that his confidential papers would be seized by the enemy, tossed his dispatches overboard in a weighted bag. Unfortunately the bag did not sink; Laurens went to the Tower of London to cool his heels; and Britain, publishing Laurens' papers, used the incident as a *casus belli* with unoffending Holland.

High adventure of course is only part of the diplomatic story of the American Revolution. The struggle between mother country and rebellious colonies transcended the bounds of a family quarrel. It became a global matter, involving great and small European powers. Surprisingly, until recently the entire story had not been pieced together by scholars. Richard B. Morris, however, has done just that. In 1965, Morris completed the formidable task of studying the manuscript collections of diplomats like John Jay and the official archives of several nations bearing upon the final negotiations of the Treaty of Paris in 1783. *The Peacemakers,* as the following selection attests, is diplomatic history at its best, dealing not only with geopolitics and dispatches, but also with the personalities of the men who shaped decisions.

For more than six embattled years, ever since the adoption of the great Declaration, Patriots in America had looked forward to the day when their erstwhile monarch would acknowledge their independence. That day finally came. On the morning of December 5, 1782, George III opened the session of Parliament with a speech from the throne. The event was witnessed by a gathering of foreign notables, including Gérard de Rayneval, and the young Vicomte de Vergennes, along with a cluster of dejected American Loyalists. Among those who managed to squeeze their way into the packed House of Lords and come close to the throne, elbow to elbow with Admiral Lord Howe, was a young New England merchant named Elkanah Watson. He had been employed to carry money and dispatches to Franklin in 1779, had tried his hand at trade in Nantes, and now had come to England with a letter of introduction from the doctor himself to Lord Shelburne.

Watson later recalled that the Parliament buildings were shrouded in a blanket of fog, appropriate to the time of year. The diamond-cut and elevated panes of glass in the House served to increase the gloom within. The spectators looked around at walls hung with dark tapestry depicting the defeat of the Spanish Armada. That event which marked the launching of the First British Empire had transpired three centuries earlier, and now the Lords were gloomily anticipating the formal admission by their King that the Empire which Elizabeth and her royal successors had created with so vast an outpouring of toil and treasure was about to be dismembered.

For two hours Lords and spectators fidgeted while they awaited the King's arrival. At last a roar of artillery announced his approach. Entering by a small door on the left of the throne, George III, clothed in royal robes, seated himself upon the chair of state, his right foot resting upon a stool. His obvious agitation quickly communicated itself to his audience. Drawing from his pocket the scroll containing his speech, the King declared that he had lost no time in giving the necessary orders to prohibit the further prosecution of offensive war upon the North American Continent. All his views and measures, he brashly insisted, had been directed "to an entire and cordial reconciliation" with the colonies. "Finding it indispensable to the attainment of this object, I did not hesitate to go the full length of the powers vested in me, and offer to declare them—"

Here George, visibly shaken and embarrassed, paused. After a moment that must have seemed to him like an eternity he resumed: "and offer to declare them *free and independent States,* by an article to be inserted in the treaty of peace."

Sacrificing every consideration of his own to the wishes and opinions of his people, George closed on a note of piety, which Edmund Burke found insufferable. He offered his "humble and ardent prayer to Almighty God" that Great Britain would not "feel the evils which might result from so great a dismemberment of the Empire, and that America may be free from the calamities which have formerly proved, in the mother country, how essential monarchy is to the enjoyment of constitutional liberty." In closing, he could not refrain from expressing the hope that religion, language, interests, and affection would "yet prove a bond of permanent union between the two countries."

The words appeared to have been dragged out of him. "He hesitated, choked, and executed the painful duties with an ill grace which does not belong to him," Watson observed. The Yankee visitor was not the only one to remark the King's embarrassment. "In pronouncing the word 'independence' the King of England did it in a constrained voice," Rayneval reported to his chief.

That evening Watson dined with the talented American-born portrait painter, John Singleton Copley, whose studio was always crowded with royalty and high nobility seeking immortality on canvas. Bostonian by birth, Copley had completed a portrait of his fellow New Englander, and painted in the background a ship bearing to America the news that independence had been acknowledged. The artist had planned a rising sun casting its rays upon the Stars and Stripes streaming from her gaff. Until the King had spoken he had not deemed it prudent to hoist the American flag in his gallery. That evening, as Watson recalled, "with a bold hand, a master's touch, and I believe an American heart," Copley attached to the ship the Stars and Stripes. Watson believed this symbolic flag-hoisting was the first occasion upon which the Stars and Stripes were raised in old England, for it was a good two months before an American ship entered the Thames estuary.

John Singleton Copley's symbolic gesture notwithstanding, the issue of American independence still seemed by no means foreclosed. For the ensuing confusion blame must fall squarely upon Shelburne's shoulders. His ambivalent public position on the score of independence, together with his failure to make a prompt disclosure of the terms of the preliminary treaty with America, served to light the fires of suspicion that the British people were being asked to make a sacrifice of great enormity.

This time the Earl, who normally paid little attention to men but much to measures, had mobilized his supporters in advance to secure their continued adherence, but he could not shut off the stormy debate which the King's address precipitated in Lords and Commons. In the Lords, Shelburne was baited by that archfoe of American independence, Viscount Stormont. Charging the Ministry with "the most preposterous conduct" and with having fallen into a situation of "the greatest imbecility," Stormont put this rhetorical question to the Lords:

"Does it not say," he asked, "that, without any condition, any qualification, any stipulation whatsoever, America shall be independent whenever France chooses to make peace with us?" In other words, the provisional treaty was "irrevocable," and the government had been so imprudent as to concede unconditional independence without equivalent, forcing "the wretched Loyalists . . . this honest, brave set of men" to be content with "a mere provision for existence, an eleemosynary support?"

Shelburne was on his feet at once. "The noble viscount," he assured the Lords, in his obsequious manner, was "mistaken in his idea of unqualified, unconditional independence being given to America." The offer was not irrevocable, he insisted, arguing that, should France not agree to peace, it could be terminated. Stormont derived a cruel pleasure from reminding Shelburne now that not too long before he had declared in Parliament that the sun of Great Britain would set when American independence was granted. Apparently, the Viscount ironically remarked, the noble lord was now of a different opinion. "That sun is set. There is not a ray of light left. All is darkness."

Shelburne's embarrassments now stemmed from his failure to lay down the line to his supporters in Commons. While Lord North, though privately disturbed by rumors that large territories had been surrendered to the Americans, was unwilling to commit himself until the articles of the provisional treaty were disclosed, the more impulsive Charles James Fox decided to bring the issue to a head. Assuming that unconditional independence was yielded by the first article of the treaty, he endorsed the recognition of America without strings attached, and Burke joined him in insisting that independence had been granted "unconditionally." Sensing the sentiment of the Opposition in Commons, young Pitt, as spokesman for the Ministry, adopted a very different line from that pursued by Shelburne in the Lords. "Unqualified recognition" of American independence, he insisted, was "the clear indisputable meaning of the provisional treaty." General Conway seconded that sentiment, and even Shelburne's man, Tommy Townshend, denied there was any equivocation in the King's speech.

With the Ministry in apparent open division on the question of whether or not the Americans had secured their independence unconditionally, the halls of Parliament continued to buzz, and rumors spread far beyond its walls. He could not go a hundred yards from the House, Fox remarked, without hearing a different interpretation put upon the intention of the King's speech than that of the Ministry. It was only to be expected, then, that when debate on the provisional treaty was resumed on December 13th, the ministers should be lashed for "inconsistency." Driven into a corner, Shelburne took refuge in the need "to keep the secrets of the King." This talk of secrecy only succeeded in making Shelburne's critics even more suspicious. The Earl of Derby demanded "a plain answer to a very plain question: Are the Americans declared to be independent or not?" Shelburne declined to enter into any explanation which in his view might endanger the country. This was not enough to quiet Fox. Five days later he excoriated Shelburne in Commons for his ambiguous course and for hiding behind the cloak of official secrecy. Burke warned the government "to avoid the slippery and unsure ground of proud silence, or of ambiguous communication," and David Hartley, long-time unofficial negotiator with Franklin, reminded Parliament that if Shelburne was consistent with his past record and "a man of honour," he simply had to be against the independence of America. Fox's motion for the production of the provisional articles was, however, rejected 219–46.

Shelburne's hollow victory, one of his last, did not abate the scandal. As Goëzmann de Thurne, the Earl's severe critic, remarked, responsible Cabinet members had declared independence irrevocable in the Commons while Shelburne himself had declared it "equivocal" in the Lords, thus shamefully exploiting these opposing interpretations to win support for the King's address in both houses.

That Pitt had caught Shelburne by surprise in declaring that independence was now irrevocable was clear from the Earl's professions to the King. Pitt went too far, Shelburne complained, and caused "some uneasiness." George III, who found the whole business with the Americans unpalatable, was quick to brand Pitt's interpretation "a mistake, for the Independence is alone to be granted for peace." He continued, "It is no wonder that so young a man should have made a slip," but counseled that it would be "best and wisest if a mistake is made openly to avow it." Stand firm in the Lords, the King ordered his First Minister.

The refusal of Pitt to confess his "mistake," combined with the continuance of Shelburne to talk equivocally on the question of independence provided the foes of the Ministry with additional ammunition to attack its chief. To them the issue over American independence seemed a glaring example of Shelburne's notorious deviousness. William Wyndham Grenville reported that the Earl had postponed a Cabinet meeting rather than risk a direct encounter with his colleagues from the Commons whose public views on American independence did not tally with his own. Indeed, it is true that Shelburne had deferred calling the Cabinet together, fearful, as he confessed, that "a cabinet of communication" might be "converted into a cabinet of discussion." From this Grenville concluded that the Earl was either "the most abandoned and direct liar upon the face of the earth, or he is deceived himself too grossly to be imagined, or the whole world is deceived." Horace Walpole was even less charitable. He commented acidly that Shelburne's "falsehood was so constant and notorious, that it was rather his profession than his instrument. It was like a fictitious violin, which is hung out of a music shop to indicate in what goods the tradesman deals; not to be of service, nor to be depended on for playing a true note." As a principal victim of Shelburne's pruning of the Civil List, Walpole could scarcely be called objective, but biased or no, his vilification of the Jesuit of Berkeley Square attained the standing of a classic.

If nobody in England, least of all Shelburne himself, was quite clear about whether or not America's independence had been unconditionally granted, the American commissioners in Paris were understandably apprehensive as a result of Parliament's reaction to the announcement of the preliminaries. The change in the attitude of the Cabinet "from affirmation to cool reserve," as Benjamin Vaughan put it, and Shelburne's public insistence that the provisional articles would cease to bind should France fail to make peace hardly contributed to the commissioners' collective peace of mind. Something of this disquiet was reflected in Benjamin Vaughan's own correspondence. Writing to his brother in America to deny the rumor that Shelburne was really an enemy of American independence, he conceded that until recently the Earl had believed that America could be recovered. Now he realized that only the American trade could be retrieved. Nonetheless, what Shelburne had done was to make an "offer not unconditionally, not a gift." Vaughan even threw out a dark hint that the tender of independence might be withdrawn should France seek to gain "something for herself, besides independence." So perturbed was Shelburne's confidant about the ambivalent position of the Ministry that he himself asked the Earl that Oswald be instructed to reassure the Americans.

Assurances to the contrary, the Americans acted anything but contented. Franklin seemed to be avoiding Vaughan; the touchy Laurens was ruffled by the manner in which the British had seen fit to publicize his release on parole; Adams was reputedly exposed to the seductions of anti-British circles in Paris; while John Jay, upset by the revelations only now made to him of the Mountstuart letter which seemed to implicate Necker in a nasty piece of double-dealing, acted extremely edgy. Vergennes sought to quiet the fears of the Americans that Parliament would revoke both the commission to negotiate the peace with them as well as recognition. Some of the "hotheads" across the Channel might indeed favor such a course, but he felt confident that the Minister would know how to snuff it out. Almost at the same moment Vaughan was urging Shelburne to end hostilities. "Your lordship probably thinks the same, but the mad English nation—!"

Although anxious about the fate of the preliminaries, the Americans during Shelburne's remaining tenure in office continued to press for incorporation in the definitive treaty of certain basic principles to which hitherto Oswald had not been authorized to accede. Prodded by Secretary Livingston to obtain the right to trade directly with the West Indies, the American commissioners were still hopeful of winning the reciprocal trade concessions that Shelburne had earlier promised. Adams wanted a stipulation of freedom of navigation, along the lines that the Neutral League and the Dutch demanded. He was prepared to enter into a mutual guarantee with the British that "no forts shall be built or garrisons maintained upon any of the frontiers in America, nor upon any of the land boundaries," a path-breaking notion not completely implemented until the later Treaty of Washington of 1871. He further urged that Bermuda be either ceded to the United States or kept unfortified and its use barred to privateers, that Sable Island off Nova Scotia be turned over to America, and that the balance of prisoners' accounts be struck and paid "according to the usages of nations."

Franklin likewise kept up the pressure on the British and advanced some far-reaching proposals to Oswald which the less adventurous Fitzherbert deemed of "an odorous nature." Outwardly the least reconciled to Britain of any of the commissioners, Franklin still argued for compensation by Britain for damages inflicted in America. This was an obvious move to counter any British proposals to ameliorate the treatment accorded the Loyalists, about whom the doctor was still "very sharp." Not wishing "to see a new Barbary rising in America, and our long extended coast occupied by piratical states," the doctor pressed for incorporation into the definitive treaty of a prohibition against privateering. He also sought to guarantee the future safety in time of war of fisherman, farmers, and all unarmed artisans or manufacturers inhabiting unfortified locations. "A good lesson to mankind at least," was Adams' cryptic comment on Franklin's proposed revision of international law. The doctor even talked of a plan for neutralizing the sugar islands of every nation, at the same time showing less than lukewarm interest in a revived proposal of Oswald for Federal Union. With Jay's backing, Franklin also proposed that the treaty of commerce, still to be negotiated between England and America, be signed at the same time as the definitive treaty, but Oswald, appreciating Shelburne's increasingly delicate situation at home, put a stop to what he privately characterized as "this premature and destructive idea." Jay subsequently proposed a three-year moratorium on the collection of debts due British creditors in America, along with the cancellation of interest accrued during the war.

These American demands, some new, some reiterated, above and beyond the preliminary articles, were so disturbing to Fitzherbert that he sounded out the Comte de Vergennes, who was not backward in expressing his disapproval of some of them, venturing his negative reaction even before France had signed her own preliminary articles. To the French court the idea of setting up the rich West Indian islands as neutral independent states, a notion by the way that Franklin shared with the former French Minister Turgot, was plain scandalous. "If urged to it," the British plenipotentiary reported, the French court "would join us in representing to the American Commissioners the monstrous injustice of introducing fresh articles into the treaty."

Shelburne later recalled that Jay and Franklin wanted England to seize the Floridas after the signing of the American preliminaries but before France and Spain had signed their own. The record seems to substantiate him. Well on in January Franklin expressed concern about the fate of West Florida and was quoted as favoring England's reconquest of the territory on the ground that it would bolster the treaty provision for the free navigation of the Mississippi by both the British and the Americans. Vaughan held out hopes that England would get the province back after the peace.

If Shelburne ended the suspense by disclosing the terms of the preliminary treaties his Ministry had made, he only succeeded in causing a new commotion. On January 27th the preliminaries to which France, Spain, and America had acceded were presented to both houses. The treaties were laid upon the table for the inspection of the members, but in deference to rules of secret diplomacy to which all European chancelleries religiously adhered when it suited their purpose, they were neither circularized nor printed. A motion for printing touched off a debate. Fox pointed to the suspicious circumstances attendant upon the preliminaries. Alderman

Wilkes provoked derisive laughter at the Ministry's expense by informing the Commons that the Lords had already ordered the treaties to be printed. The question was quickly carried without a division.

Outside the halls of Parliament the various interest groups affected by the preliminaries now bestirred themselves. The Canadian fur merchants, joined by the Loyalists, laid down a barrage of barbed questions about the cessions in North America. Governor William Franklin asked, "Why were the forts in Indian territories surrendered to the Americans without consulting the Indians?" Oswald riposted neatly. "Your father, Doctor Franklin," he informed him, "insisted on a boundary being drawn. The Doctor ran his finger along the map to indicate the desired boundaries. And what," concluded Oswald, with becoming humility, "could *I* object to a man of Dr. Franklin's influence and authority?" Other critics voiced fears that the northern boundary of the United States would give complete ascendancy in the Ohio Valley to American trade and proposed that portions of the upper valley be given Canada in return for opening the St. Lawrence to free navigation by the Americans. The concessions to France and America in the Newfoundland fisheries were contested by merchants trading to that area as well as by those who feared that if the English fishery declined, the nation would lose its "nursery for seamen." Even Benjamin Vaughan joined the critics of the treaty, privately urging upon Shelburne some modification of the northeastern boundary, which, he correctly contended, was "incompletely, irregularly, and clumsily defined," and drawn without his being consulted.

Other complaints poured in on Whitehall. From the prized West Indies, where even small islands were considered valuable properties not lightly sacrificed, came a deputation of Tobago planters demanding an extension of the time limit given them to sell their plantations, permission to export their sugar to England, and a stipulation assuring them the free exercise of their Protestant faith. West India merchants requested the Ministry to make a pact with Spain covering the restoration of runaway slaves. The logwood merchants, foreshadowing what was to be a long and tedious struggle, asked for a defined and extended settlement area in the Bay of Honduras for the British woodcutters, as well as for Southern Loyalists, who might settle there, and complained that the Mosquito Shore was never a part of Spanish territory. Finally, the East India Company was alert to what it considered the military risks implicit in the concessions to the French in India.

The most piteous cries were raised by the Loyalists, and the preliminaries with America inspired bitter recriminations. "The misery which American independence has brought to individuals is inexpressable," declared one of the victims, "and I assure you that I am one of the most ill-used." Of all the American commissioners, Benjamin Franklin was the least sympathetic to their appeals. In a satirical trifle he wrote soon after the signing of the preliminaries the doctor told how Lion, King of the Forest, influenced by evil counselors, condemned his faithful dogs without a hearing, while a mongrel race, corrupted by royal promises of great rewards, deserted the honest dogs and joined their enemies. Now, with the good dogs victorious, the mongrels, barred from returning, claimed the reward that had been promised them. To settle the question a council of beasts was held. The wolves and foxes sided with the mongrels, but the horse, arguing that the King had been misled by bad ministers "to war unjustly upon his faithful subjects," persuaded the council to reject the mongrels' demand. Franklin never saw fit to revise the fable.

Contrariwise, Benjamin Franklin's natural son William was at that very moment rallying the leading Loyalists in London, who laid siege to Shelburne House and stormed Parliament to secure compensation for their losses. William Franklin contended that the preliminary treaty would not redress their grievances, an argument that was substantially borne out by events. It was in fact to be the British government, not the

American states, upon whom the burden was to fall of providing substantial compensation to the Tories. In a somewhat special category were the descendants of William Penn, who were most assiduous in pressing their claims. Ignoring Oswald's advice, Lady Juliana Penn, widow of Thomas, the founder's second son, swooped down on Paris and buttonholed Jay and Franklin, winning their backing for an adjustment of Penn family claims for property which had been confiscated. Skillful diplomacy resulted in escalating the payments for the vacant and unappropriated lands in Pennsylvania formerly belonging to the family, for which the Pennsylvania legislature had already made a settlement.

The issue of confiscation posed certain larger social questions which the revolutionary ferment brought to the fore. As one American correspondent reminded Lady Juliana, any proposals in the peace negotiations to restore Loyalist estates would not apply to the proprietary lands. These were "taken from the Proprietarys," he remarked, "not in a way of confiscation, but upon principle of policy and expedience" that "no subject" should possess an estate of such extent "supposing it dangerous to the public that so much property should rest in the hands of one family." Some people may not have wanted to be reminded that the War for Independence was also a revolution, but the American commissioners never forgot it for a moment.

Emboldened by the hue and cry set off outside Parliament's walls by the printing of the preliminaries, the enemies of the administration launched a full-scale attack, with the opening volley fired off in Parliament on February 17th. The terms confirmed the Opposition's darkest suspicions that the peace negotiations had been mishandled. "The moment America was out of the question," Sir Gilbert Elliot observed, "Samson lost the lock of his strength, and the natural weakness of the Ministry appeared immediately."

The hostile or disaffected Lords, beginning with the Earl of Carlisle, whose own clumsy efforts toward conciliating

America had long ago backfired, riddled the American preliminaries. Carlisle, Walsingham, and Lord Townshend found fault with the Canadian boundary, charged that Canada was now insecure, the fur trade sacrificed, and faith broken with the Indians. Viscount Sackville insisted that "the immense district of country which supplied us with masts was gone." Considering these weaknesses, and in addition the lack of reciprocity in the fishing concession, and the threat that the yielding of St. Pierre and Miquelon to the French posed to the English fishery, Townshend found cause to remark that the Americans "had evidently been too cunning for us in the negotiation," and had been an "overmatch for Oswald," of whom Stormont spoke contemptuously as "that extraordinary geographer and politician."

The most punishing blows were dealt by two Cabinet defectors, Richmond and Keppel. The latter had quit the Ministry as soon as the preliminaries were signed while the Duke chose to stay at the Ordnance but withdrew from the Cabinet. Both now argued that the terms Shelburne obtained were unnecessarily humiliating in view of the brightened military prospects of Britain and the comparative inferiority of the French and Spanish fleets.

The bombardment against the battered Ministry continued without letup until the early hours of the eighteenth. That evening Shelburne replied, drawing upon memoranda provided by Lord Grantham and more closely upon an elaborate brief prepared by Benjamin Vaughan, who was now back in London, and apparently acting as the Earl's confidential secretary. Standing on free-trade ground, the Earl defended his sacrifices in America. Missing from the speech was some of the vision of a future reconciliation between England and America that Vaughan had caught in his correspondence with Shelburne, as well as Shelburne's own private notion that the preliminaries foreshadowed changes in imperial relations and trade policy. The House in its black mood would doubtless have rejected such prospects as totally unrealistic. The Earl assured the Loyalists of the generosity of England, while conceding that "a part must be wounded, that the whole of the Empire may not perish." Shelburne chose to make his main stand, however, on the exhausted state of the nation, the tottering of public credit, the deterioration of the navy, its ships unclean, undermanned, its naval stores exhausted, its cordage rotten, and its magazines depleted. Critics then and since have pounced on this argument as a prime specimen of Shelburne's disingenuous line, and have insisted that Shelburne did not paint a credible picture, that this puerile navy bore little resemblance to the magnificent fleet that Howe took into Gibraltar or Rodney maneuvered at the Saints. His critics notwithstanding, Shelburne had caught the popular mood of war weariness and the universal desire for a peace, however temporary it might prove. His eloquence won the day for the Address on the Peace, with a majority of thirteen in the Lords.

A very different fate awaited the Shelburne Ministry in Commons. Fox attacked the terms given France in India, Burke assailed the abandonment of the Loyalists and the surrender of the Middle West, and North denounced the cessions as "unfortunate" and "improvident." North's speech provided one hilarious moment. While he was on his feet a dog that had strayed into the House started to bark. Amid shouts of "Hear! hear!" North joined the general laughter. Addressing the chair, he remarked, "Sir, I was interrupted by a new Speaker, but as his argument is concluded, I will resume mine."

Against this strong current Shelburne's lieutenants, Tommy Townshend and young Pitt, made little headway. On the morning of February 18th an amendment proposed by Cavendish to leave out of the Address expressions that might be construed as approving the peace and to substitute a declaration to take it into consideration was carried by a vote of 224 to 208. The edifice was crumbling. How to denounce the peace while still accepting it as a necessary evil now became the chief preoccupation of Shelburne's enemies, aside from jockeying for power. On February 21st they proposed to the Commons a series of resolutions accepting the peace as necessary, approving the grant of independence to the United States as being in conformity with the wishes of Parliament, while condemning the concessions to the enemy as being greater than the comparative strength and actual situation of the belligerents warranted. Another all-night debate ensued, and the vote of censure was carried by the margin of 207–190.

The vote of censure disclosed to the diplomatic observers as well as the rest of the world the preposterous and implausible combination of opposites who had joined forces to bring down their more farsighted, if politically maladroit, rival. His scepter slipping from his grasp, Shelburne had made indirect approaches both to Lord North and to Charles James Fox. The suitor was rudely rebuffed because the objects of his sudden affection were caught up in a heady flirtation of their own. Boreas and Reynard, as Burke nicknamed the pair, united to destroy the Ministry and to set up a successor government in which they expected to divide the spoils. The first appeared easier to achieve than the second. Pitt's desperate effort to defeat the resolutions of censure had failed despite his castigation of "the unnatural coalition." "If this ill-omened marriage is not already solemnized," he warned the Commons, "I know a just and lawful impediment, and, in the name of public safety, I here forbid the banns." In disregard of this solemn interdiction the ill-mated pair entered upon their illicit union.

Two days after the vote of censure Shelburne resigned. "Whence came the idea that the moment a minister loses a question in Parliament he must be displaced?" John Jay inquired in a letter to Benjamin Vaughan. To answer would require a chapter on the rise of the notion of responsible ministries. To the formulation of that Constitutional precept Shelburne himself now made an indispensable contribution. True, young Pitt in similar circumstances followed a different course a year later, but Shelburne's seemingly impulsive action was prompted in no small part by personal pique enkindled by suspicion that he had been double-crossed by the King and let down by his own immediate followers. By no means insensitive to his personal unpopularity, the Earl was shrewd enough to realize that his talk of sweeping reforms, including trade liberalization, had badly frightened the standpatters and that his administrative economies had pinched the pocketbooks of still others. In short, if a scapegoat had to be chosen to bear the onus of a humiliating peace, the retiring First Lord of the Treasury was the ideal target.

Ironic if belated tribute to the skill with which Shelburne had negotiated the peace in his own country's best interest was grudgingly paid by the other belligerents, who proceeded to pick all sorts of flaws in the preliminaries. "The very points which are found fault with here," wrote Grantham plaintively to Sir James Harris, "are those which do not give satisfaction to France." Across the Channel the opposition faction of the Duc de Choiseul marshaled its forces to bring down the Comte de Vergennes, who was particularly excoriated for the paucity of the spoils France retrieved in India. Alarms were sounded that England, having lost America, would now undertake a vast expansion in India. France's course, then, was not to withdraw her troops and ships from that distant area, but to look upon the Indian articles as nothing more than stopgap terms. Vergennes faced additional criticism for ending the war without regaining Canada, and for not having insisted that St. Pierre and Miquelon be fortified, a step which was advised less out of fear of England than from concern over competition and encroachment upon French preserves by American fishermen.

To add to Vergennes' discomfiture, the Dutch blamed him for signing the preliminaries without looking out for their interests. Despite heavy pressure from the French, the obstinate Hollanders continued to insist on Negapatam, offering in its stead lands on the Sumatran coast, and remained adamant about conceding to the English the free navigation of Eastern waters.

The Spaniards were far more affronted by the terms of the

preliminaries than the French. Aside from their chagrin over Gibraltar, they were hardly reconciled to the American settlement made without their participation. Three issues between Spain and America still divided the parties: recognition of the United States, conceding America her Western territorial claims, and allowing her the free navigation of the Mississippi. That winter the Marquis de Lafayette was in Spain on a diplomatic mission carrying the endorsement of the American commissioners, who viewed his departure with barely concealed relief. Spain still recoiled from independence, fearful that England and America, as Goëzmann de Thurne astutely remarked, would soon stir up a revolution in her own restless dominions. Indeed, Floridablanca made no secret of his view that the independence of the United States was a "misfortune." Nevertheless, Lafayette managed to persuade that cautious and crusty diplomat to invite Carmichael to a diplomatic dinner, the first overt recognition of the new nation on Spain's part. Lafayette also wrung from Floridablanca an implied conditional recognition of the boundaries as settled between England and America in their preliminaries. "It is His Majesty's intention to abide for the present by the limits established" by the Anglo-American preliminaries, Floridablanca told the Marquis. "Yet the King intends to inform himself particularly whether it can be in any way inconvenient or prejudicial to settle that affair amicably with the United States."

The Spanish court had opened the door a crack. Once more Aranda took up with Jay the issues in dispute. Whether or not it was temperamentally impossible for the reserved American and the volatile Spaniard ever to see eye to eye, which was Montmorin's opinion, or because the differences were so fundamental, the Spanish government had second thoughts about leaving the negotiations in the Conde's hands. What is more, Spain refused to turn Natchez over to the Americans, despite the fact that this predominantly English-speaking community was located fifty miles north of the 31st parallel. Through

Vergennes Spain conducted backstage negotiations with the British to retain it. The restoration by the British of West Florida to Spain knocked the props from under the American case for the free navigation of the Mississippi to its mouth, as little support could be found in international law upholding the right of one power to navigate a river both of whose banks were held by another power. Such a rule would have permitted Spain the unhampered navigation of the Tagus to Lisbon and the subjects of Joseph II the freedom of shipping down the Scheldt to the sea. True, the Americans claimed all the rights that the British had held when West Florida was under their domain, but the French court offered them little or no encouragement. In frustration and annoyance, Jay wisely decided to put off and then to decline an invitation to return to Spain for face-to-face negotiations, and these issues remained unsettled at the peacemaking.

Seeing his negotiations with Jay founder on the rock of rival national interests, Aranda reputedly drew up at this time and submitted to his King a secret memorial pointing out the dangers that the new American nation posed to the Spanish Empire, and proposing as a counterweight to American expansion and annexation that Spain turn over all her colonies except Puerto Rico and Cuba to royal princes, exerting regal powers in their respective domains, while the Spanish King assumed the title of Emperor. The Spanish realms would be united by offensive and defensive alliances and enjoy trade reciprocity, which Aranda was prepared to open to French trade but not to the British. Much has been written about the genuineness of this memoir. It has been suggested that it was concocted years later by Manuel de Godoy, a political enemy of Aranda, in order to discredit the Conde. Incontestably, though, Aranda had already gone on record warning that the United States, though a pygmy in infancy, would some day become the colossus of the West and a formidable menace to Spain's possessions. In 1786, three years after the memoir was allegedly written, Aranda did propose to establish one infante in Spanish America, not three. Despite doubts that will not down on the legitimacy of Aranda's memorial, his sentiments on the effects of American independence were no secret from his government.

The critics of the peacemaking notwithstanding, the major architects of the preliminaries among England's foes took the news of Shelburne's fall badly. Vergennes put it to rancorous party spirit, and kept up a cordial correspondence with the Earl after he left office, as did the Abbé Morellet, much to the succeeding Ministry's annoyance. In fact, distrust of England's intentions about peace were so thick that the Marquis de Moustier, France's ambassador to the Court of St. James's, set up entirely on his own an espionage service in British ports until he was rebuked for his zeal by Vergennes. The Americans were equally uneasy now about the good faith of Parliament toward the preliminaries. Although they never really trusted Shelburne completely, they recognized him as a reformer of their own stripe. They knew that the Earl sought to reform the tax structure, get more work out of civil servants, increase and equalize Parliamentary representation, hold more frequent elections, and extend the suffrage by allowing all landowners to vote, even though he never had the strength to risk a showdown in Parliament. Vaughan was even encouraged to ask Franklin what he thought about extending the suffrage, and the old Revolutionary, though the preliminaries had not yet been signed, had no compunctions about passing on through Shelburne's intermediary the advice that Parliaments should be elected by all the people, and that the only way the lower classes would rise in England would be by elevating them in education and political responsibility.

Now that they had brought about his downfall, Shelburne's enemies, it soon became clear, were putting his peacemaking in jeopardy and scuttling the major part of his reform program, notably the liberal trade policy on which the prospects of long-range peace and prosperity heavily depended. "We have demolished the Earl of Shelburne," Edmund Burke commented following the vote of censure, "but in his fall he has pulled down a large piece of the building." Burke's partisan diagnosis would have placed the onus for the ensuing confusion upon the victim rather than the victors, but he admitted ruefully that he could not tell what direction affairs would take. "For once I confess," he conceded, giving us a glimpse of the later anti-Revolutionary Burke, "I apprehend more from the madness of the people than from any other cause."

An extraordinary interregnum, or more precisely "interministerium," of seven weeks followed Shelburne's fall, during which the peace negotiations were virtually suspended. Grantham clung to the Foreign Office as long as possible, behaving, as Shelburne remarked, like "a sick man who could not get over his illness." George III made desperate efforts to avert a North-Fox Ministry. The previous year he had actually drafted an abdication message and held his royal yacht in readiness for a fortnight. Now, sooner than yield, he would "go to Hanover," he threatened. Rather than accept a coalition including Fox, he would accept North, or Pitt, or Gower, or "Mr. Thomas Pitt or Mr. Thomas anybody." Young Pitt shrewdly declined, regarding the moment unpropitious to head a Ministry. Thurlow, Gower, and others resisted the lures of the Treasury. North refused to break with Fox, and in the end George had to swallow the bitter pill of the coalition, with the Duke of Portland as its titular head, and Charles James Fox as Foreign Secretary.

Aside from his politics, Charles James Fox had long been a thorn in the side of George III. He had deliberately cultivated the spoiled Prince of Wales and encouraged him in his willful and dissolute course. It has been remarked that the Prince had the best possible excuse for being a Whig, "for his father had ruled him exactly as he ruled the Bostonians, and with as little success." Fox, whose financial circumstances had been desperate, had recouped much of his losses at the gaming club of Brooks's. Thence, after rising fashionably late, the disheveled leader would repair with a levee of his hard-drinking, high-playing followers. Their irreverent jests about their monarch, to which the Prince contributed his share, were not confined to the club's walls, and rumor had it that George had vowed that "he would have no peace till his son and Fox were secured in the Tower." Like so many other of his threats George failed to carry this one out. On April 2nd Fox and North kissed hands as Secretaries of State, but the King remained unreconciled, making no secret of his aversion to the new Foreign Secretary in undiplomatic remarks to the French ambassador.

In the new Ministry the Duke of Portland was no more than a cipher, and Lord North interfered not at all in the business of the peacemaking, which Fox henceforth dominated. No greater contrast could be imagined between the temperate, immaculate, and even fawning Shelburne and his undisciplined but charming rival. Having gained office by forcing a vote of censure of Shelburne's preliminaries, Fox was under obligation to make good his charges that Shelburne's peace made one "sicken at its very name," because it was "more calamitous, more dreadful, more ruinous than war could possibly be."

Fox's first move was to make a clean sweep of Shelburne's plenipotentiaries and agents in Paris. David Hartley, member from Hull, long-time correspondent of Franklin, and advocate of Anglo-American reunion, replaced Oswald, although Franklin himself would have been quite "content," as he privately expressed it, "to have finished with Mr. Oswald, whom we always found very reasonable." The Duke of Manchester, the newly appointed ambassador to Paris, replaced a thoroughly disillusioned Fitzherbert as plenipotentiary to conclude peace with Holland and make definitive treaties with France and Spain, and Vergennes found the replacement "as cunning as he is weak and callous." The King was doubtless happy to see the end of Vaughan's solicitous activities in Paris, for he considered Shelburne's confidant "so void of judgment that it is fortunate he has had no business, and the sooner he returns to his family the better; indeed the fewer engines the better, and those of the most discreet kind."

Aside from bringing in new faces, Fox found the peacemaking heavy going. He was sticky, negative, obstructive, but unable to obtain radical revisions in the preliminary terms. While he conceded that public faith required that the preliminaries be ratified, he made no bones in talks with foreign diplomats of his discontent with Shelburne's achievements. To Comte d'Adhémar, who succeeded Moustier as French ambassador to London, he damned "those devils" who had made the preliminaries, denouncing Shelburne and Grantham as "pusillanimous ministers without any shred of character." Peace had been bought dearly, he complained because "those villainous persons have tied my hands in every conceivable manner." Fox held out stubbornly against giving the French exclusive fishing rights in Newfoundland, and secured from Vergennes the acceptance of the word "concurrent" instead of "exclusive." He also won such trivial concessions as the freedom of Protestants on Tobago to exercise their religion "privately." A few declarations and counterdeclarations as to commerce and India completed the settlement with the French.

Fox soon locked horns with the Spaniards over the status and geographical limits of the logwood settlements in Honduras. The logwood cutters were concerned about obtaining a large and permanent foundation for the mahogany trade and retaining all the logwood rivers formerly possessed as well as opening up fresh channels of supply. Manchester finally obtained a minor adjustment of the northern and western boundaries, but he was forced to accept Grantham's stipulation that the British abandon their settlements on the Mosquito Shore. Nothing whatever came of Fox's notion of securing some lands in northern Florida for the Georgia Loyalists to form a buffer between the Spanish and American dominions.

Against the Dutch Fox held more trumps in his hand than against the other belligerents. Nevertheless his tenacity came as a surprise to Netherlanders, who had assumed that the "man of the people" would do everything he could to support the Patriot faction in Holland, which he had earlier held in such high esteem. Turning his back on his long professed sentiments, Fox felt that he could drive a harder bargain than did Shelburne since the Dutch were in a tight corner. First of all, though, he had to get free of a trap of his own making. In the spring of 1782 he had proposed as Foreign Secretary the acceptance of Russia's offer to mediate between Great Britain and the Dutch on the basis of the Anglo-Dutch Treaty of 1674, and he had secured the Cabinet's endorsement of a proposal to recognize the principles of the Armed Neutrality. With a general peace imminent, Shelburne saw no necessity for making so lavish a concession, nor for having Russia mediate with the Netherlands.

The Dutch clung to three demands without being in a military posture to secure a single one of them. They insisted that all their captured colonies be returned, that Great Britain acknowledge the principles of the Armed Neutrality, and that the British pay damages for all captures made during the war in violation of neutral rights. They were particularly insistent on the restitution of Negapatam and on opposing the Eastern seas to the free navigation of the British. The latter concession the East India Company deemed essential if the British were to trade freely with the Spice Islands and the Moluccas. Fox appeared willing to bargain over Negapatam, proposing half jokingly that the French yield Tobago in return for the Indian post, or that the Dutch turn over Demerara in Dutch Guiana or the southern portion of Sumatra, though the last proposal was in effect vetoed by the East India Company directors. Even John Adams, staunch friend of the Dutch Patriot faction, intervened through Hartley to persuade the British to show some moderation.

Talk about equivalents dragged on. The Dutch envoys

pointed out that the constitution of their republic would not permit them to conclude a definitive treaty without first gaining the approval of the various provinces. Finally, Vergennes notified the Dutch that France was about to sign a definitive peace. Bereft of the backing of their ally, the Dutch had no course but to capitulate. The concessions England gained proved of considerable value for the future of the Empire. Negapatam gave a *point d'appui* for the British smuggling trade to the island of Ceylon, and the Dutch concession of the right to trade and navigate freely in Eastern waters opened a path for Britain's penetration in Malaysia. In substance, however, Fox did not improve upon the terms that Shelburne and Vergennes had previously agreed upon for the Dutch.

In no aspect of the peacemaking was Fox's meddling more inept and its consequences more mischievous than in his negotiations with the Americans. A leading critic of the American War from the moment news had come of the shots fired on Lexington green, Fox had earned the antipathy of the King and the North Ministry by the fervor of his advocacy of American independence. So far as the American settlement was concerned, he might have been expected to rise above personal and party rancor and to recognize that Shelburne's liberal inclinations looking toward *rapprochement* deserved hearty endorsement and implementation. Quite the contrary proved the case. Although he never challenged the grant of American independence and in any event could not take back what had already been given up, he would not budge another inch.

After the preliminaries the major outstanding issue between the Americans and the British concerned the trade settlement. Shelburne had maintained that his treaties proved that "we prefer trade to dominion," and that a peace was good "in the exact proportion that it recognizes" the principle of free trade. True, his own Cabinet had rejected the article drafted by John Jay providing for complete reciprocity between England and

America on the ground that the executive had no authority to alter the operation of the Navigation Laws. It was understood, however, that such matters would be covered by a treaty of commerce, and the preamble to the provisional articles declared the intention of putting the principle of reciprocity into effect between the two nations.

Supported by some British merchants, a small coterie of Americans in London, including Elkanah Watson and the apostate Silas Deane, whom the American commissioners shunned as a moral leper, sought to drum up sentiment for liberalizing commerce with the former colonies. Shelburne's adviser on trade, John Pownall, counseled that special legislation would be needed to carry out this principle. A bill was accordingly drafted permitting American produce for the time being to enter British ports on the same footing as though British-owned, while treating American ships carrying such produce as those of other foreign states. During this interim period the bill would have permitted American ships to carry American goods to British colonies and islands in America and to export any goods whatsoever from such British possessions. Duties and charges would in both cases be the same as for British-owned merchandise, transported by British ships and crews.

By the time the bill was introduced Shelburne was already out of office, and Pitt, still holding on as Chancellor of the Exchequer, assumed responsibility for steering the measure through the House. When the bill came up to the House on March 7th, Pitt proved a lukewarm advocate, while its opponents were thoroughly aroused. Fox advocated caution. He deemed the bill to infringe upon England's commercial treaty with Russia, which accorded that power most-favored-nation treatment. Burke compared the proposed legislation to a one-sided courtship. "Great Britain was extremely fond in her wooing, and in her love-fit was ready to give largely; whereas, to his knowledge, America had nothing to give in return."

It was William Eden, offended by Shelburne's obvious disregard, who proceeded to demolish the proposal. His arguments reflected a careful reading of a tract just published, entitled *Observations on the Commerce of the American States.* Its author, Lord Sheffield, marshaling an imposing array of statistics, argued that Americans must be treated as foreigners and not permitted to enjoy those branches of the carrying trade with the Empire in which they had previously participated, notably the trade in foodstuffs and timber with the British West Indies. Hewing to the Sheffield line, Eden attacked the bill as introducing "a total revolution in our commercial system," and warned that the Americans would monopolize the supply of provisions to the West Indies to the ruin of the provision trade of Ireland and the disadvantage of the sugar refiners of England. He painted a disturbing picture of American ships returning from British ports, their holds stuffed with tools and emigrant artificers, and he appealed to the patriotism of his listeners, arguing that by this concession England would lose her great nursery of seamen, would languish in peace and be helpless in war. The bill was sent to Committee, where it was altered beyond recognition.

With the Shelburne project moribund, the Fox-North coalition, from its inception in April, was confronted with the need to set guidelines for reopening trade with America. According to Henry Laurens, who had returned to England for his health, Fox showed "a disposition to proceed to business with us with liberality and effect," and rumors spread that not only trade reciprocity but dual citizenship was in contemplation. The coalition had accepted Eden's amendment to the Shelburne bill, vesting discretionary power in the King in Council to regulate all such matters for a limited period, in effect giving the new Ministry a free hand to work out a trade program *ad interim.* The Ministry then had no one else to blame but itself for making a shambles of its own negotiations in Paris.

When, toward the end of April, the American commissioners sat down with the bespectacled David Hartley in the latter's apartment at the Hôtel d'York they were confronted with a well-meaning liberal of unsullied probity, whom Adams in an uncharitable mood found "talkative and disputatious and not always intelligible," a negotiator apparently oblivious to the rising tide in England against trade concessions to America. The emasculation of Shelburne's trade bill notwithstanding, both sides went through the motions. The Americans carefully prepared propositions which they submitted to Hartley, and he in turn advanced counterproposals. These American propositions Hartley described as professing "one simple and invariable principle for the basis of their negotiations, viz., reciprocity; reciprocity upon any terms whatsoever, from the narrowest limits to the utmost extent of mutual intercourse and participation."

In deference to instructions from Congress to secure, if possible, the direct trade with the British West Indies the American commissioners proposed to Hartley on April 29th that the rivers, harbors, and ports of both countries, including areas under the dominion of Great Britain, be opened to the citizens of the other. Hartley "approved of it greatly," the American commissioners later reported, but he earned a stinging rebuke from his chief for his generosity. Fox insisted that Hartley had not attended to his instructions, and that only American ships laden with *American produce* be admitted to British ports. To compound Hartley's mortification, the Foreign Minister enclosed a copy of an Order in Council issued the previous day, May 14th, permitting *unmanufactured* goods of American production to be imported into England in British or American ships, but saying nothing about manufactures from the States. A shamefaced Hartley passed on this Order in Council to the Americans. As might be expected, they proceeded to denounce as discriminatory this denial on the part of Britain of the admission of American manufactures into England in American ships. In retrospect John Adams castigated the proclamation as "the first link in that great chain of Orders in Council which have been since stretched and extended, till it has shackled the commerce of the globe."

Hartley defended his position with dignity, and warned Fox that it was his "firm conviction the American principle of equal reciprocity and the restrictive principle of the British Acts of Navigation must come to issue." To reconcile the Ministry's point of view with that of the Americans he made a counterproposal on May 21st, suggesting, as a temporary expedient, that both parties return to the conditions of trade regulation existing at law before the start of the American Revolution. He would have allowed American trade with the West Indies, but confined American exports therefrom to the produce of the islands.

"Can you sign in case we agree?" the Americans asked. Hartley admitted he could not. "Then we think it improper to proceed to consider it until after you obtain the consent of your Court." Hartley argued eloquently with Fox for some affirmative action on the part of the Ministry. "As surely as the rights of mankind have been established by the American War, so surely will all the Acts of Navigation of the world perish and be buried amongst occult qualities. . . . Throw out a loose and liberal line," he urged. With Anglo-American friendship as his longer-range objective, Hartley predicted that the American States would "be the foundations of great events in the new page of life."

Fox, the fiery revolutionary, now sought to chill Hartley's liberal fervor with the reminder that "literall reciprocity is impossible as much from their engagements as from our system of navigation." The best he could do would be to permit trade between the United States and the West Indies, but he was not prepared to admit West Indian commodities brought to Great Britain in American vessels.

Hartley came up with still another compromise, one that would permit Americans to trade between the islands and

Canada, a proposition which the Americans quickly accepted. Fox let the proposal lie on his desk unanswered. Nothing came of this proposal, nor of John Jay's propositions that British subjects be barred from exporting slaves into America, "it being the intention of the said States entirely to prohibit the importation thereof," and that trade between America and Ireland be liberated from prewar restrictions.

Virtually ignored henceforth by the Ministry, Hartley, whose "zeal exceeded his authority," as the commissioners later attested, was forced to concede that "prejudices" in England were so strong that a relaxation of the Navigation Laws could never be undertaken without a full Parliamentary inquiry. Vergennes put the matter aptly when he remarked to Adams that Fox "was startled at every clamour of a few merchants." The final rebuff came on July 2nd, when an Order in Council was issued barring American ships from the West Indian trade. Its author, William Knox, a long-time public official and die-hard Tory, claimed that the order, which he had first drafted as a bill, entitled him to have engraved upon his tombstone a tribute for "having *saved the navigation of England.*" The appearance of this order "convulsed the negotiation in Paris," Hartley reported in despair. "Mr. Hartley," John Adams remarked, "is probably kept here if he was not sent at first merely to amuse us, and to keep him out of the way of embarrassing the coalition." In his chagrin Adams struck out wildly, with the French court and American apostates in England his special targets. True, the Comte de Vergennes was by no means displeased by the breakdown of the British-American trade negotiations, for he and his aides at that very moment were engaged in consultations with John Jay's contrary brother, Sir James, to promote Franco-American trade relations at Britain's expense. With quite adverse inclinations, John Jay reputedly was hostile to encouraging imports into the United States of luxury products from France. It was neither the Comte nor Sir James Jay, however, who blocked a trade agreement with England.

Rather must credit go to the forces mobilized by Sheffield & Company, a combination too awesome to be defied by their government.

If Adams was correct and the coalition had been formed at the gaming tables and conducted itself "upon no other than gambling principles," it had shown a timidity in the face of odds which one normally does not associate with gamblers. By its behavior the coalition had opened up a grievous and festering wound in Anglo-American relations. The Orders in Council, along with the demise of the Hartley negotiations, disclosed that the shooting war was to be succeeded by one of intense commercial rivalry between the belligerents. All sorts of interest groups had been marshaled to oppose Shelburne's program of trade liberalization, and although British shipping and manufacturing interests would reap a short-term harvest, the British West Indian planters, now forced to pay exorbitant prices for salt, fish, and timber from Canada and Honduras, with the cheaper supplies from New England cut off, would suffer mortal injury by this impairment of their competitive position. Fox still mumbled about a separate trade treaty with America, not "under the eye of France," but his heart was no longer in the business, if it ever really had been, and time was running out for him. The following year, when the irrepressible Hartley was in Paris to exchange ratifications of the peace treaty, he once more put out feelers to the Americans for a commercial convention. Pitt's youthful Foreign Secretary, the Marquess of Carmarthen, peremptorily ordered him home. In turning his back upon Shelburne's liberal trade principles, Pitt, the Earl's protégé, also chose to swim with the tide, and to uphold rivalry and exclusion in the place of cooperation and the prospect of federal union.

Aside from the issues of trade, all the belligerents, even the reluctant Dutch, had virtually come to terms. On August 8th the plenipotentiaries of the belligerent powers, excepting the United States, whose envoys expressed no desire to be present, assembled at the home of Mercy d'Argenteau to learn the proposed final terms of peace. To the chagrin of the titular mediators a trivial if dignified role had been assigned them by Vergennes. The Comte had made no secret to the other belligerents of his wish that the treaties be settled by the parties themselves, a wish that Fox fully shared. The latter's fears that the mediators might try to introduce the new maritime code into the body of the definitive treaties seemed well founded, for the mediators made motions to that end. Vergennes stopped them in their tracks. Despite his lip-service dedication to the cause of neutral rights, he now made it clear that he did not want to embarrass England when the moment of reconciliation between the two nations seemed at hand. Fox hastened to make a parallel response to the mediators. As for the American treaty, the British made it known that they did not wish mediators to interfere in their private concerns, while the Americans, having lost none of their suspicions of the mediators, told Hartley that they preferred to conclude without them, a preference implicitly endorsed by Vergennes himself.

On August 16th Franklin reported to Vergennes that the British Ministry, not agreeing to any propositions made "either by us or by their Minister here," had instead sent over a plan for a definitive treaty, which consisted merely of the preliminaries formerly signed, along with short introductory and concluding paragraphs, confirming and putting into effect the preliminary articles. "My colleagues seem inclined to sign this with Mr. Hartley, and so to finish the affair," he added.

As the great moment drew near the British plenipotentiaries asked for instructions on the presents to be made to the ministers of the different nations participating in the signing in accordance with custom. Fox asked the King, and George, with little enthusiasm, replied, "Give whatever the French do." "This will do very well with regard to the mediators," Fox informed Manchester, "but what are we to do with the four Americans?" It was customary to give diamond-encased portraits of the monarch in whose name the present was made, but Fox thought that the Americans would prefer money to pictures. He was hardly so rash as to presume that they would be flattered with a jeweled portrait of George III, whose rule they had foresworn. Perhaps a thousand pounds apiece, he suggested, would be "thought a great deal," an amount which Manchester and Hartley deemed "very handsome and satisfactory." Hartley made a point of mentioning this to Franklin, but neither the doctor nor his colleagues made an entry of any such transaction. Since it was the season for gifts, the Abbé Morellet was rewarded by Vergennes at Shelburne's prompting with a handsome pension, a beneficence which did not sit well with Fox. One other conciliatory gesture was made toward the Americans, this time by their implacable adversary, Charles III of Spain. Ten days before the final signings Carmichael was presented to the King and royal family at San Ildefonso in his capacity of chargé d'affaires of the United States.

Almost until the moment of signing, as delay followed delay, mutual suspicions festered. Then an element of tragic mystery intruded itself into the final preparations. In an especially peevish mood, George III let it be known that he was discontented with the pace which the Duke of Manchester had set in Paris and took special exception to the Duke's secretary, Maddison. On the eve of the signing, Maddison was taken violently ill and died of poisoning within two days. Whether the secretary had taken his own life in a mood of despondency or was the victim of foul play, his death added a macabre note to the closing rites that ended the war.

The date for those closing rites was finally set. Word came to Franklin from Vergennes on August 29th. The Comte, so Rayneval informed the doctor, "has directed me to say that nothing ought to prevent your signing at Paris on Wednesday next, the day proposed for the signature of the other treaties." Rayneval requested that the signing with Hartley take place at nine o'clock in the morning so as to give time for a courier to be dispatched to Versailles with word of the event, as the

Comte was "desirous of being informed of the completion of your labors at the same time with his own."

On the morning of September 3rd, after some last-minute consultations in anticipation of another hitch, the Americans at Hartley's invitation repaired to the British commissioner's lodgings at the Hôtel d'York. That edifice, standing in one of the most crowded streets in the Quartier Latin, close by the venerable Hôpital de la Charité (since demolished to make way for a big white medical school building), no longer serves as a residential hotel, but houses the publishing firm of Firmin Didot. It would be another six years before Louis Jacques Daguerre would make his bow on the world stage, and in the absence of on-the-spot photography we must accept a witness secondhand to the event, Benjamin West's celebrated painting of the signing. This renowned canvas perpetuates an historical image which is incorrect in two particulars. It includes Henry Laurens among the American signers, along with Jay, Franklin, Adams, and the secretary to the American delegation, William Temple Franklin. Laurens was actually in England at the time, and Franklin's grandson was not accorded the honor of attesting the final signings. The artist had in fact sketched in the cast of characters who participated in the preliminaries, hoping that his commemorative painting would not need to be altered, but he left a large blank space on the right-hand side of the canvas to paint in either Richard Oswald and Caleb Whitefoord, or, if he had chosen to update it, David Hartley. Blind of one eye and conscious of his rather repelling physiognomy, Oswald was notoriously shy about sitting for any portraits, and declined on this occasion. For West to have painted in David Hartley instead would have involved re-doing the left side of the canvas. The bespectacled Hartley did pose, however, for Romney, who painted him seated before a copy of the treaty. Indeed, it was perhaps fitting that West's painting was never finished, because, for the Americans, the definitive signing was anticlimactic.

That same afternoon the Duke of Manchester signed the

treaties with France and Spain at Versailles. Separate declarations certifying the role of the mediators were affixed to both the French and Spanish treaties and signed by Comte Mercy for Joseph II, and by Bariatinski and Markov for Catherine. Everything was done with dispatch. The last signature was affixed by three that afternoon. The previous day in Paris Manchester had signed the preliminaries with the Dutch, who begged off signing definitively.

On the very evening of the signing of the definitive treaties a company of Americans, including Matthew Ridley and Thomas Barclay, a Philadelphia merchant and American Consul General in France, sat down to dinner with Lafayette and the Marquis de Castries at Versailles. Conversation turned on future trade relations between the two countries. The Americans were shocked to hear the Minister of Marine remark, apropos of the French West Indies, "Our colonies are our slaves, the greater part of which would have to be destroyed." To the court circle at Versailles the official ending of this world war brought not even a glimmer of the new era in the relations of colonies and metropolis which the War of the American Revolution had inaugurated.

To the delays which had put off the signing and to the event itself George III, who had lost an empire, professed equal indifference. Contrariwise, the Comte de Vergennes did not conceal his relief and gratification. His strength sapped by the protracted negotiations, his nerves strained by Cabinet intrigues behind his back by traditional foes joined by the Queen herself, he avowed to Montmorin, "The end was for so long a time the unique object of my solicitude."

But this was not the end of it. Despite the signings, the insistent question remained unanswered: Would there be peace? Idealists like David Hartley envisioned "the fairest prospects," "reciprocal advantage," and a joining of hearts and hands by Britons and Americans "in one common cause for the reunion of all our ancient affections and common interests." More realistic statesmen, thinking of the shorter term, were far less confident, for both in the Old World and the New there was ground for concern about the shape of things to come.

For Further Reading

Samuel Flagg Bemis, *The Diplomacy of the American Revolution* (1935) is the standard general treatment of its subject, but revealing too is Richard W. Alstyne, *Empire and Independence: The International History of the American Revolution* (1965). Important aspects of diplomatic history are treated in Edward S. Corwin, *French Policy and the American Alliance of 1778* (1916), Gerald Stourzh, *Benjamin Franklin and American Foreign Policy* (1954), and Isabel de Maderiaza, *Britain, Russia, and the Armed Neutrality of 1780* (1962).

There are several modern surveys of the military history of the War for Independence; perhaps the best brief study is Willard M. Wallace, *Appeal to Arms* (1951). Also recommended are John C. Miller, *Triumph of Freedom, 1775–1783* (1948); Piers Mackesy, *The War for America, 1775–1783* (1964), written from the British perspective; Howard H. Peckham, *War for Independence* (1958), and George F. Scheer and Hugh F. Rankin, *Rebels and Redcoats* (1957), which is heavily interlaced with extracts from eyewitness accounts. John R. Alden's *American Revolution* (1954) gives considerable attention to non-military aspects of the war, as does his larger and more recent *History of the American Revolution* (1969), which includes the prewar and the Confederation periods as well as the war years.

The contributions of the military leaders on both sides can most easily be understood through two collections of essays edited by George Athan Billias: *George Washington's Generals* (1964), and *George Washington's Opponents* (1969). Book-length biographies that stress their subject's role in the war are volumes three through five of Douglas S. Freeman's

George Washington (7 vols., 1948–1957); Esmond Wright, *George Washington and the American Revolution* (1957); James Thomas Flexner, *George Washington in the American Revolution* (1968); Bernard Knollenberg, *Washington and the Revolution* (1940); Theodore Thayer, *Nathanael Greene: Strategist of the American Revolution* (1960); Don Higginbotham, *Daniel Morgan: Revolutionary Rifleman* (1961); North Callahan, *Henry Knox, Washington's General* (1958); Charles P. Whittemore, *A General of the Revolution: John Sullivan of New Hampshire* (1961), and Samuel E. Morison, *John Paul Jones* (1959). And on the British side: William B. Willcox, *Portrait of a General: Sir Henry Clinton . . .* (1964), and Troyer S. Anderson, *The Command of the Howe Brothers During the American Revolution* (1935). For the life of the general who fought on both sides, see Willard M. Wallace, *Traitorous Hero* (1954), and James T. Flexner, *The Traitor and the Spy* (1953).

Long neglected by historians, the loyalists have recently come in for a good deal of attention. Supplementing the earlier study by Claude H. Van Tyne, *The Loyalists in the American Revolution* (1902), are William H. Nelson, *The American Tory* (1961); Paul H. Smith, *Loyalists and Redcoats* (1964); Wallace Brown, *The King's Friends* (1966), and North Callahan, *The Tories of the American Revolution* (2 vols., 1963, 1967).

Other special topics are well covered in Benjamin Quarles, *The Negro in the American Revolution* (1961); Allan Nevins, *The American States During and After the Revolution* (1924); Carl Van Doren, *Mutiny in January . . .* (1943), and J. Franklin Jameson, *The American Revolution Considered as a Social Movement* (1926).

A useful reference book on the Revolution is Mark M. Boatner, *Encyclopedia of the American Revolution* (1966). Richard B. Morris and Henry Steele Commager, eds., *The Spirit of Seventy-Six* (2 vols., 1958), is the outstanding anthology of primary sources.

The Constitution as an Economic Document

Robert E. Brown

The Constitution of the United States remains, after a century and three-quarters, much the same as it emerged from Convention Hall. Only twenty-five amendments have been added—most of which clarify rather than alter the intentions of the Founding Fathers—so that the fundamental law of the land remains a product of the eighteenth century. The Constitution's historical origins are therefore of more than academic interest. How one interprets the momentous process of drafting and ratifying the Constitution determines, and is determined by, one's concept of the very meaning of America.

Over the years two broad and conflicting views have been developed. On the one hand, historians like George Bancroft and John Fiske followed the lead provided by the Constitution's adherents in 1787–1789: the new form of government established by the famous

Source: Robert E. Brown, *Charles Beard and the Constitution: A Critical Analysis of "An Economic Interpretation of the Constitution"* (Princeton, N.J.: Princeton University Press, 1956), pp. 92–111. Reprinted by permission of Princeton University Press.

document was essential for the preservation of national independence, personal liberty, and private property—goals fought for during the American Revolution. According to the authors of the Federalist Papers and to the later "nationalist" historians, the time of chaos and weak central government following the Revolution, the so-called Critical Period, made necessary the changes brought forward in 1787. The Constitution was therefore a political act by selflessly patriotic men.

On the other hand, some historians have challenged this view of the Constitution. Instead they see the Constitution as a counterrevolution, a reaction against, not a continuation of, the earlier Revolution movement. More often than not, historians of this school look for economic causation, with emphasis on the private interests of the Founding Fathers.

The leading historian of this second school was Charles Austin Beard (1874–1948). More than a half century ago Beard wrote *An Economic Interpretation of the Constitution of the United States* (1913). At the time most critics either hailed the book as a perceptive and realistic appraisal of the forces that produced the Constitution or condemned his venture as perverse and unpatriotic. Today the work still provokes strong feelings, and historians and political scientists find it difficult to discuss the Constitution without first dealing with the Beardian interpretation.

What did Beard say? Simply that previous commentators had overlooked the importance of economic motives in the drafting and ratifying of the great charter in 1787–1789. Hitherto, he averred, historians had concentrated on the drafters' political theory and rhetoric. All very well and good; yet surely other considerations animated supporters of the Constitution. To Beard, writing in an era of considerable labor and agrarian unrest, it seemed inconceivable that economic self-interest—an integral part of most human motivation, as James Madison had pointed out in the Federalist Papers—had been ignored while the Constitution was being formed. Beard argued that the movement for the Constitution in 1787 was generated by a small and active group of men who represented "personality" (that is, non-landed property) interests. He concluded that the delegates to the Constitutional Convention were chosen undemocratically as were those who participated in the various state ratifying conventions. These delegates represented the minority personalty interests. The resultant document itself was economic in nature, designed to protect the interests of those who drafted it. "The whole people" did not create the Constitution, nor did abstract political principles of patriotism or nationalism play the most important energizing roles. Economic self-interest, Beard proposed, was the key.

These overall conclusions had the merit of simplicity and force. Certainly they were persuasive to a generation of historians. Such prominent scholars as Vernon Louis Parrington, Robert Livingston Schuyler, and Arthur Meier Schlesinger, Sr., in large measure endorsed Beard's views, as did a majority of the authors of American history college textbooks.

These scholars accepted Beard's interpretation on far more firm a basis than its rhetorical strength. Much of what Beard said, after all, had been said earlier by others. Beard's research techniques and the method he used in presenting his evidence, however, were "revolutionary." He used the then relatively unexplored records of the Treasury Department to determine the security holdings of the Constitution's drafters. Using this information as his primary data, Beard then constructed a brief economic biography for each of the Constitutional Convention's delegates. In a long and apparently objective chapter Beard presented these case histories to his readers, ending his account with a summary that tallied the socioeconomic characteristics shared by the delegates, a summary that seemed to prove his thesis of economic motivation.

Beard's "scientific" method and unimpassioned presentation of his evidence long went unchallenged. The first major book-length criticism of Beard's thesis did not appear until 1956, forty-three years after publication of *An Economic Interpretation.* But in the past decade other scholars have joined the attack. Their criticisms are varied and telling: Beard exaggerated the importance of James Madison's *Federalist* No. 10; he selected his data to support his contention, suppressing or ignoring contrary evidence; he misunderstood the difference between economic "interpretation" and "determinism"; he "proved" his thesis of economic motivation in 1787 in part by using evidence, such as the list of security holders, that postdated the historical events of drafting and ratification, and he assumed that which he was to have proved.

The flaws in Beard's thesis cannot be overlooked, although many scholars still accept his basic contention. Robert E. Brown, a leading interpreter of democratic practices in early America, indicates in the following selection some of the flaws in Beard's approach and conclusions.

The Constitution as an Economic Document

*H*aving proved to his own satisfaction that the delegates to the Convention were the representatives of personalty, Beard then went on to show that the Constitution was fundamentally an economic rather than a political document, designed above all else to protect personalty from the leveling attacks of democracy. The true nature of the Constitution is not apparent on the surface, he said, for it contains no property qualifications for voting and does not outwardly recognize economic groups or confer special class privileges. Only if we study the newspapers and correspondence of the time, or read *The Federalist* or the debates in the Convention, do we begin to understand the true nature of the Constitution. Our understanding is broadened by a study of such items as the structure of government or the balance of power, powers conferred on the federal government and denied the state governments, and the economics of international politics. These will convince us, said Beard, that the Constitution was not a piece of abstract legislation reflecting no group interests or economic antagonisms. It was "an economic document drawn with superb skill by men whose property interests were immediately at stake; and as such it appealed directly and unerringly to identical interests in the country at large" (p. 188).

We have already had occasion to note Beard's questionable use of Madison and *The Federalist* No. 10, but we need to examine more fully his interpretation of *The Federalist* in this chapter because he relied much on this source for his interpretation. Here, declared Beard, is presented in relatively brief and systematic form an economic interpretation of the Constitution by the men best qualified to expound the political science of the new government. In fact, he said, *The Federalist* was "the finest study in the economic interpretation of politics which exists in any language." When we combine this with his previous opinion that Madison's political philosophy in No. 10 was "a masterly statement of the theory of economic determinism in politics" (p. 15), we begin to appreciate Beard's concept of the importance of *The Federalist.*

The first question to be answered then is whether *The Federalist* presents merely an "economic interpretation of politics." Can Jay's arguments on the need for a stronger union as protection from foreign enemies, presented in Nos. 2 to 5, be considered strictly economic? Was the danger of civil war between the states, as expounded by Hamilton, all due to economic causes? Is an appeal for the preservation of liberty and justice simply an appeal to man's economic instincts? Were all the criticisms of the Confederation and all the attempts to allay fears about the form and powers of the new government or freedom of the press purely economic?

My answer to these questions is no, and I have little doubt

that anyone who reads *The Federalist* without a propensity for the economic interpretation of history would find many noneconomic arguments in this document. This is not to deny that Hamilton, Madison, and Jay appealed to economic interests. On the contrary, there were many such appeals, as there naturally would be to a people the vast majority of whom were middle-class property owners. But nationalism and the fear of foreign domination can have a much broader appeal than merely the economic, and especially to a people who have just emerged from under British imperialism. We know there are people who have some concern over whether or not they have a voice in the selection of their governors, a matter certainly connected with the form of government. There have been studies showing that laboring men support their unions not merely because the unions work for better wages and hours, but also because they help to give the worker status as a human being. How much simpler life would be if people did operate strictly from economic motives.

But even if we granted that *The Federalist* appealed only to the economic man, which, of course, we do not, this still would not support the Beard thesis that *personal* property was responsible for the Constitution. If he had said that Hamilton, Madison, and Jay based their appeal on the protection of *property in general,* Beard would have been correct as far as he went. There are appeals to economic interests, *all kinds* of economic interests—merchants, farmers, moneylenders, land speculators, artisans, everybody. Hamilton, Madison, and Jay were astute politicians. They knew then, just as politicians know now, that a winning combination under popular government must appeal to many groups and many interests. They were too astute to think that the Constitution could be adopted by an appeal to only 3.7 per cent of the country's property, even if the appeal had been all economic. But as I have said before, why would farmers not be interested in expanded markets for their products, or in a government that could open western lands for settlement and the Mississippi as an outlet for western products? And why would artisans and mechanics not vote for a government that would protect them from foreign competition? But all this is not to say that *The Federalist* appealed only to economic instincts, and especially that it appealed only to personalty interests.

Then we return again to Beard's version of Madison's political philosophy in *The Federalist* No. 10 as the underlying political science of the Constitution. Madison *did say* that the most important function of government was to protect the diversity in the faculties of men, from which the rights of property originate, but he *did not say,* as the Beard thesis does, that the only property to be protected was personal property. Madison divided society both horizontally into those with and without property and vertically into various kinds of property interests, such as a landed interest, a moneyed interest, a manufacturing interest, a mercantile interest, and many others. In other words, he assumed not that these personalty interests would combine against agriculture, but that each had its own objectives and must be protected from the predatory actions of the others. This ability to ignore the influence of the landed interest and what it wanted by way of property protection was one of Beard's greatest failures. Furthermore, Madison was talking about the future, when there would be a landless proletariat; not about 1787, when the small farmers dominated the country.

A second point about Madison, as I have said before, is that he was not an economic determinist in *The Federalist* No. 10. He believed that there were many reasons for conflicts in society—religious differences, attachments to different leaders and different political ideas, and even frivolous contentions —and that the purpose of government was to control all these conflicting groups, whether religious, political, economic, or other. If this had not been true, Madison should have remained a Federalist rather than becoming a Republican.

In the light of Beard's emphasis on *The Federalist* No. 10, it is of some consequence to see what Madison believed as revealed by his statements in the Constitutional Convention and elsewhere. On occasion he talked of horizontal divisions in society—creditor vs. debtor, rich vs. poor—but in the same breath he included other divisions—followers of different demagogues and different religions, as well as landed, mercantile, manufacturing, and moneyed interests. Especially he said the landed interest oppressed the mercantile interest, and holders of one species of property oppressed holders of other species. In speaking of the rich and poor, however, he said he was talking about a future day when American society would resemble that of Europe, not about society as it existed in 1787. In fact, he claimed that the divisions in American society in 1787 were vertical rather than horizontal. The country was divided into three classes, the landed, commercial, and manufacturing, he said, with the latter two being very small compared with the landed interest. Farmers had more in common with each other, regardless of where they lived in the country, than they did with merchants or manufacturers, even if the latter were the farmer's neighbors. Each group had its rights, and the interests of one should not be sacrificed to the interests of another. Or again he declared that the landed interest was predominant, and should retain the power to check other groups when in the future America resembled Europe and had a propertyless laboring class. This does not look like special consideration for personalty.

Sometimes Madison talked in terms of regional or sectional conflicts, in which apparently he thought that the various interests of one section combined to oppose similar interests in another section. He spoke of the division of eastern, middle, and southern states, or of commercial and noncommercial states. He even believed that people would have attachments to their states, and that therefore there was a conflict of interests between large and small states. But then he contradicted himself by saying that states had different manners, habits, and prejudices (all of which might be noneconomic), which prevented the combination of large states such as Massachusetts, Pennsylvania, and Virginia. In short, Madison included many of the ideas found in *The Federalist*—all eighty-five numbers of it.

Having enumerated all these divisions in society, Madison finally got around to what he considered the most fundamental of all—and the one which actually proved to be the most fundamental. This was the division between slave and free states, between North and South. He contended that the states were divided in interests depending on whether or not they had slaves. The North against the South formed the great division in the United States, he said, and the great danger to the general government was this opposition of great northern and southern interests, as the sectional voting in Congress had demonstrated. Later he declared that he had always conceived the great difference of interests in the United States to be between the two sections. And finally he went so far as to say that it was pretty well understood in the Convention that the real difference of interests lay not between large and small states but between northern and southern, with the institution of slavery and its consequences forming the line of demarcation.

So we can use Madison to prove many things, in addition to what Beard said he proved. Given the Civil War, it would be better to use him as a basis for a political philosophy of sectionalism rather than economic class determinism.

Even if Beard had used No. 10 accurately, he would still have had to show that it was more important to the people at the time than the other eighty-four numbers of *The Federalist*. Perhaps some of the farmers actually believed that a stronger government would benefit them, as *The Federalist* suggested, by opening up western lands for settlement and by expanding the market for farm products. Perhaps the artisans and mechanics believed that a stronger government would protect the sale of their products by use of a tariff as they had asked in their petitions and as *The Federalist* promised would happen. The fact is that most of the people must have believed some of these arguments, for most of them had the vote, and we can assume that they did not vote for a government which would promote only the interests of personalty.

It follows from what has been said, then, that the balance of powers, or checks and balances, in the Constitution were not there for the reasons attributed by Beard. The Beard thesis follows the line that personalty was under attack and that it designed a system of checks and balances by which the majority, presumably including the propertyless, the debtors, and those with very little property, could not override the rights of the minority—"which minority is of course composed of those who possess property that may be attacked" (p. 160). The way to insure the rights of this minority, said Beard, was to have a government in which the different interests could check each other and thus head off any pernicious attacks. The House of Representatives, he continued, came from those people who were enfranchised, which did not include the disfranchised "mass of men"; the Senate was elected by state legislatures which were themselves based on property qualifications; and the president was to be chosen by electors, which would make him one step removed from the electorate. Different terms of office for each would make a complete overturn in the government impossible at any given time. Then the keystone of the whole structure was a Supreme Court which was not elected, which held office during good behavior rather than at pleasure, and which had the final power of checking the other branches of the government by declaring laws unconstitutional.

If the class structure was not what Beard said it was, the corollary follows that checks and balances were likewise not as he pictured them. As I have already demonstrated, men in the Convention believed that there were all sorts of interests in the country, horizontal class interests, vertical property groups, states' rights, slave and free interests, and many others. Of course it is true that checks and balances were designed to allow these different interests to restrain each other. But we must remember that as recent colonists, the people in 1787 had experienced a system of government in which they did not have sufficient constitutional checks and balances. Even Jefferson believed that the main fault in the Virginia constitution was its failure to provide checks to a legislative tyranny by pitting different interests against each other. As for the Senate's being elected by state legislatures, we must remember that one of the big issues in the Convention was whether the government was to be national or federal, and those who advocated a federal government insisted that the Senate be elected by state legislatures to protect state interests. So while some looked on the Senate as a safeguard for property, others looked on it as the branch which would represent the states. Again, as I have said, some men did not think the people would accept a national government by giving up equal rights for states in the Senate.

That the judiciary, as a "check," was appointed during good behavior is not unusual. In fact, the very reverse is true, if we assume, as I do, that the Revolution was designed primarily to keep the prevailing social order rather than to change it. The colonies and states had long been accustomed to appointed judges. Furthermore, one of their strongest complaints against the British had come after 1760 when the British attempted to appoint judges during pleasure rather than during good behavior. The colonists had protested that their lives and property would not be safe in the hands of a judge who could be removed at the pleasure of the king.

And finally, the authors of *The Federalist* were not simply justifying checks and balances. What they had to do was to assure the people that the Constitution really provided for checks and balances, for its critics claimed that it did not do this. In fact, *The Federalist* pointed out that the Constitution had the same system of checks and balances that the state constitutions had, especially that of New York, which had one of the better systems of checks. One of the complaints of the colonists had been that they did not have checks on the

British government, so checks and balances were nothing new.

A few quotations from the *Records* of the Convention will demonstrate what the members themselves thought of checks and balances. Madison said, as we have seen, that the landed interest dominated at the time; but in the future, when America resembled Europe, the landed interest would be outnumbered and it should have the power to check other interests. The North Carolina delegates believed that the Constitution was devised in such a way to protect the interests of North Carolina's citizens. Gerry agreed with Madison that the majority would violate justice if they had an interest in doing so, but he did not think there was any temptation for this in America because of cheap land. Charles Pinckney thought there were three groups, landed, professional, and commercial, that they were mutually dependent on each other, and really had only one great interest in common. All that was needed, therefore, was to distribute powers of government in such a way as to provide a degree of permanency to the government —i.e., by checks and balances. Gerry said the people had two great interests—land and commerce (including stockholders). Since the people were chiefly composed of the landed interest, to draw both House and Senate from the people would not provide security for commerce. Wilson answered that the election of the Senate by state legislatures would not reduce the power of the landed interest, for landed interests controlled state legislatures and there was no reason to suppose that they would choose someone different for the Senate. Mason believed the purpose of the Convention was to devise a system that would obtain and preserve the protection, safety, and happiness of the people, and even Hamilton said the great question was the kind of government which would be best for the happiness of the country. King gave personal protection and security of property as one great object of government, while Hamilton said there were three concerns of government—agriculture, commerce, and revenue. There must be equality in the Senate to protect the small states, said

Sherman, for states, like individuals, had their peculiar habits and usages. Madison even proposed a check and balance system between slave and free states, for he considered the conflict between them to be the main conflict in American society. "I do not, gentlemen, trust you," declared Bedford, and he went on to say that any group with power would probably abuse it, and that the small states must be protected from the large.

So there were many views of society expressed in the Convention and many reasons given for checks and balances besides the protection of property and especially personal property. We cannot simply take one delegate's view, and only one of his many opinions, and say "This represents the thinking of the Convention," as Beard did.

After disposing of these elements of the check and balance system, Beard went on to give the reasons why another check on democracy, property qualifications for voting and office-holding, was omitted from the Constitution. Again the reason was economic, not political, and Beard's argument runs as follows: The personalty interests represented in the Convention could not see any "safeguard at all in a freehold qualification against the assaults on vested personalty rights which had been made by the agrarians in every state." On the other hand, they could not have gotten a personalty qualification written into the Constitution even if they had desired. The reason: "there would have been no chance of securing a ratification of the Constitution at the hands of legislatures chosen by freeholders, or at the hands of conventions selected by them" (p. 166). Distrusting the freeholders and unable to get the kind of voting qualifications they wanted, these personalty interests preferred to omit all property qualifications from the Constitution. Beard hastened to add, however, that there was really "little risk to personalty" in leaving the question of voting qualifications to the states, for there were other checks in the Constitution itself and most of the states already had voting qualifications (p. 168). Thus is the omission of property qualifications from the Constitution explained in terms of personalty interests.

The argument sounds plausible, so let us examine the evidence that Beard used to prove it, as well as some of the evidence in the *Records* that he might have used.

It is quite true, as Beard said, that Madison believed a small quantity of land as a qualification would be no security and a large quantity would exclude the representatives of those who were not landowners. But what else did Madison say about the franchise? He said "it was politic as well as just that the interests & rights of every class should be duly represented & understood in the public Councils. It was a provision everywhere established that the Country should be divided into districts & representatives taken from each, in order that the Legislative Assembly might equally understand & sympathise, with the rights of the people in every part of the Community. It was not less proper that every class of Citizens should have an opportunity of making their rights be felt & understood in the public Councils." These classes he defined as "the landed, the commercial, & the manufacturing," and he wished that some qualification besides land could be devised to protect the interests of the last two. But he did not say that commercial and manufacturing interests were to be protected at the expense of landed interests. As I have said before, he also wanted to make sure that the landholders were able to protect their interests in the future when there would be a majority without land. In short, it was both politic and just for all groups to have a voice in government—which is not economic determinism, and especially economic determinism with a personalty flavor.

Later Madison elaborated even more fully on his views of the suffrage, again without supporting the Beard generalization. He said the right to vote was fundamental in a republican constitution. If this right were confined to property, persons would be oppressed, and if it were confined to persons, property would be oppressed. Both property and personal rights must be protected. Limiting the vote to freeholders would violate the vital principle of free government that those bound by laws should help make them. Madison even came to the conclusion, which is certainly not the result of an economic interpretation, that if the choice ever came between universal suffrage and limitation of voting to people with property, the decision would have to be for universal suffrage at the expense of property. But, he continued, the United States had a precious advantage in the actual distribution of property, especially land, and in the universal hope of acquiring property, for this created much sympathy in the country for property. This, it seems to me, comes dangerously close to a political philosophy based on such old-fashioned principles as justice and right.

From the standpoint of historical method, Beard's generalization that "the other members also knew that they had most to fear from the very electors who would be enfranchised under a slight freehold restriction" (p. 165) and his citation of the *Records,* II, 201ff. for his reference constitute a misuse of evidence. If we turn to those pages of the *Records,* what do we find? Gouverneur Morris wanted to "restrain the right of suffrage to freeholders," who would approve the restriction because nine-tenths of the people were freeholders. Merchant Fitzsimons seconded his motion. Wilson did not want any qualifications in the Constitution because it would be difficult to make a uniform rule for all the states, the Convention should avoid innovations, and it would be hard and disagreeable for persons who could vote for state legislators to be excluded from voting for the national legislature. Ellsworth favored the qualifications as they were in the states, for the people would not adopt the Constitution if it disfranchised them. Mason agreed. Eight or nine states allowed others besides freeholders to vote, and what would these people say if they were disfranchised? Butler agreed with Ellsworth and Mason that both freeholders and nonfreeholders should vote, but Dickinson wanted a restriction to freeholders "as the best guardians of liberty." Ellsworth then declared that every man who paid a tax should vote for the representatives who were to levy taxes, and this would certainly mean freeholders. Then Mason went beyond his original position and declared that not only should freeholders and other property owners have the vote, but also "every man having evidence of attachment to & permanent common interest with the Society ought to share in all its rights & privileges." The electorate would not be restricted to freeholders or owners of other kinds of property but would include the parents of children, who obviously had a stake in society. Mason was really trying to break down the accepted idea that *only* freeholders could be trusted with the vote. Even Madison, Beard's great foundation stone for his personalty interpretation, said that "the freeholders of the Country would be the safest depositories of Republican liberty," and he implied that he would favor a restriction of the suffrage if he were sure that such a change would be accepted in those states "where the right was now exercised by every description of people." To cite this evidence as proof that the Convention delegates feared the enfranchised small freeholders is gross misrepresentation.

The same misrepresentation carries over into Beard's citation of a part of Gorham's statement (p. 165) to bolster his own generalization that the delegates feared the freeholder vote. Gorham *did not* say that he feared the vote of freeholders. What he was doing was attempting to head off the move by some of the delegates to restrict voting to freeholders because they thought freeholders were really the only ones to be trusted with the vote. To counteract this argument, Gorham said he had never seen any inconvenience from allowing nonfreeholders to vote, a practice long tried in this country. He cited the elections in Philadelphia, New York, and Boston, where merchants and mechanics voted, to show that these nonfreeholders were just as capable of making good choices in elections as were the freeholders. Nowhere did Gorham say or imply that he feared the freeholders as voters.

Whether the historical method permits such a use of evidence is something that each reader must decide for himself. But if it does, the time has come for us to redefine it.

Numerous other statements made in the Convention emphasize the absurdity of attributing the absence of property qualifications in the Constitution to personalty influences. George Mason proposed a landed qualification for members of Congress and exclusion from Congress of anyone having unsettled accounts with the United States. Gouverneur Morris called this a scheme of the landed against the moneyed interest, and maybe it was. But we must remember that Morris was one of the most vocal advocates of the freehold qualification for voters, which could also be a scheme of the landed against the moneyed interest. John Dickinson, another proponent of the freehold qualification, sided with Morris against Mason. On the other hand Gerry, one of the few real representatives of personalty, was ready not only to support Mason's motion requiring land as a qualification, but to go much further than Mason. The delegates simply were not consistent, for if Morris and Dickinson favored personalty, as Beard claimed, they should have championed a personalty instead of a freehold qualification for voting, and security holder Gerry should never have backed Mason.

If the omission of property qualifications from the Constitution was not due to the delegates' fear of freeholders and their inability to get the kind of qualifications they wanted, what is the explanation?

John Dickinson offered two reasons, one based on interest, one based on principle. He was against "any recital of qualifications [for office] in the Constitution. . . . The best defense lay in the freeholders who were to elect the Legislature. . . . He doubted the policy of interweaving into a Republican constitution a veneration for wealth. He had always understood that a veneration for poverty & virtue, were the objects of republican encouragement. It seemed improper that any man of merit should be subjected to disabilities in a Republic where merit was understood to form the great title to public trust, honors & rewards."

Like Madison, even Dickinson could talk in terms of "principles" rather than economic interest, though he certainly did not ignore the latter. Of course, if one argued that the delegates had tongue in cheek when they talked principles, but really meant what they said when they discussed economic interests, we would still need the evidence under the historical method.

As a matter of fact, the two reasons for the exclusion of property qualifications from the Constitution were political, not economic, and they are not difficult to find in the *Records*.

One reason was that there were different qualifications in effect in different states and the delegates simply could not agree on a uniform qualification that would be satisfactory to all. Some wanted a freehold, others wanted to include any property, and a few would eliminate practically all qualifications. There was no great opposition to property qualifications for voting either in the Convention or in the country at large, for as Dickinson and Morris said, nine-tenths of the people were freeholders and would be pleased if voting were restricted to freeholders. But while most of the delegates favored a voting qualification, they could not agree on what that qualification should be. Ellsworth explained the situation as follows: "The different circumstances of different parts of the U.S. . . . render it improper to have either uniform or fixed qualifications." Wilson said it "was difficult to form any uniform rule of qualifications for all the states," and Rutledge said the committee considering the matter had omitted qualifications "because they could not agree on any among themselves."

The second reason for omitting property qualifications from the Constitution was also political—the delegates were simply afraid that any innovations on this point might result in the rejection of the Constitution. Wilson wanted to avoid "unnecessary innovations," while Ellsworth thought the prevailing state qualifications were sufficient, and that "the people [would] not readily subscribe to the Natl. Constitution, if it should subject them to be disfranchised." Men who wished for innovations on this point certainly were ignoring force of habit, declared Mason, for what would "the people say, if they should be disfranchised." Franklin did not want to displease the common people by disfranchising them, for they had contributed much during the late war. Sons of substantial farmers would not be pleased at being disfranchised, he said, and if the common people were "denied the right of suffrage it would debase their spirit and detach them from the interest of the country." Defending the habitual right of merchants and mechanics to vote, Gorham declared: "We must consult their rooted prejudices if we expect their concurrence in our propositions." Rutledge explained why the committee had omitted the qualifications by saying its members could not agree among themselves for fear of displeasing the people if they made the qualifications high or having the qualifications be worthless if they were low.

Since there were no personalty qualifications for voting in the Constitution, and since, as Beard said, the landed interests would control ratification either by state legislatures or by special conventions, the big question is this: Why was the Constitution ratified by the landed interests if it was designed to protect personalty? Beard never answered this question.

Inconsistencies and the drawing of unjustified conclusions soon become obvious when we attempt to follow the tortuous trail of the Beard thesis into the powers conferred on the federal government. Why did rural interests have to be conciliated on the point of direct taxes to prevent manufacturing states from shifting the tax burden to sparsely settled agricultural regions, if these rural regions were not represented in the Convention? Does the quotation from the North Carolina delegates (p. 169) prove the influence of personalty? No. The delegates said they had protected "the Southern states in general and North Carolina in particular" on the tax question, but this represents a sectional or state interest, not personalty. These delegates were also looking out for the interests of North Carolina farmers, who, incidentally, had, on the average, land twice the value of that of the people in New England. And why did Hamilton have to conciliate "the freeholders and property owners in general" if the Convention represented personalty? Then there are the questions of whether military power and nationalism have nothing but economic connotations, even though everyone admits that economic factors accompany both.

One key to an understanding of the Constitutional Convention was provided by Beard himself in his discussion of the control of commerce (p. 175). His earlier use of petitions signed by mechanics and manufacturers was evidence that these skilled artisans wanted protection from foreign competition just as does organized labor today. But his final sentence in the paragraph is the important one—that merchants and manufacturing interests achieved commercial benefits, but "they paid for their victory by large concessions to the slave-owning planters of the south." This is only one example of what is so evident to anyone who reads the *Records* without preconceptions. There were a multitude of conflicting interests in the Convention, some economic and some not, and there simply had to be a great deal of compromising of interests for anything to be achieved. As one delegate said, he did not trust the other gentleman, and they all did everything possible to insure that their interests and principles got a hearing and that others' were checked as much as possible. Nobody could have his own way completely.

That the Constitution did not confer on Congress the power to make direct attacks on property is not to be wondered at (p. 176). Given the America of 1787, in which most men owned property, the reverse would have been the more astonishing. A constitution which permitted an attack on property would not have received a hearing in a country that had fought a revolution for the preservation of life, liberty, and property. One of the colonists' chief complaints against Britain had been that the British, on whom the colonists had no check, were endangering the property rights of colonists. The opponents of the Constitution were not opposed to the protection of property rights. After all, were not the Antifederalists responsible for the adoption of the first ten amendments, and did not Articles IV, V, and VII provide for additional protection of property which these Antifederalists did not think the Constitution provided?

If Madison was any authority, and Beard seemed to think he was, then Beard greatly exaggerated the importance of agrarianism in the country (pp. 178–79). Beard used the term, not to mean agricultural, but to designate men who favored an equal or a more nearly equal distribution of land. Madison stated in the Convention that as yet there had not been any agrarian attempts in the country.

Some interesting and significant points on obligation of contracts which Beard did not include in his discussion of the contract clause as a protection for personalty (pp. 179–83) were brought out in the *Records*. For instance, when King moved to add a clause prohibiting the states from interfering in private contracts, Gouverneur Morris objected. And his argument—shades of Oliver Wendell Holmes!—was that "within the State itself a majority must rule, whatever may be the mischief done among themselves." Even Madison had his doubts about restricting the states on contracts, and Mason was strongly against it. Wilson then resolved the controversy with this answer: "The answer to these objections is that *retrospective* interferences only are to be prohibited." Instead of the original motion, then, the restriction was made that the state legislatures could not pass "retrospective laws," that is, ex post facto laws, and on this issue Connecticut, Maryland, and Virginia voted no. Later, however, Dickinson said he had examined Blackstone's *Commentaries on the Laws of England* and found that "ex post facto" related only to criminal cases, and that legislatures could still pass retrospective laws in civil cases. So the prohibition against violation of contracts was included, but to the members this meant only contracts already made. It did not in any way restrict the right of legislatures to provide the conditions under which future contracts could be made.

Given this situation, Beard's account of Chief Justice John Marshall and the contract clause (pp. 181–83) was completely invalid, and could easily have been corrected by a reference to the *Records*. Beard said Marshall "doubtless" understood the full import of the obligation-of-contract clause better than any man of that generation. In 1827 the Supreme Court passed on the question of whether a bankrupt law which applied to contracts made after its passage impaired the obligation of those contracts. The majority on the Court upheld the law, but Marshall took "the high ground" that a contract was a contract and could not be changed by external legislation. Then Beard said that Marshall should have known what the framers of the Constitution intended better than any man on the Supreme Court, that is, that the Founding Fathers intended to ban "all legislation which affected personalty adversely." If the *Records* have any validity, this was not true. The majority of the Court which upheld the right of states to impair the obligation of *future contracts* was simply following the stated intent of the Founding Fathers as recorded in the *Records*. This explains why there was so little opposition to the Constitution on this particular score.

The *Records* also gave a different version of paper money than that given by Beard, who implied that the adoption of the Constitution would put an end to paper money (pp. 178–80). He failed to point out that the adoption of restrictions against future emissions of paper money by the states did not annihilate paper money in the states or invalidate contracts that were to be paid in paper money. As Davie told the North Carolina convention: "The Federal Convention knew that several states had large sums of paper money in circulation, and that it was an interesting property, and they were sensible that those states would never consent to its immediate destruction, or ratify any system that would have that operation. The mischief already done could not be repaired: all that could be done was, to form some limitation to this great political evil. As the paper money had become private property, and the object of numberless contracts, it could not be destroyed or intermeddled with in that situation, although its baneful tendency was obvious and undeniable. It was, however, effecting an important object to put bounds to this growing mischief. If the states had been compelled to sink the paper money instantly, the remedy might be worse than the disease. As we could not put an immediate end to it, we were content with prohibiting its future increase, looking forward to its entire extinguishment when the states that had an emission circulating should be able to call it in by gradual redemption."

This puts the paper money restriction in quite a different light, just as the *Records* put the contract clause in a different light. State legislatures did not have to retire the paper money that was circulating, and contracts in paper money were still valid. As long as the paper money party controlled the state legislature, that party could keep bills of credit in circulation. Parties to contracts could still make contracts in paper money, even if the legislature could not make paper money a legal tender, and in the future both parties to a contract would know the conditions under which the contract was to be fulfilled. This, too, explains the lack of opposition to the bills of credit clause. Further research in a later period would show how long bills of credit circulated in the states and whether state legislatures did not, in effect, get around the Constitutional restriction by chartering state banks which issued bank notes, just as the colonists attempted to set up private land banks to replace the British-extinguished public banks.

In the last section of the chapter (pp. 183–88), Beard used Hamilton to prove a point that Hamilton did not prove, namely, that foreign and domestic controversies are based primarily on commercial antagonisms. What Hamilton appears to have been doing in *The Federalist* No. 6 was to convince the people that commerce was as important as other causes in the fomenting of wars. Hamilton was too realistic to make commerce the most important factor in war. The causes of hostility among nations were innumerable, he declared—love of power, desire of preeminence and dominion, desire for territory, jealousy of power, desire for equality and safety, and commercial rivalry, as well as private passions stemming from attachments, enmities, interests, hopes, and fears of leading individuals in their own communities. Even the caprices of women had caused wars. Sometimes countries engaged in wars contrary to their true interests, motivated by momentary passions and immediate interests rather than by general considerations of policy, utility, or justice. Men were subject to impulses of rage, resentment, jealousy, avarice, and other irregular and violent propensities. Was not the love of wealth as important a passion as love of power and glory, Hamilton asked? He implied that love of power and glory was important, and certainly he did not confine wealth to personalty. Hamilton did not rule out policy, utility, and justice as motivations, nor did he necessarily represent the views of other men in the Convention and the country at large.

So to prove that the Constitution was "an economic document drawn with superb skill by men whose property interests were immediately at stake," Beard had to violate the concepts of the historical method in many ways. These ran the gamut from omission to outright misrepresentation of evidence, and included the drawing of conclusions from evidence that not only did not warrant the conclusions but actually refuted them. To say that the Constitution was designed in part to protect property is true; to say that it was designed only to protect property is false; and to say that it was designed only to protect *personalty* is preposterous.

For Further Reading

The long and heated controversy over the intentions of the Founding Fathers can be approached effectively by reading John Fiske's *Critical Period in American History* (1888), then Charles A. Beard's *An Economic Interpretation of the Constitution,* and finally one or two of the modern critical works, such as Forrest MacDonald, *We the People: The Economic Origins of the Constitution of the United States* (1958), Lee Benson, *Turner and Beard* (1960), or Richard Hofstadter, *The Progressive Historians: Turner, Beard, Parrington* (1968). Among recent studies that do not adopt the Beardian approach are Benjamin F. Wright, *Consensus and Continuity, 1776–1787* (1958), Catherine Drinker Bowen, *Miracle at Philadelphia* (1966), and Clinton Rossiter, *1787: The Grand Convention* (1966).

That Beard's economic emphasis is not altogether rejected nor altogether invalid is clear from Jackson Turner Main, *The Anti-Federalists: Critics of the Constitution, 1781–1788* (1961), and Forrest MacDonald, *E Pluribus Unum: The Formation of the American Republic, 1776–1790* (1965).

The events of the Confederation period, out of which the Constitution emerged, have been analyzed by many authors, most notably by Fiske, cited above, who saw the national experiment on the verge of disaster; Merrill Jensen, who in *The New Nation: A History of the United States during the Confederation, 1781–1789* (1950) finds the nation functioning well under the Articles of Confederation; Andrew C. McLaughlin, *The Confederation and The Constitution* (1905), whose position is closer to Fiske's than Jensen's, and most recently by Forrest MacDonald (cited above) and Gordon Wood, *The Creation of the American Republic* (1969). Important light is also shed on the period in biographies of the Founders.

Among the reliable and readable lives of Alexander Hamilton are the volumes by John C. Miller (1959), Broadus Mitchell (2 vols., 1957, 1962), and Nathan Schachner (1946); of John Adams by Page Smith (1962) and Gilbert Chinard (1933); of Jefferson by Dumas Malone (3 vols. to date, 1948–1962) and Nathan Schachner (2 vols., 1951); of George Washington by D. S. Freeman (7 vols., 1948–1957), and James T. Flexner (3 vols. to date, 1965–1969); and of James Madison by Irving Brant (6 vols., 1941–1961). Shays' Rebellion, the most dramatic event between the Peace of Paris and the Convention, is well analyzed in Marion L. Starkey, *A Little Rebellion* (1954), and in Robert J. Taylor, *Western Massachusetts in the Revolution* (1954).

Attempts to understand the Confederation and Constitution rest ultimately on the documents left by the Founding Fathers and their contemporaries. In addition to Max Farrand, ed., *Records of the Federal Convention* (4 vols., 1911–1937), the most accessible collections are A. T. Prescott, *Drafting the Federal Constitution* (1941); Jonathan Elliot, *The Debates in the Several State Conventions on the Adoption of the Federal Constitution* (5 vols., 1836–1945); and C. C. Tansill, *Documents Illustrative of the Formation of the Union* (1927). Vital also are the papers of Madison, Jay, Hamilton, Franklin, Adams, Jefferson, Washington, James Wilson, and others, and, of course, the Federalist Papers.

Bureaucratic Strife in Washington's Cabinet

Leonard D. White

A lasting dualism in American history has been symbolized by Alexander Hamilton and Thomas Jefferson. As schoolboys once recited:

Jefferson said, "the many!,"
Hamilton said, "the few!"
Like opposite sides of a penny were those exalted two.
If Jefferson said "It's black, sir!," Hamilton cried, "Its' white!"
But twixt the two, our Constitution started working right.

The personal rivalry was transformed into the nation's first partisan struggle as Hamilton's Federalist faction and the Jeffersonian Republicans vigorously competed for control of the government in the dozen years following the adoption of the Constitution. No party battle in our history has matched this contest in mutual distrust, violent invective, and destructiveness to na-

Source: Leonard D. White, *The Federalists: A Study in Administrative History* (New York: The Macmillan Company, 1948), pp. 210–236. Reprinted by permission of The Macmillan Company.

tional unity. After Jefferson's election to the presidency, he made several gestures toward cooperation with his opponents, declaring in his inaugural address: "Every difference of opinion is not a difference of principle. We have called by different names brethren of the same principle. We are all Republicans, we are all Federalists." Although the contentions continued, the Jeffersonians grew steadily stronger in all sections, and the Federalists never again held national power. The philosophical battle has been more enduring.

On the broadest level the adjective "Hamiltonian" has come to describe an attitude that favors extension of central governmental power, stability, and (often) rule by the few and able. "Jeffersonian," on the contrary, now denotes a view that promotes individual liberty, the rights of the states, and rule by the many. For example, commentators have suggested that certain political leaders "favored Hamiltonian ends achieved by Jeffersonian means." This type of neat labeling of course is a convenient shorthand; but insofar as it represents stereotypical thinking it also tends to create confusion. The confusion is not diminished when one consults American historical treatments of either of these two men or of the period in which they lived. The reason for this is simple: no label can sum up a man. As human beings, Hamilton and Jefferson were not always consistent, not always Hamiltonian or Jeffersonian, as the case might be.

There have been many accounts written of the Hamilton-Jefferson "conflict" and of the Federalist period generally. As a result, there is a vast literature on drafting, ratifying, and interpreting the Constitution; on the rise of political factions or parties; on the formulation of national fiscal and foreign policies; on the roles of individuals like Washington, Hamilton, Jefferson, Adams, and Madison; on specific events such as the Whisky Rebellion, the Jay Treaty, the XYZ Affair, and the Alien and Sedition Acts; and on the general philosophic principles of the Federalists and their opponents. Much of the literature is repetitive, too much reflects the political bias of the authors who have themselves identified too closely with Hamilton or Jefferson.

Recently, however, a political scientist has chronicled the political history of the Federalist era from another viewpoint. In 1948, Leonard D. White published *The Federalists: A Study in Administrative History*. White, a student of public administration, a former member of the United States Civil Service Commission, and a past president of the American Political Science Association, conceived of this work as the first in a multi-volume series recounting the administrative history of the United States federal government. He lived to complete four of the volumes, bringing the story up to 1901.

Administrative history generally has not been a popular topic for either the historian or for the lay reader. Perhaps historians, with an eye for the dramatic and episodic, have found it difficult to see significance in the humdrum of bureaucratic life. Yet the current awareness of bureaucracy, of institutions, of organizational structure, and of the governmental process—interests which men like White reflected and helped create—has made these aspects of life worthy of historical inquiry. White has demonstrated that such inquiries can be both systematic and readable.

The selection that follows deals with the Hamilton-Jefferson feud. White first emphasizes Hamilton's interference in his colleague's departmental prerogatives and then details Jefferson's reaction, demonstrating his thorough mastery of the primary sources of the period—a characteristic that is one of his strongest assets and marks him as an able scholar familiar with both the historians' and political scientists' techniques. The narrator has also been able to remain neutral as he tells his story, and he has managed, throughout *The Federalists*, to blend traditional political history with a multitude of fresh details concerning how government actually operated during the momentous days of the early republic. For these qualities his study has earned a high place in the historical literature on the Federalist period.

Interdepartmental Relations

In an era when the departments numbered only three, when their duties were relatively "plain and simple," and when personal contact between Secretaries and the Chief Executive was frequent, it might be supposed that the relations between departments would be equally "plain and simple." In fact the problem of coordinating the operations of different agencies at points where they touched or overlapped arose at once.

The structure of the federal system was not at fault. The lines of responsibility to the Chief Executive were clearly established and during Washington's administration were unchallenged. Responsibility within the departments to the Secretaries was equally undoubted. Administrative work was carefully assigned to one of the three departments, the principal exception being the operation of the sinking fund, a joint responsibility of a board comprising the Secretaries of Treasury and State and the Attorney General. As he left the Treasury, Hamilton noted the accepted rule in a letter to Washington.

> These observations proceed on the supposition that the President has adopted in principle and practice, the plan of distributing all the particular branches of the public service, except that of the law, among the three great departments; a plan which is believed to be founded on good reasons.

The rule did not touch the problem of coordination. No department, however closely contained, lived in a world of its own. Often two or more had a legitimate interest in a given field of administration, and one sometimes performed services for others. The necessity of coordinating and harmonizing activities was implicit in even as simple an administrative structure as that of 1790 to 1800.

The lines of demarcation between departments were drawn only by the broad descriptions of the duties of each in laws that left unanswered many problems of jurisdiction—for example, should the Post Office be assigned to Treasury as a revenue-producing agency or to State, as the recognized home of domestic affairs? Should correspondence with American diplomats abroad concerning foreign loans be carried on by Treasury or by State? Should correspondence with territorial governors about Indians be dealt with by State or by War? Should the enforcement of an embargo fall to State or to Treasury?

These questions were answerable only by experience within the departments and by presidential direction. On the whole, with the exception of procurement, the provision of services by one department for others gave rise to no perplexing problems. The adjustment of overlapping interests in a single area of public affairs was more difficult, especially in the field of foreign relations. Conflict between State and Treasury at this point brought out some carefully considered statements of policy.

INTERDEPARTMENTAL SERVICES

There were several cases in which one agency provided service for another or others, in the capacity that may be called auxiliary. The most notable example was the Attorney General, whose duty it was to give legal advice to other departments upon their request. Another example was the Post Office, which was the principal medium of communication between the central and field offices of the federal government, and between the states and Philadelphia. While there were constant complaints about the service in general, there was no concerted effort to improve it. The departments suffered in official silence.

The purchase of army supplies by the Treasury represented

a more formal type of interdepartmental service. Initiated by Hamilton in 1792, it was abandoned in 1798 because it divided responsibility for War Department business. The Treasury also developed the accounting system for other departments, as well as for itself; there is no evidence of objection by the departments. On the other hand, the initial examination of claims and bills against the departments by the Treasury was resisted and eventually a departmental accountant was set up in War and in Navy.

At the very moment of their conflict over neutrality enforcement, the two department heads of State and Treasury agreed to employ the collectors of customs as the means of distributing passports to American vessels engaged in foreign trade. Jefferson politely requested Treasury to assist him and Hamilton promptly consented: "It will be equally agreeable to me, that they be transmitted either directly from your office, or through this department. If you prefer the latter, which I shall with pleasure facilitate," etc. There was equal readiness by State to accommodate Treasury with respect to foreign loans through the agency of William Short and others. Short, as an American diplomat, was to correspond with Jefferson; but in fact Hamilton wrote him directly on foreign loans, apparently with Jefferson's knowledge and consent.

The duties imposed upon the Secretary of State in 1796 to register land grants made by the Treasury were purely ministerial and gave rise to no dissension. At a lower level of organization a widespread problem of coordination existed in principle between the district attorneys, whose duty it was generally to prosecute for crimes and offenses against federal laws, and other law enforcement officers, especially customs and excise, whose duty it was to prosecute for violation of the customs laws. The Department of State was the central office to which the district attorneys looked for instructions and general supervision, while the customs officers were of course attached to the Treasury. No instance has come to our attention of correspondence between the Treasury Department and the district attorneys on legal business of concern to the Treasury. Apparently there was no intrusion upon the authority of the Department of State.

CONFLICT IN FOREIGN AFFAIRS

It was Jefferson's misfortune not to arrive at the seat of government until March 22, 1790, a full six months after Hamilton had taken office. In this interval Hamilton had not only gone far in organizing the Treasury and setting up its far-flung field service, he had also—*faute de mieux*—taken the initiative in the foreign field. To the United States, Great Britain had sent an unaccredited agent, Major George Beckwith, who arrived in October 1789. Beckwith and Hamilton immediately engaged in conversations with Washington's knowledge and approval. The contact was also made known to Jefferson upon his appearance in New York. Until George Hammond arrived in October 1791 as the regularly accredited British minister, Beckwith kept in close touch with Hamilton. With the establishment of regular diplomatic agents, it might be presumed that negotiations and contacts would have been consolidated into the Department of State; but this was not to happen. Hammond clearly understood the French bias of Jefferson and the British sympathies of Hamilton. In 1793 Hammond wrote to London that "he preferred to make most of his communications privately to Hamilton and to have relations with Jefferson only when absolutely necessary."

This invasion of his special province was of course not concealed from so astute a person as Jefferson. As early as the spring of 1792 (five months after Hammond's arrival) Jefferson was smarting under Hamilton's aggressiveness. "It was observable," he wrote on March 11, 1792, "that whenever at any of our consultns anything was proposed as to Gr. Br. Hamilton had constantly ready something which Mr. Hammond had communicated to him, which suited the subject, and proved the intimacy of their communications: insomuch that I believe he communicated to Hammond all our views &

knew from him in return the views of the British Court." There can be no doubt that Jefferson's negotiations with Hammond were weakened by Hamilton's private exchange of opinions with the British minister. Hamilton did not hesitate to rewrite Jefferson's dispatches, as matters of foreign policy came up for Cabinet discussion. The tone of diplomatic exchanges between the United States and both Great Britain and France was set more nearly by Hamilton than by the Secretary of State.

Hamilton recognized the delicacy of his situation in the field of foreign affairs. Long after Jefferson had resigned, Hamilton told Washington his view of the instructions Jefferson had written for Jay on his mission to Great Britain.

> The truth, unfortunately, is, that it is in general a crude mass, which will do no credit to the administration. This was my impression of it at the time; but the delicacy of attempting too much reformation in the work of another head of department, the hurry of the moment, and a great confidence in the person to be sent, prevented my attempting that reformation.

The clash of opinion between Jefferson and Hamilton concerning American foreign policy came to a head in early 1793 when news of war between France and Britain reached the United States. Hamilton had already assured Hammond of his intent to hold the United States to a neutral course; this view coincided with Washington's. A Cabinet meeting was held on April 19, 1793. "Jefferson opposed neutrality on principle, and was defeated. He urged delay, and was again defeated. He then argued the matter on constitutional grounds. The President had no powers, without the consent of Congress, to take such a step as was contemplated." Jefferson was unable to carry the day except in matters of phraseology; here he succeeded in having the word, neutrality, omitted from the text. He affixed his signature to the Proclamation of Neutrality on April 22, 1793. Hamilton, helped greatly by

Genêt's tactless course, had triumphed in Jefferson's own domain.

The method of enforcement of the Proclamation of Neutrality, a strictly administrative problem, further strained the relations between the two Secretaries. Hamilton immediately prepared a circular letter to the collectors of customs instructing them (in Jefferson's paraphrase) "to superintend their neighborhood, watch for all acts of our citizens contrary to laws of neutrality or tending to infringe those laws, & inform him of it; & particularly to see if vessels should be building pierced for guns." The next day (May 5, 1793) Washington wrote Hamilton that he wanted to speak to him about the circular, and on the following day the President showed it to Jefferson. Washington then returned the circular to Hamilton for further consultation with Randolph and Jefferson, and wrote Hamilton a note indicating his disposition not to take measures which might check shipbuilding and further to refrain from adopting measures that were not "indispensably necessary."

The animus in the situation appears in a letter from Jefferson to Randolph, May 8, 1793. In this communication Jefferson raised objections to the whole proposal.

> . . . the Collectors of the customs are to be made an established corps of spies or informers against their fellow citizens, whose actions they are to watch in secret, inform against in secret to the Secretary of the Treasury, who is to communicate it to the President. . . . This will at least furnish the collector with a convenient weapon to keep down a rival, draw a cloud over an inconvenient censor, or satisfy mere malice & private enmity.
>
> The object of this new institution is to be to prevent infractions of the laws of neutrality, & preserve our peace with foreign nations. Acts involving war, or proceedings which respect foreign nations, seem to belong either to the department of war, or to that which is charged with the affairs of foreign

> nations. But I cannot possibly conceive how the superintendance of the laws of neutrality, or the preservation of our peace with foreign nations can be ascribed to the department of the treasury, which I suppose to comprehend merely matters of revenue. It would be to add a new & a large field to a department already amply provided with business, patronage, & influence. . . .

As an alternative means of enforcing neutrality Jefferson proposed to rely on the grand juries, "the constitutional inquisitors & informers of the country." And then in a postscript he added a characteristic Jeffersonian suggestion: "P.S. I understood Col. H. yesterday that he should confer with the President on the subject of our deliberation. As that is not exactly the channel thro' which I would wish my objections to be represented, should the President mention the subject to you I will thank you to communicate to him this note, or it's substance."

Washington neatly solved the dispute by directing the Attorney General (not the Secretary of State, the normal channel) to instruct the district attorneys to require from the collectors of the several ports information of all infractions of neutrality; and by implication to report directly to him, not to either Secretary. Hamilton's circular was not approved—at this time.

The enforcement of neutrality rapidly became a major problem as the French boldly sought to use American ports for their purposes, and the most effective means of action was clearly not a grand jury. The governors of the states were requested to seize any offending vessels and generally to guard against violations of neutrality. On July 8, 1793, the three Cabinet members met in Washington's absence to consider a letter from Governor Mifflin of Pennsylvania, calling their attention to the brigantine, *Little Sarah,* outfitted and armed in the port of Philadelphia, then lying in the river between the city and Mud Island and perhaps ready to sail. The Governor asked for instructions. Hamilton and Knox advised immediate measures to set up a battery on Mud Island and if necessary to use coercion to prevent her sailing until the President could be consulted. Jefferson dissented.

Governor Mifflin immediately asked for the loan of four cannon to mount on Mud Island, and the whole problem was reviewed with the President at a Cabinet meeting on July 15. The President was greatly disturbed; he had assumed that the governors would detect violations "in embryo & stop them when no force was requisite or a very small party of militia wd. suffice"; he doubted whether he had power to establish permanent guards; and he was opposed to dispersing cannon "all over the U. S." According to Jefferson's account, the President delayed his decision until Jefferson had withdrawn, but after reprimanding Knox for putting the loan of cannon in motion, Washington finally agreed.

The dangers involved in reliance upon the governors, evidenced to Washington in this episode, brought him back to Hamilton's initial proposal. On July 29, 1793, Washington asked the Cabinet to consider the expediency of directing the customs officers to supervise the observation of the Neutrality Proclamation. "Unless this, or some other *effectual* mode is adopted to check this evil in the first stage of its growth, the Executive of the U States will be incessantly harassed with complaints on this head, and probably when it may be difficult to afford a remedy." On August 4, instructions were issued to the collectors of customs, three months after Hamilton had originally suggested this course of action. The Treasury triumphed again in what Jefferson chose to consider the domain of foreign affairs.

Jefferson may well have felt annoyed, if not outraged, by Hamilton's activities in foreign problems. As a former minister to the King of France, dealing intimately with the course of diplomatic affairs of Europe and America, he ranked high among Americans entitled to speak on foreign policy with authority. Hamilton had never been to Europe, was personally unacquainted with the European courts, was without experience in diplomacy—and was head of a department concerned with revenue. But foreign policy involved the kind of question on which Washington insisted upon the opinions of his Cabinet in preference to advice of the Secretary of State alone. Jefferson suffered from the fact that his departmental problems as a matter of course came up for collective deliberation; Hamilton's usually could be settled by conference with the President alone. Furthermore, Hamilton's fiscal policy depended for its success upon peace; and he could therefore claim a competence to discuss foreign policy from the standpoint of his admitted fiscal responsibilities. Despite these considerations, Jefferson believed that Hamilton was invading his prerogatives, and eventually told the President as much.

VIEWS OF JEFFERSON, HAMILTON, AND RANDOLPH

Jefferson, as Secretary of State, asserted his devotion to the rule of noninterference of one department with another. In defense of his conduct in his relations with Hamilton, he wrote to Washington:

> When I embarked in the government, it was with a determination to intermeddle not at all with the legislature, & as little as possible with my co-departments. . . . The second part of my resolution has been religiously observed with the war department; & as to that of the Treasury, has never been farther swerved from than by the mere enunciation of my sentiments in conversation, and chiefly among those who, expressing the same sentiments, drew mine from me. If it has been supposed that I have ever intrigued among the members of the legislature to defeat the plans of the Secretary of the Treasury, it is contrary to all truth. . . .

Hamilton suggested a different guide to departmental relations, the *rule of common concert* in view of common responsibility to the President. Jefferson recorded Hamilton's concept in his *Anas* at the point where he entered his recollections of the assumption controversy.

> He [i.e., Hamilton] observed that the members of the administration ought to act in concert, that tho' this question was not of my department, yet a common duty should make it a common concern; that the President was the center on which all administrative questions ultimately rested, and that all of us should rally around him, and support with joint efforts measures approved by him. . . .

This was in 1790. In October 1792, Hamilton stated fully his view of the proper relationship of one department head to another and to the President. Despite its length, the passage must be quoted *in extenso*.

> The position must be reprobated that a man who had accepted an office in the Executive Department, should be held to throw the weight of his character into the scale, to support a measure which in his conscience *he disapproved, and in his station had opposed*—or, that the members of the administration should form together *a close and secret* combination, into whose measures the profane eye of the public should in no instance pry. But there is a very obvious medium between *aiding* or *countenancing,* and *intriguing* and *machinating* against a measure; between opposing it in the discharge of an official duty, or volunteering an opposition to it in the discharge of no duty; between entering into a close and secret combination with the other members of an administration, and being the active leader of an opposition to its measures.
>
> The true line of propriety appears to me to be the following: A member of the administration, in one department, ought only to *aid* those measures of another which he approves—where he disapproves, if called upon to *act officially,* he ought to manifest his disapprobation, and avow his opposition, but out of an official line he ought not to interfere *as long as he thinks fit to continue a part of the administration.*

When the measure in question has become a law of the land, especially with a direct sanction of the chief magistrate, it is peculiarly his duty to acquiesce. A contrary conduct is inconsistent with his relations as an officer of the government, and with a due respect as such for the decisions of the Legislature, and of the head of the executive department. The line here delineated, is drawn from obvious and very important considerations. The success of every government—its capacity to combine the exertion of public strength with the preservation of personal right and private security, qualities which define the perfection of a government, must always naturally depend on the energy of the executive department. This energy again must materially depend on the union and mutual deference which subsists between the members of that department, and the conformity of their conduct with the views of the executive chief.

Difference of opinion between men engaged in any common pursuit, is a natural appendage of human nature. When only exerted *in the discharge of a duty,* with delicacy and temper, among liberal and sensible men, it can create no animosity; but when it produces officious interferences, dictated by no call of duty—when it volunteers a display of itself in a quarter where there is no responsibility, to the obstruction and embarrassment of one who is charged with an immediate and direct responsibility, it must necessarily beget ill-humor and discord between the parties. Applied to the members of the executive administration of any government, it must necessarily tend to occasion, more or less, distracted councils, to foster factions in the community, and practically to weaken the government.

Moreover, the heads of the several executive departments are justly to be viewed as auxiliaries to the executive chief. Opposition to any measure of his, by either of those heads of departments, except in the shape of frank, firm, and independent advice to himself, is evidently contrary to the relations which subsist between the parties. And it cannot well be controverted that a measure becomes his, so as to involve the duty of acquiescence on the part of the members of his administration, as well by its having received his sanction in the form of a law, as by its having previously received his approbation.

To much of this Jefferson would have agreed. Indeed he observed more than once that he had loyally carried out policies as a member of the government which he deeply disapproved, the President's policy having taken a direction different from his own. He denied, as we have seen, Hamilton's charge that he interfered with the Treasury. He never developed as fully as Hamilton, however, his concept of the proper relationship of one department to another.

On January 2, 1794, Edmund Randolph stepped into Jefferson's post in the State Department. He had been a firsthand witness of the progressive deterioration of relations between Treasury and State, and took immediate steps to prevent a repetition. To keep interdepartmental relations clear and wholesome he wrote the following letter to his two colleagues in Treasury and War.

> I have just taken the oath of Office, which reminds me that I am brought into a nearer relation to your department than hitherto. While official men are under no less an obligation than others, to live in harmony; there are too many opportunities for misconception and misrepresentations to interrupt it. I have therefore prescribed this rule for myself: that if any thing, supposed to be done in the other departments, shall create dissatisfaction in my mind, I will check any opinion, until I can obtain an explanation, which I will ask without reserve. By these means I shall avoid the uneasiness of suspicion; and I take the liberty of requesting, that the same line of conduct be pursued with respect to myself.

These were the principal efforts to state general rules or procedures to govern the relations of one department to another. Both Hamilton's concept of concerted action on matters which had received presidential approval and Jefferson's formula of departmental self-sufficiency had their place, but neither was destined to secure a degree of acceptance sufficient to prevent in later years a long history of interdepartmental disputes and feuds.

The Hamilton-Jefferson Feud

On September 11, 1789, Alexander Hamilton took the oath of office as first Secretary of the Treasury. On March 22, 1790, Thomas Jefferson entered upon his duties as Secretary of State. By the summer of 1792, open warfare had broken out between these powerful members of the Cabinet. On August 23, 1792, President Washington wrote to Jefferson, and three days later to Hamilton, begging each of them for mutual forbearance lest their bitter quarrels "tare the Machine asunder" and disrupt the Union of the States. His appeal was in vain; Jefferson resigned his office December 31, 1793, and Hamilton, who had already told the President of his desire to resign, finally left office on January 31, 1795.

The great issues of policy, domestic and foreign, which occasioned this historic quarrel are well known. Jefferson cherished the ideal of an agricultural society; Hamilton a balanced economy calling for substantial development of manufactures, banking, corporations, and cities. Jefferson had an ardent faith in the masses; Hamilton had little. Jefferson favored little government and that mostly in the states and their smallest subdivisions; Hamilton needed a national government capable of energetic direction of the public economy to produce the balanced system he believed essential. Jefferson stood in principle for the predominance of popular legislative bodies; Hamilton expounded the theory and practice of executive leadership. In foreign affairs, Jefferson was attached to France and to the beneficent influence which he saw in the French Revolution, while Hamilton admired English institutions, feared the consequences of the Revolution, and believed that the interests of the United States required above all the maintenance of good relations with Great Britain. These conflicts of policy in matters both domestic and foreign were fundamental, and fatal to effective collaboration.

The administrative phases of the great duel between Hamilton and Jefferson are less well known. When Jefferson and Hamilton met in New York in March 1790, they were comparative strangers. They had seen each other briefly during their service in the Continental Congress in 1783, but Jefferson had been out of the country for five years as the American minister in Paris, while Hamilton had been in the midst of the struggle to frame a constitution and to secure its adoption. Neither could have had a clear perception of the ideas of the other as, with Washington, they faced the problems of the future.

Jefferson's welcome in New York was friendly. He wrote, "The President received me cordially, and my Colleagues & the circle of principal citizens, apparently, with welcome." There was a round of dinners and the new Secretary of State felt at home. Hamilton later recorded his early opinion of Jefferson as one of very great esteem, and Washington could have had no concern as to the ability and willingness of his principal advisers to cooperate effectively.

The first substantial break over public policy occurred in February 1791, when Jefferson declared Hamilton's plan to establish the Bank of the United States beyond the power of Congress to enact. Hamilton's success in convincing Washington of the constitutionality of the bank bill persuaded Jefferson that Hamilton had to be watched and controlled. Jefferson's fear of Hamilton's dominance was well founded. Hamilton recognized no limits to the extension of his official activity and influence. The War Department fell into his orbit; and foreign policy had such an essential connection with his fiscal and domestic plans that he threw himself into diplomatic negotiations with the same attention he gave to financial operations. Hamilton's friendly biographers as well as his critics acknowledge this trait. Oliver wrote:

> it is none the less true, not only that he threw the net of his department as widely as possible over the waters, but that his activity extended and his influence predominated far outside the limits of his own office. Every important proposal brought forward by his colleagues was minuted and reviewed by Hamilton, and it may be added that a large number, if not the majority, of these proposals were offered at his instigation, and were drawn upon lines which he had already sketched out. From the beginning to the end of his official career the cabinet was literally overwhelmed by his wide interest and untiring industry; and although in a short time his insistence provoked a violent resentment in certain quarters, in the main issues his policy prevailed, and the government submitted to the force of his will, whether the various ministers liked it or not.

Hamilton's active intervention in the field of foreign affairs, a field peculiarly Jefferson's, set off an administrative feud that was to dominate the scene from 1791 to 1793. The story of Jefferson's attempts at defense, his attack on Hamilton, Hamilton's counterattack, Washington's intervention, and the ultimate solution by the road of resignation makes a fascinating, if not a happy tale.

JEFFERSON AND THE TREASURY

Beginning in the spring of 1791 and continuing through 1792 one line of attack after another was opened on the Treasury to reduce Hamilton's influence. None succeeded, but their cumulative effect was to destroy Hamilton's capacity to move forward. The first assault was on the departmental level, Jefferson seeking to place his friends in the Treasury Department or to break up the Department itself.

Coxe vs. Wolcott. So far as has been ascertained, Jefferson's first move against Hamilton occurred on April 17, 1791.

Nicholas Eveleigh, the Comptroller of the Treasury, died on April 16. Jefferson sought to secure the appointment of his successor. Neither Jefferson nor Hamilton wasted a moment.

On April 17 Jefferson wrote the President, who was then on his southern trip, enclosing an application from Tench Coxe, Assistant to the Secretary of the Treasury. On the same day, Hamilton wrote Washington recommending Wolcott, then Auditor, and went out of his way to observe that, "I am influenced by information that other characters will be brought to your view by weighty advocates." Immediately on his return to Mount Vernon, Washington acknowledged Hamilton's letter and authorized him to inform Wolcott of the President's intention to appoint the latter as Comptroller.

Jefferson took a bold step in undertaking, without consultation with Hamilton, to forward the appointment of Coxe to the second position in the Treasury Department. He apparently was assured of Coxe's personal loyalty at this early date, although the tie was not generally known until later. Jefferson, however, exposed himself to an almost certain rebuff from the President, whose decision would naturally be governed primarily by the advice of the head of the department concerned. Jefferson also laid bare to Hamilton his intrigue to place his own man in the center of Hamilton's department —a challenge which the Secretary of the Treasury was not likely to overlook.

Pickering vs. Paine. A second occasion of the same sort occurred in the summer of 1791 when Samuel Osgood resigned as Postmaster General. Jefferson and Randolph tried to persuade Washington to appoint Thomas Paine, who was then in France. They knew well what they were doing—as Randolph observed, "It seemed to be a fair opportunity for a declaration of certain sentiments." Washington's action in appointing the unyielding Federalist, Timothy Pickering (on Hamilton's recommendation), was a clear enough answer.

Transfer of the Post Office. Failing in this attempt, Jefferson made a bolder effort in 1792. On February 20, the President approved an act of Congress putting the Post Office on a permanent basis. Jefferson seized the occasion to attempt to persuade the President to transfer the Post Office from Hamilton's domain to his. In two meetings with the President on February 28 and 29 he presented a plan "for doubling the velocity" of the posts. The record of the conversations is revealing of the administrative and political rivalry of Hamilton and Jefferson.

> I . . . observed . . . that I had hitherto never spoke to him on the subject of the post office, not knowing whether it was considered as a revenue law, or a law for the general accommodation of the citizens; that the law just passed seemed to have removed the doubt, by declaring that the whole profits of the office should be applied to extending the posts & that even the past profits should be refunded by the treasury for the same purpose: that I therefore conceived it was now in the department of the Secretary of State: that I thought it would be advantageous so to declare it for another reason, to wit, that the department of treasury possessed already such an influence as to swallow up the whole Executive powers, and that even the future Presidents (not supported by the weight of character which himself possessed) would not be able to make head against this department. That in urging this measure I had certainly no personal interest, since, if I was supposed to have any appetite for power, yet as my career would certainly be exactly as short as his own, the intervening time was too short to be an object. My real wish to avail the public of every occasion during the residue of the President's period, to place things on a safe footing. . . .

Jefferson's request for the Post Office was one to which Washington could not have acceded without disrupting his Cabinet and he naturally followed the rule of not disturbing status quo. There is no record of any formal reply to Jefferson's proposal; it was quietly shelved and perhaps never came to Hamilton's attention. The only response of which there remains a record is an indirect one over six months later when

Washington acceded to Jefferson's desire to place the Mint in the State Department. The President added in his letter: "The Post Office (as a branch of Revenue) was annexed to the Treasury in the time of Mr. Osgood; and when Col. Pickering was appointed thereto, he was informed . . . that he was to consider it in that light. . . ."

Jefferson retired from the State Department in possession of the Mint but not of the Post Office. A curious turn was given to his effort to capture the Post Office when Hamilton proposed, a year and a month later when he resigned as Secretary of the Treasury, to exchange it for the Mint. By this time a convinced Federalist was in the State Department; but Hamilton also recognized what Jefferson had privately urged upon Washington earlier, that the Post Office was becoming something other than a revenue office.

Control of the Mint. Whether to assign the Mint to the Treasury as a subordinate fiscal unit, or to the Department of State as the general agency for home affairs was another debatable issue. Congress apparently was undecided; the President turned it over to Jefferson. Washington's letter to Jefferson suggests the opportunistic quality of his decision: "If from relationship, or usage in similar cases . . . the Mint does not appertain to the Department of the Treasury I am more inclined to add it to that of State than to multiply the duties of the other."

In view of the nature of the work of the Mint, Hamilton could hardly have failed to see in this decision a defeat. He suggested in 1795 that the Mint properly belonged in the Treasury, as a "most material link in the money system of the country," but Washington did not disturb the existing arrangement. On this point Jefferson was victor.

Division of the Treasury Department. How far Jefferson was prepared to go to reduce the power of the Treasury Department is revealed by his proposal to Madison in August 1793. Jefferson had already submitted his resignation, and had been told by Washington that Hamilton also intended to retire.

Jefferson now suggested to Madison splitting the Treasury. "It would be the moment for dividing the Treasury between two equal chiefs of the customs and Internal Taxes, if the Senate were not so unsound." Federalist predominance in the upper House precluded success in this direction. In fact, at every point that Jefferson tried to break down the internal cohesion of the Treasury Department, he failed. Meanwhile he was deeply engaged in another series of moves against Hamilton through the House of Representatives—seeking to end the practice of referring matters to heads of departments and to keep Secretaries from the floor of the House; and setting on foot, with Giles and Madison, a hostile investigation of Hamilton's management of funds. The temper of the skirmish is disclosed in Madison's private letter to Jefferson early in 1794 referring to the charges against the Secretary of the Treasury, "His trial is not yet concluded."

Jefferson's Conversations with the President. In private conversations and letters throughout 1792 Jefferson pursued his campaign against Hamilton directly with the President, attacking his fiscal policy and the integrity of some of his supporters in Congress. The record of these meetings is supplied by Jefferson himself. On February 28 and 29, 1792, he had long conferences with Washington in which he protested against the power of the Treasury. He complained about the issuance of paper money by the Bank, more than hinted at corruption among members of the House, and especially warned Washington against subsidies for manufactures, as proposed in Hamilton's Report on Manufactures. In May 1792 he wrote a long letter to the President at Mount Vernon, in which appears the most complete exposition of his charges. He asserted that an artificial debt had been created beyond the power of the country ever to pay, that the excise tax was odious, that the interest rate on government obligations was excessive, that the meager stock of coins would soon be exported, to be replaced by paper money, and that there was a "corrupt squadron" in Congress. He alleged that Hamilton sought to establish a monarchy, and spoke darkly about the danger of southern secession. In July he repeated these charges in a private conversation with the President.

In midsummer 1792 Jefferson induced Colonel George Mason of Virginia to lay before Washington similar criticisms of the fiscal policy of the government. The President immediately communicated their substance to Hamilton in a letter of his own, referring to the criticisms as coming from "sensible and moderate men." Hamilton responded with a detailed defense, point by point, and nothing further was heard of them. He was not, however, unaware of the source from which they came.

Later in 1792 Jefferson privately accused Hamilton of having monarchy in contemplation, through the means of a "corps of interested persons who should be steadily at the orders of the Treasury." Washington insisted there were hardly ten men of consequence who supported monarchy, defended the government's fiscal policy, and scouted the existence of a "corrupt squadron" in Congress. At the same time he begged Jefferson not to retire, since he "thought it important to preserve the check of my opinions in the administration in order to keep things in their proper channel & prevent them from going too far."

Attack in the Press. The persistence of Jefferson in seeking to destroy an adversary whose policy he believed fatal was not exhausted by his efforts to divide the Treasury, to weaken Hamilton in the House, or to undermine his standing with the President. He also turned to the press. With his knowledge and approval, Madison arranged to bring Philip Freneau to Philadelphia to start a newspaper. Jefferson appointed Freneau to the position of translating clerk in the State Department and in October 1791, the *National Gazette* made its first appearance. It soon became the vehicle for attacks upon the policy of the government, upon Hamilton, and eventually upon Washington. These attacks were often bitter in their character and deeply irritated Washington.

As early as August 1792, the President referred in a private letter to "the Seeds of discontent, distrust, and irritations which are so plentifully sown. . . ." On May 23, 1793, he could no longer forbear complaining openly to Jefferson, according to whose account "he said he despised all their attacks on him personally, but that there never had been an act of the government, not meaning in the Executive line only, but in any line which that paper had not abused. . . . He was evidently sore & warm, and I took his intention to be that I should interpose in some way with Freneau, perhaps withdraw his appointment of translating clerk to my office. But," Jefferson added, "I will not do it." In short, Jefferson was untiring in his attempts to defeat Hamilton and to drive him from the government. Until the summer of 1792 the President chose to ignore their quarrels; but Hamilton was less restrained in carrying the attack to his opponent.

HAMILTON COUNTERATTACKS

During 1790 and 1791 Hamilton was driving forward his program of fiscal reconstruction, defending himself in Congress through his friends in the two Houses, and in Cabinet discussions dominating both domestic and foreign policy, on the whole supported by the independent judgment of Washington. It was not until the summer of 1792 that he openly fought Jefferson in the *Gazette of the United States.* He was not, however, unaware of what he called "malicious intrigues to stab me in the dark."

Before noting the papers in the *Gazette,* it is in order to point out an earlier move by Hamilton to block Jefferson's effort to secure his designation (as Secretary of State) as successor to the presidency in case of death or disability of both the President and Vice President. Debate on the bill to define the succession to the presidency first took place in the House on January 10 and 13, 1791, with inconclusive results. The Federalist leaders proposed the Chief Justice of the Supreme Court; Madison and others stood for the Secretary of State.

The discussion was resumed by the next Congress; the Senate passed a bill devolving the succession upon the President of the Senate, pro tempore, and then the Speaker of the House. Jefferson's friends again fought for the Secretary of State. By the close margin of 27 to 24 the Federalists prevailed, although the vote can hardly yet be called a party division. The debate was renewed on February 9 and 10, 1792, and this time the House acted in favor of the Secretary of State. But the Senate refused to budge from its preference and on February 21 the House receded. Jefferson lost.

Hamilton's share in Jefferson's defeat was subsequently avowed by him in his letter to Edward Carrington. "You know," he wrote, "how much it was a point to establish the Secretary of State, as the officer who was to administer the Government in defect of the President and Vice-President. Here, I acknowledge, though I took far less part than was supposed, I ran counter to Mr. Jefferson's wishes; but if I had had no other reason for it, I had already experienced opposition from him, which rendered it a measure of self-defence." Jefferson was doubtless fully aware of the opposition of the Secretary of the Treasury.

In the face of the attacks by Freneau in the *National Gazette* Hamilton was less restrained than Washington. In a series of letters to the *Gazette of the United States* beginning in July and ending in December 1792, he charged Jefferson with initial opposition to the Constitution, with opposition to almost all the important measures of the administration, especially the provisions concerning the debt, public credit, and the Bank of the United States, with a desire to depress the national authority, with a willingness to pay French debts at the expense of the Dutch, with the clandestine circulation of "foul and pestilent whispers," and with exhibiting a "caballing, self-sufficient, and refractory temper," as well as with the sponsorship of Freneau. Hamilton asserted openly that his objective was to expose "a public officer who is too little scrupled to embarrass and disparage the government of which he is a member. . . ." The country was treated to the extraordinary spectacle of the Secretary of the Treasury openly attacking the Secretary of State in the newspapers, while a translating clerk in the Department of State castigated the Secretary of the Treasury.

The President Intervenes

For the most part Washington had ignored the controversy in his official family, but this unseemly publicity forced him to take cognizance of the deep rift which had developed. From the relative peace of Mount Vernon he wrote Jefferson on August 23, 1792:

> How unfortunate, and how much it is to be regretted then, that whilst we are encompassed on all sides with avowed enemies and insidious friends, that internal dissensions should be harrowing and tearing our vitals. The last, to me, is the most serious, the most alarming, and the most afflicting of the two. And without more charity for the opinions and acts of one another in Governmental matters, or some more infallible criterion by which the truth of speculative opinions, before they have undergone the test of experience, are to be forejudged than has yet fallen to the lot of fallibility, I believe it will be difficult, if not impracticable, to manage the Reins of Government or to keep the parts of it together: for if, instead of laying our shoulders to the machine after measures are decided on, one pulls this way and another that, before the utility of the thing is fairly tried, it must, inevitably, be torn asunder. And, in my opinion the fairest prospect of happiness and prosperity that ever was presented to man, will be lost, perhaps for ever!
>
> My earnest wish, and my fondest hope therefore is, that instead of wounding suspicions, and irritable charges, there may be liberal allowances, mutual forbearances, and temporising yieldings on *all sides*. Under the exercise of these, matters will

> go on smoothly, and, if possible, more prosperously. Without them every thing must rub; the Wheels of Government will clog; our enemies will triumph, and by throwing their weight into the disaffected Scale, may accomplish the ruin of the goodly fabric we have been erecting.

Three days later he followed this appeal with a similar letter to Hamilton, and on September 9, both Secretaries responded at length, in terms which must have caused Washington to despair of reconciliation. While Hamilton offered to embrace any opportunity to heal or terminate the differences which existed, he declared that he was "the deeply injured party," declined to recede for the present from the "retaliations which have fallen upon certain public characters," and asserted that he had been "an object of uniform opposition from Mr. Jefferson . . . [and] the frequent subject of the most unkind whispers and insinuations. . . ." He declared Jefferson was bent upon his subversion and the subversion of the government.

In a lengthy reply Jefferson acknowledged that he utterly disapproved of the system of the Secretary of the Treasury, which he believed was calculated to undermine the republic by corrupting the legislative branch and making it docile to the Treasury. He asserted, with truth, that Hamilton had forced acceptance of his views concerning France and England which, Jefferson said, were not only "exactly the reverse" of his own but "inconsistent with the honor & interest of our country." He pointedly asked "which of us has . . . stepped farthest into the controul of the department of the other?" He did not conceal that he knew Hamilton was the author of the papers in the *Gazette of the United States*, and defended himself against Hamilton's charges, denying especially that he influenced, "directly or indirectly," the opinions expressed in Freneau's *National Gazette*. He allowed, however, that he took for granted that Freneau would give "free place to pieces written against the aristocratical & monarchical principles," although he urged Washington to believe that he did not expect "any criticisms on the proceedings of government." As to his course of action, he took note of his intention to retire after the fall elections (1792) and meanwhile to refrain from newspaper controversy until he became a private citizen.

Despite this unpromising exchange of letters Washington persisted in his efforts to restore unity among his advisers. Jefferson recorded on February 7, 1793, that the President informed him privately that he had proposed a "coalescence" and that Hamilton had expressed his willingness. When the President and Jefferson met on October 1, 1792, at the breakfast table of Mount Vernon, Washington sought to mediate between his Cabinet members. Jefferson was obdurate in his accusations and Washington finished the conversation with "another exhortation" against Jefferson's threatened retirement. After reaching Philadelphia he sent Washington letters to clear up his record concerning the Constitution. In reply Washington expressed his "sincere esteem and regard for you both," and asked plaintively why "shd. either of you be so tenacious of your opinions," and repeated his ardent "wish that some line could be marked out by which both of you could walk."

No such line could be found.

Resignations

How difficult Washington's task was can be appreciated by the views which Hamilton and Jefferson held of each other. Both left considered judgments, as well as less considered criticisms. Jefferson summed up his final estimate of Hamilton in these words.

> Hamilton was indeed a singular character. Of acute understanding, disinterested, honest, and honorable in all private

> transactions, amiable in society, and duly valuing virtue in private life, yet so bewitched & perverted by the British example, as to be under thoro' conviction that corruption was essential to the government of a nation. . . .

Hamilton's mature views about Jefferson are contained in letters written at the height of the contested election of 1800, when no one could be certain whether Burr or Jefferson would become President. He wrote Gouverneur Morris, "If there be a man in the world I ought to hate, it is Jefferson." To James A. Bayard he wrote a long estimate of the character of his political enemy.

> Perhaps, myself the first, at some expense of popularity, to unfold the true character of Jefferson, it is too late for me to become his apologist. Nor can I have any disposition to do it.
>
> I admit that his politics are tinctured with fanaticism; that he is too much in earnest in his democracy; that he has been a mischievous enemy to the principal measures of our past administration; that he is crafty and persevering in his objects; that he is not scrupulous about the means of success, nor very mindful of truth, and that he is a contemptible hypocrite. But, it is not true, as is alleged, that he is an enemy to the power of the Executive, or that he is for confounding all the powers in the House of Representatives. It is a fact, which I have frequently mentioned, that, while we were in the administration together, he was generally for a large construction of the Executive authority, and not backward to act upon it in cases which coincided with his views. Let it be added, that in his theoretic ideas, he has considered as improper the participations of the Senate in the Executive authority. I have more than once made the reflection, that viewing himself as the reversioner, he was solicitous to come into the possession of a good estate. Nor is it true, that Jefferson is zealot enough to do any thing in pursuance of his principles, which will contravene his popularity or his interest. He is as likely as any man I know, to temporize; to calculate what will be likely to promote his own reputation and ad-

> vantage, and the probable result of such a temper is the preservation of systems, though originally opposed, which being once established, could not be overturned without danger to the person who did it. To my mind, a true estimate of Mr. Jefferson's character warrants the expectation of a temporizing, rather than a violent system. That Jefferson has manifested a culpable predilection for France, is certainly true; but I think it a question, whether it did not proceed quite as much from her *popularity* among us as from sentiment; and in proportion as that popularity is diminished, his zeal will cool. Add to this, that there is no fair reason to suppose him capable of being corrupted, which is a security that he will not go beyond certain limits. . . .

The denouement was not long delayed. The newspaper battle came to an end at the close of 1792; the assault on Hamilton in the House of Representatives opened at once and came to a head in the decisive vote on the Giles resolutions in February 1793. On April 19, 1793, was reached the crucial decision on foreign policy in favor of neutrality between France and Great Britain—a defeat for Jefferson in his own field. Hamilton, pursuing Washington's policy, practically took over the Department of State so far as its major moves were concerned. On July 31, 1793, Jefferson handed in his resignation, and in September left for Monticello, returning for a few weeks in the autumn. His resignation became effective on December 31, 1793. On New Year's eve he must have brooded over an unhappy sequence of frustration and defeat.

For Further Reading

John C. Miller's *The Federalist Era* (1960) provides an excellent introduction to the political history of the United States during the administrations of the first two Presidents, as does an earlier and longer work by Nathan Schachner, *The*

Founding Fathers (1954), which despite its title treats the same period. Washington's eight years in office are dissected in great detail in the final volume of Douglas Southall Freeman's biography of *George Washington* (7 vols., 1948–1957), the pertinent volume completed by John A. Carroll and Mary W. Ashworth. The administration of John Adams is admirably covered in Stephen Kurtz, *The Presidency of John Adams* (1957).

Probably the most lasting outgrowth of the Federalist years, the emergence of a two-party political system, has received much attention since World War II. Key studies include Joseph Charles, *The Origins of the American Party System* (1956); Noble E. Cunningham, *The Jeffersonian Republicans: The Formation of Party Organization, 1789–1801* (1957); Manning J. Dauer, *The Adams Federalists* (1953), William N. Chambers, *Political Parties in a New Nation: The American Experience, 1776–1809* (1963), and Richard Hofstadter, *The Idea of a Party System* (1969). Older works that still have value are Charles A. Beard, *Economic Origins of Jeffersonian Democracy* (1915), and Claude G. Bowers, *Jefferson and Hamilton: The Struggle for Democracy in America* (1925). A good brief survey is Morton Borden, *Parties and Politics in the Early Republic, 1789–1815* (1967). Norman K. Risjord has edited a useful anthology of important writings in *The Early American Party System* (1969).

Other aspects of the Federalist period have also received competent treatment by modern historians. Two studies of the Alien and Sedition Acts can be recommended: James Morton Smith, *Freedom's Fetters* (1956), and John C. Miller, *Crisis in Freedom* (1951). On the revolt of Pennsylvania farmers against the federal tax on whisky, see Leland D. Baldwin, *Whiskey Rebels* (1939). R. A. Rutland, *The Birth of the Bill of Rights* (1955), tells of one important episode in constitutional history. Diplomatic events are covered in Bradford Perkins, *The First Rapprochement: England and the United States, 1795–1805* (1953); Alexander DeConde, *En-*

tangling Alliance (1958); Samuel Flagg Bemis, *Jay's Treaty* (1923) and *Pinckney's Treaty* (1926), and Felix Gilbert, *To the Farewell Address* (1961; reissued in paperback as *Beginnings of American Foreign Policy*).

Despite a tendency to favor unquestioningly the man they have written about, the relations between Jefferson and Hamilton—the principal non-presidential figures of the decade before 1800—can best be studied in biographies. Major works on Hamilton include Broadus Mitchell's *Alexander Hamilton: The National Adventure* (1962) and John C. Miller's *Alexander Hamilton: Portrait in Paradox* (1959); on Jefferson the best recent study is Dumas Malone, *Jefferson and the Ordeal of Liberty* (1962).

A fine short collection of primary readings has been edited by Noble E. Cunningham, Jr., as *The Early Republic, 1789–1828* (1968).

American Ideals in the Age of Jefferson

Henry Adams

*O*ne eminent American historian has called Henry Adams' nine-volumed *History of the United States of America During the Administrations of Jefferson and Madison* (1889–1891) "the finest piece of historical writing in our literature." This judgment may not seem surprising; the *History* was written by a man who himself was a part of the national story. An Adams could be no mere historian; and Henry Adams (1838–1918) was far more: scion of two Presidents, diplomatist, literary critic, novelist, and philosopher. He came from a family of historians and makers of history. Moreover he moved with the great, lived within the shadow of the White House, and, with his brothers Brooks and Charles Francis, Jr., belonged to the intellectual elite of his day.

Yet Adams himself rated his historical work low. He thought the *History* negligible; it was a disagreeable task unwisely undertaken and inconclusively completed. Indeed, he valued more highly his two novels, *Democracy*

Source: Henry Adams, *History of the United States of America During the Administrations of Jefferson and Madison,* 9 vols. (1889–1891), vol. I, pp. 156–184.

(1880) and *Esther* (1884). Adams' assessment of his own work cannot be dismissed as the standard self-deprecatory attitude of an author; there is no reason to doubt his sincerity. Why then do historians dispute Adams' conclusions by assigning his work to a prominent place in American historical literature? The answer lies in the differing standards applied by the author and his admiring critics.

Adams was disappointed that his narrative account of the Jefferson and Madison years failed to demonstrate the universal laws of history. He had started his searches with the notion that, if he were absolutely open-minded and permitted the facts to speak for themselves, some sort of ineluctable pattern would emerge. But the facts did not speak for themselves; recounting historical sequences did not provide the key to the past. Adams had mastered the "standard" approach to history, but he considered the triumph hollow.

Dissatisfied with narrative history, rejected by his political contemporaries, and alienated by the materialism of post-Civil War America, Henry Adams added pessimism to his familial heritage of skepticism and candor. The combination of these qualities led him to spurn his grandfather's eighteenth-century vision of the inevitability of progress. As a substitute, he proposed that the so-called second law of dynamics (the law of inevitable dissolution of energy) be applied to human society as well as to the physical universe. In his last years he prophesied the imminent stagnation, or entropy, of human society. Man collectively would run out of steam; retrogression, not progress, was his fate. Adams —with such a gloomy prognosis of human destiny, with such a genteel distaste for late-nineteenth-century America, and with such a conviction that old modes of life (including "old school" historical writing) had succumbed to the onslaught of a scientific, mechanistic civilization—could not but dismiss his own historical work as insignificant.

Needless to say, Adams' prophecies did not materialize;

he failed in his strict application of the scientific muse to history. The wonder is not that he failed to find universal laws of history; nor is it strange that he should have deprecated his own work. What is amazing is that this prickly, complicated, and pessimistic man should have succeeded so well as a historian. The first six chapters of the *History*—one of which is reprinted below—are unsurpassed as examples of imaginative social history. The remaining volumes of the work, moreover, are noteworthy in their coverage of political and diplomatic events.

Few scholars since Adams' time have believed it necessary or dared to go over the trail he blazed. The research he conducted, both in the United States and in foreign archives; the literary grace with which he wrote; the relative degree of objectivity which informs the work; and the breadth of the author's scope—all have daunted later generations of historians. Only recently have scholars begun to expand our understanding of the period. The story of the War of 1812 has been retold several times in the past three decades; of equal significance has been the emphasis of several historical analysts on political party development during 1801–1828. Yet Adams' *History* stands as a colossus, as it were, casting its shadow over the Jefferson and Madison eras, and signifying ironically: this is Adams' country.

Nearly every foreign traveller who visited the United States during these early years, carried away an impression sober if not sad. A thousand miles of desolate and dreary forest, broken here and there by settlements; along the sea-coast a few flourishing towns devoted to commerce; no arts, a provincial literature, a cancerous disease of negro slavery, and differences of political theory fortified within geographical lines, —what could be hoped for such a country except to repeat the story of violence and brutality which the world already knew by heart, until repetition for thousands of years had wearied and sickened mankind? Ages must probably pass before the interior could be thoroughly settled; even Jefferson, usually a sanguine man, talked of a thousand years with acquiescence, and in his first Inaugural Address, at a time when the Mississippi River formed the Western boundary, spoke of the country as having "room enough for our descendants to the hundredth and thousandth generation." No prudent person dared to act on the certainty that when settled, one government could comprehend the whole; and when the day of separation should arrive, and America should have her Prussia, Austria, and Italy, as she already had her England, France, and Spain, what else could follow but a return to the old conditions of local jealousies, wars, and corruption which had made a slaughter-house of Europe?

The mass of Americans were sanguine and self-confident, partly by temperament, but partly also by reason of ignorance; for they knew little of the difficulties which surrounded a complex society. The Duc de Liancourt, like many critics, was struck by this trait. Among other instances, he met with one in the person of a Pennsylvania miller, Thomas Lea, "a sound American patriot, persuading himself that nothing good is done, and that no one has any brains, except in America; that the wit, the imagination, the genius of Europe are already in decrepitude;" and the duke added: "This error is to be found in almost all Americans,—legislators, administrators, as well as millers, and is less innocent there." In the year 1796 the House of Representatives debated whether to insert in the Reply to the President's Speech a passing remark that the nation was "the freest and most enlightened in the world,"—a nation as yet in swaddling-clothes, which had neither literature, arts, sciences, nor history; nor even enough nationality to be sure that it was a nation. The moment was peculiarly ill-chosen for such a claim, because Europe was on the verge of an outburst of genius. Goethe and Schiller, Mozart and Haydn, Kant and Fichte, Cavendish and Herschel were making way for Walter Scott, Wordsworth and Shelley, Heine and Balzac, Beethoven and Hegel, Oersted and Cuvier, great physicists, biologists, geologists, chemists, mathematicians, metaphysicians, and historians by the score. Turner was painting his earliest landscapes, and Watt completing his latest steam-engine; Napoleon was taking command of the French armies, and Nelson of the English fleets; investigators, reformers, scholars, and philosophers swarmed, and the influence of enlightenment, even amid universal war, was working with an energy such as the world had never before conceived. The idea that Europe was in her decrepitude proved only ignorance and want of enlightenment, if not of freedom, on the part of Americans, who could only excuse their error by pleading that notwithstanding these objections, in matters which for the moment most concerned themselves Europe was a full century behind America. If they were right in thinking that the next necessity of human progress was to lift the average man upon an intellectual and social level with the most favored, they stood at least three generations nearer than Europe to their common goal. The destinies of the United States were certainly staked, without reserve or escape, on the soundness of this doubtful and even improbable principle, ignoring or overthrowing the institutions of church, aristocracy, family, army, and political intervention, which long experience had shown to be needed for the safety of society. Europe might be right in thinking that without such safeguards society must come to an end; but even Europeans must concede that there was a chance, if no greater than one in a thousand, that America might, at least for a time, succeed. If this stake of temporal and eternal welfare stood on the winning card; if man actually should become more virtuous and enlightened, by mere process of growth, without church or paternal authority; if the average human being could accustom himself to reason with the logical processes of Descartes and Newton!—what then?

Then, no one could deny that the United States would win

a stake such as defied mathematics. With all the advantages of science and capital, Europe must be slower than America to reach the common goal. American society might be both sober and sad, but except for negro slavery it was sound and healthy in every part. Stripped for the hardest work, every muscle firm and elastic, every ounce of brain ready for use, and not a trace of superfluous flesh on his nervous and supple body, the American stood in the world a new order of man. From Maine to Florida, society was in this respect the same, and was so organized as to use its human forces with more economy than could be approached by any society of the world elsewhere. Not only were artificial barriers carefully removed, but every influence that could appeal to ordinary ambition was applied. No brain or appetite active enough to be conscious of stimulants could fail to answer the intense incentive. Few human beings, however sluggish, could long resist the temptation to acquire power; and the elements of power were to be had in America almost for the asking. Reversing the old-world system, the American stimulant increased in energy as it reached the lowest and most ignorant class, dragging and whirling them upward as in the blast of a furnace. The penniless and homeless Scotch or Irish immigrant was caught and consumed by it; for every stroke of the axe and the hoe made him a capitalist, and made gentlemen of his children. Wealth was the strongest agent for moving the mass of mankind; but political power was hardly less tempting to the more intelligent and better-educated swarms of American-born citizens, and the instinct of activity, once created, seemed heritable and permanent in the race.

Compared with this lithe young figure, Europe was actually in decrepitude. Mere class distinctions, the *patois* or dialect of the peasantry, the fixity of residence, the local costumes and habits marking a history that lost itself in the renewal of identical generations, raised from birth barriers which paralyzed half the population. Upon this mass of inert matter rested the Church and the State, holding down activity of thought. Endless wars withdrew many hundred thousand men from production, and changed them into agents of waste; huge debts, the evidence of past wars and bad government, created interests to support the system and fix its burdens on the laboring class; courts, with habits of extravagance that shamed common-sense, helped to consume private economics. All this might have been borne; but behind this stood aristocracies, sucking their nourishment from industry, producing nothing themselves, employing little or no active capital or intelligent labor, but pressing on the energies and ambition of society with the weight of an incubus. Picturesque and entertaining as these social anomalies were, they were better fitted for the theatre or for a museum of historical costumes than for an active workshop preparing to compete with such machinery as America would soon command. From an economical point of view, they were as incongruous as would have been the appearance of a mediæval knight in helmet and armor, with battle-axe and shield, to run the machinery of Arkwright's cotton-mill; but besides their bad economy they also tended to prevent the rest of society from gaining a knowledge of its own capacities. In Europe, the conservative habit of mind was fortified behind power. During nearly a century Voltaire himself—the friend of kings, the wit and poet, historian and philosopher of his age—had carried on, in daily terror, in exile and excommunication, a protest against an intellectual despotism contemptible even to its own supporters. Hardly was Voltaire dead, when Priestley, as great a man if not so great a wit, trying to do for England what Voltaire tried to do for France, was mobbed by the people of Birmingham and driven to America. Where Voltaire and Priestley failed, common men could not struggle; the weight of society stifled their thought. In America the balance between conservative and liberal forces was close; but in Europe conservatism held the physical power of government. In Boston a young Buckminster might be checked for a time by his father's prayers or commands in entering the path that led toward freer thought;

but youth beckoned him on, and every reward that society could offer was dangled before his eyes. In London or Paris, Rome, Madrid, or Vienna, he must have sacrificed the worldly prospects of his life.

Granting that the American people were about to risk their future on a new experiment, they naturally wished to throw aside all burdens of which they could rid themselves. Believing that in the long run interest, not violence, would rule the world, and that the United States must depend for safety and success on the interests they could create, they were tempted to look upon war and preparations for war as the worst of blunders; for they were sure that every dollar capitalized in industry was a means of overthrowing their enemies more effectively than a thousand dollars spent on frigates or standing armies. The success of the American system was, from this point of view, a question of economy. If they could relieve themselves from debts, taxes, armies, and government interference with industry, they must succeed in outstripping Europe in economy of production; and Americans were even then partly aware that if their machine were not so weakened by these economies as to break down in the working, it must of necessity break down every rival. If their theory was sound, when the day of competition should arrive, Europe might choose between American and Chinese institutions, but there would be no middle path; she might become a confederated democracy, or a wreck.

Whether these ideas were sound or weak, they seemed self-evident to those Northern democrats who, like Albert Gallatin, were comparatively free from slave-owning theories, and understood the practical forces of society. If Gallatin wished to reduce the interference of government to a minimum, and cut down expenditures to nothing, he aimed not so much at saving money as at using it with the most certain effect. The revolution of 1800 was in his eyes chiefly political, because it was social; but as a revolution of society, he and his friends hoped to make it the most radical that had occurred since the downfall of the Roman empire. Their ideas were not yet cleared by experience, and were confused by many contradictory prejudices, but wanted neither breadth nor shrewdness.

Many apparent inconsistencies grew from this undeveloped form of American thought, and gave rise to great confusion in the different estimates of American character that were made both at home and abroad.

That Americans should not be liked was natural; but that they should not be understood was more significant by far. After the downfall of the French republic they had no right to expect a kind word from Europe, and during the next twenty years they rarely received one. The liberal movement of Europe was cowed, and no one dared express democratic sympathies until the Napoleonic tempest had passed. With this attitude Americans had no right to find fault, for Europe cared less to injure them than to protect herself. Nevertheless, observant readers could not but feel surprised that none of the numerous Europeans who then wrote or spoke about America seemed to study the subject seriously. The ordinary traveller was apt to be little more reflective than a bee or an ant, but some of these critics possessed powers far from ordinary; yet Talleyrand alone showed that had he but seen America a few years later than he did, he might have suggested some sufficient reason for apparent contradictions that perplexed him in the national character. The other travellers —great and small, from the Duc de Liancourt to Basil Hall, a long and suggestive list—were equally perplexed. They agreed in observing the contradictions, but all, including Talleyrand, saw only sordid motives. Talleyrand expressed extreme astonishment at the apathy of Americans in the face of religious sectarians; but he explained it by assuming that the American ardor of the moment was absorbed in money-making. The explanation was evidently insufficient, for the Americans were capable of feeling and showing excitement, even to their great pecuniary injury, as they frequently proved; but in the foreigner's range of observation, love of money was the most conspicuous and most common trait of American character. "There is, perhaps, no civilized country in the world," wrote Félix de Beaujour, soon after 1800, "where there is less generosity in the souls, and in the heads fewer of those illusions which make the charm or the consolation of life. Man here weighs everything, calculates everything, and sacrifices everything to his interest." An Englishman named Fearon, in 1818, expressed the same idea with more distinctness: "In going to America, I would say generally, the emigrant must expect to find, not an economical or cleanly people; not a social or generous people; not a people of enlarged ideas; not a people of liberal opinions, or toward whom you can express your thoughts free as air; not a people friendly to the advocates of liberty in Europe; not a people who understand liberty from investigation and principle; not a people who comprehend the meaning of the words 'honor' and 'generosity.'" Such quotations might be multiplied almost without limit. Rapacity was the accepted explanation of American peculiarities; yet every traveller was troubled by inconsistencies that required explanations of a different kind. "It is not in order to hoard that the Americans are rapacious," observed Liancourt as early as 1796. The extravagance, or what economical Europeans thought extravagance, with which American women were allowed and encouraged to spend money, was as notorious in 1790 as a century later; the recklessness with which Americans often risked their money, and the liberality with which they used it, were marked even then, in comparison with the ordinary European habit. Europeans saw such contradictions, but made no attempt to reconcile them. No foreigner of that day—neither poet, painter, nor philosopher—could detect in American life anything higher than vulgarity; for it was something beyond the range of their experience, which education and culture had not framed a formula to express. Moore came to Washington, and found there no loftier inspiration than any Federalist rhymester of Dennie's school.

> Take Christians, Mohawks, democrats and all,
> From the rude wigwam to the Congress hall,—
> From man the savage, whether slaved or free,
> To man the civilized, less tame than he:
> 'Tis one dull chaos, one unfertile strife
> Betwixt half-polished and half-barbarous life;
> Where every ill the ancient world can brew
> Is mixed with every grossness of the new;
> Where all corrupts, though little can entice,
> And nothing's known of luxury but vice.

Moore's two small volumes of Epistles, printed in 1807, contained much more so-called poetry of the same tone,—poetry more polished and less respectable than that of Barlow and Dwight; while, as though to prove that the Old World knew what grossness was, he embalmed in his lines the slanders which the Scotch libeller Callender invented against Jefferson:—

> The weary statesman for repose hath fled
> From halls of council to his negro's shed;
> Where, blest, he woos some black Aspasia's grace,
> And dreams of freedom in his slave's embrace.

To leave no doubt of his meaning, he explained in a footnote that his allusion was to the President of the United States; and yet even Moore, trifler and butterfly as he was, must have seen, if he would, that between the morals of politics and society in America and those then prevailing in Europe, there was no room for comparison,—there was room only for contrast.

Moore was but an echo of fashionable England in his day. He seldom affected moral sublimity; and had he in his wanderings met a race of embodied angels, he would have sung of them or to them in the slightly erotic notes which were so well received in the society he loved to frequent and flatter. His remarks upon American character betrayed more temper than truth; but even in this respect he expressed only the common feeling of Europeans, which was echoed by the Federalist society of the United States. Englishmen especially indulged in unbounded invective against the sordid character of American society, and in shaping their national policy on this contempt they carried their theory into practice with so much energy as to produce its own refutation. To their astonishment and anger, a day came when the Americans, in defiance of self-interest and in contradiction of all the qualities ascribed to them, insisted on declaring war; and readers of this narrative will be surprised at the cry of incredulity, not unmixed with terror, with which Englishmen started to their feet when they woke from their delusion on seeing what they had been taught to call the meteor flag of England, which had burned terrific at Copenhagen and Trafalgar, suddenly waver and fall on the bloody deck of the "Guerriere." Fearon and Beaujour, with a score of other contemporary critics, could see neither generosity, economy, honor, nor ideas of any kind in the American breast; yet the obstinate repetition of these denials itself betrayed a lurking fear of the social forces whose strength they were candid enough to record. What was it that, as they complained, turned the European peasant into a new man within half an hour after landing at New York? Englishmen were never at a loss to understand the poetry of more prosaic emotions. Neither they nor any of their kindred failed in later times to feel the "large excitement" of the country boy, whose "spirit leaped within him to be gone before him," when the lights of London first flared in the distance; yet none seemed ever to feel the larger excitement of the American immigrant. Among the Englishmen who criticised the United States was one greater than Moore,—one who thought himself at home only in the stern beauty of a moral presence. Of all poets, living or dead, Wordsworth felt most keenly what he called the still, sad music of humanity; yet the highest conception he could create of America was not more poetical than that of any Cumberland beggar he might have met in his morning walk:—

> Long-wished-for sight, the Western World appeared;
> And when the ship was moored, I leaped ashore
> Indignantly,—resolved to be a man,
> Who, having o'er the past no power, would live
> No longer in subjection to the past,
> With abject mind—from a tyrannic lord
> Inviting penance, fruitlessly endured.
> So, like a fugitive whose feet have cleared
> Some boundary which his followers may not cross
> In prosecution of their deadly chase,
> Respiring, I looked round. How bright the sun,
> The breeze how soft! Can anything produced
> In the Old World compare, thought I, for power
> And majesty, with this tremendous stream
> Sprung from the desert? And behold a city
> Fresh, youthful, and aspiring! . . .
> Sooth to say,
> On nearer view, a motley spectacle
> Appeared, of high pretensions—unreproved
> But by the obstreperous voice of higher still;
> Big passions strutting on a petty stage,
> Which a detached spectator may regard
> Not unamused. But ridicule demands
> Quick change of objects; and to laugh alone,
> . . . in the very centre of the crowd
> To keep the secret of a poignant scorn,
> . . . is least fit
> For the gross spirit of mankind.

Thus Wordsworth, although then at his prime, indulging in what sounded like a boast that he alone had felt the sense sublime of something interfused, whose dwelling is the light of setting suns, and the round ocean, and the living air, and the blue sky, and in the mind of man,—even he, to whose moods the heavy and the weary weight of all this unintelligible world was lightened by his deeper sympathies with nature and the soul, could do no better, when he stood in the face of American democracy, than "keep the secret of a poignant scorn."

Possibly the view of Wordsworth and Moore, of Weld, Dennie, and Dickens was right. The American democrat possessed little art of expression, and did not watch his own emotions with a view of uttering them either in prose or verse; he never told more of himself than the world might have assumed without listening to him. Only with diffidence could history attribute to such a class of men a wider range of thought or feeling than they themselves cared to proclaim. Yet the difficulty of denying or even ignoring the wider range was still greater, for no one questioned the force or the scope of an emotion which caused the poorest peasant in Europe to see what was invisible to poet and philosopher,—the dim outline of a mountain-summit across the ocean, rising high above the mist and mud of American democracy. As though to call attention to some such difficulty, European and American critics, while affirming that Americans were a race without illusions or enlarged ideas, declared in the same breath that Jefferson was a visionary whose theories would cause the heavens to fall upon them. Year after year, with endless iteration, in every accent of contempt, rage, and despair, they repeated this charge against Jefferson. Every foreigner and Federalist agreed that he was a man of illusions, dangerous to society and unbounded in power of evil; but if this view of his character was right, the same visionary qualities seemed also to be a national trait, for every one admitted that Jefferson's opinions, in one form or another, were shared by a majority of the American people.

Illustrations might be carried much further, and might be drawn from every social class and from every period in national history. Of all presidents, Abraham Lincoln has been considered the most typical representative of American society, chiefly because his mind, with all its practical qualities, also inclined, in certain directions, to idealism. Lincoln was born in 1809, the moment when American character stood in lowest esteem. Ralph Waldo Emerson, a more distinct idealist, was born in 1803. William Ellery Channing, another idealist, was born in 1780. Men like John Fitch, Oliver Evans, Robert Fulton, Joel Barlow, John Stevens, and Eli Whitney were all classed among visionaries. The whole society of Quakers belonged in the same category. The records of the popular religious sects abounded in examples of idealism and illusion to such an extent that the masses seemed hardly to find comfort or hope in any authority, however old or well established. In religion as in politics, Americans seemed to require a system which gave play to their imagination and their hopes.

Some misunderstanding must always take place when the observer is at cross-purposes with the society he describes. Wordsworth might have convinced himself by a moment's thought that no country could act on the imagination as America acted upon the instincts of the ignorant and poor, without some quality that deserved better treatment than poignant scorn; but perhaps this was only one among innumerable cases in which the unconscious poet breathed an atmosphere which the self-conscious poet could not penetrate. With equal reason he might have taken the opposite view,—that the hard, practical, money-getting American democrat, who had neither generosity nor honor nor imagination, and who inhabited cold shades where fancy sickened and where genius died, was in truth living in a world of dream, and acting a drama more instinct with poetry than all the avatars of the East, walking in gardens of emerald and rubies, in ambition already ruling the world and guiding Nature with a kinder and wiser hand than had ever yet been felt in human history. From this point his critics never approached him,—

they stopped at a stone's throw; and at the moment when they declared that the man's mind had no illusions, they added that he was a knave or a lunatic. Even on his practical and sordid side, the American might easily have been represented as a victim to illusion. If the Englishman had lived as the American speculator did,—in the future,—the hyperbole of enthusiasm would have seemed less monstrous. "Look at my wealth!" cried the American to his foreign visitor. "See these solid mountains of salt and iron, of lead, copper, silver, and gold! See these magnificent cities scattered broadcast to the Pacific! See my cornfields rustling and waving in the summer breeze from ocean to ocean, so far that the sun itself is not high enough to mark where the distant mountains bound my golden seas! Look at this continent of mine, fairest of created worlds, as she lies turning up to the sun's never-failing caress her broad and exuberant breasts, overflowing with milk for her hundred million children! See how she glows with youth, health, and love!" Perhaps it was not altogether unnatural that the foreigner, on being asked to see what needed centuries to produce, should have looked about him with bewilderment and indignation. "Gold! cities! cornfields! continents! Nothing of the sort! I see nothing but tremendous wastes, where sickly men and women are dying of home-sickness or are scalped by savages! mountain-ranges a thousand miles long, with no means of getting to them, and nothing in them when you get there! swamps and forests choked with their own rotten ruins! nor hope of better for a thousand years! Your story is a fraud, and you are a liar and swindler!"

Met in this spirit, the American, half perplexed and half defiant, retaliated by calling his antagonist a fool, and by mimicking his heavy tricks of manner. For himself he cared little, but his dream was his whole existence. The men who denounced him admitted that they left him in his forest-swamp quaking with fever, but clinging in the delirium of death to the illusions of his dazzled brain. No class of men could be required to support their convictions with a steadier faith, or pay more devotedly with their persons for the mistakes of their judgment. Whether imagination or greed led them to describe more than actually existed, they still saw no more than any inventor or discoverer must have seen in order to give him the energy of success. They said to the rich as to the poor, "Come and share our limitless riches! Come and help us bring to light these unimaginable stores of wealth and power!" The poor came, and from them were seldom heard complaints of deception or delusion. Within a moment, by the mere contact of a moral atmosphere, they saw the gold and jewels, the summer cornfields and the glowing continent. The rich for a long time stood aloof,—they were timid and narrow-minded; but this was not all,—between them and the American democrat was a gulf.

The charge that Americans were too fond of money to win the confidence of Europeans was a curious inconsistency; yet this was a common belief. If the American deluded himself and led others to their death by baseless speculations; if he buried those he loved in a gloomy forest where they quaked and died while he persisted in seeing there a splendid, healthy, and well-built city,—no one could deny that he sacrificed wife and child to his greed for gain, that the dollar was his god, and a sordid avarice his demon. Yet had this been the whole truth, no European capitalist would have hesitated to make money out of his grave; for, avarice against avarice, no more sordid or meaner type existed in America than could be shown on every 'Change in Europe. With much more reason Americans might have suspected that in America Englishmen found everywhere a silent influence, which they found nowhere in Europe, and which had nothing to do with avarice or with the dollar, but, on the contrary, seemed likely at any moment to sacrifice the dollar in a cause and for an object so illusory that most Englishmen could not endure to hear it discussed. European travellers who passed through America noticed that everywhere, in the White House at Washington and in log-cabins beyond the Alleghanies, except for a few Federalists, every American, from Jefferson and Gallatin down to the poorest squatter, seemed to nourish an idea that he was doing what he could to overthrow the tyranny which the past had fastened on the human mind. Nothing was easier than to laugh at the ludicrous expressions of this simple-minded conviction, or to cry out against its coarseness, or grow angry with its prejudices; to see its nobler side, to feel the beatings of a heart underneath the sordid surface of a gross humanity, was not so easy. Europeans seemed seldom or never conscious that the sentiment could possess a noble side, but found only matter for complaint in the remark that every American democrat believed himself to be working for the overthrow of tyranny, aristocracy, hereditary privilege, and priesthood, wherever they existed. Even where the American did not openly proclaim this conviction in words, he carried so dense an atmosphere of the sentiment with him in his daily life as to give respectable Europeans an uneasy sense of remoteness.

Of all historical problems, the nature of a national character is the most difficult and the most important. Readers will be troubled, at almost every chapter of the coming narrative, by the want of some formula to explain what share the popular imagination bore in the system pursued by government. The acts of the American people during the administrations of Jefferson and Madison were judged at the time by no other test. According as bystanders believed American character to be hard, sordid, and free from illusion, they were severe and even harsh in judgment. This rule guided the governments of England and France. Federalists in the United States, knowing more of the circumstances, often attributed to the democratic instinct a visionary quality which they regarded as sentimentality, and charged with many bad consequences. If their view was correct, history could occupy itself to no better purpose than in ascertaining the nature and force of the quality which was charged with results so serious; but nothing was more elusive than the spirit of American democracy. Jefferson, the literary representative of the class, spoke chiefly for Virginians, and dreaded so greatly his own reputation as a visionary that he seldom or never uttered his whole thought. Gallatin and Madison were still more cautious. The press in no country could give shape to a mental condition so shadowy. The people themselves, although millions in number, could not have expressed their finer instincts had they tried, and might not have recognized them if expressed by others.

In the early days of colonization, every new settlement represented an idea and proclaimed a mission. Virginia was founded by a great, liberal movement aiming at the spread of English liberty and empire. The Pilgrims of Plymouth, the Puritans of Boston, the Quakers of Pennsylvania, all avowed a moral purpose, and began by making institutions that consciously reflected a moral idea. No such character belonged to the colonization of 1800. From Lake Erie to Florida, in long, unbroken line, pioneers were at work, cutting into the forests with the energy of so many beavers, and with no more express moral purpose than the beavers they drove away. The civilization they carried with them was rarely illumined by an idea; they sought room for no new truth, and aimed neither at creating, like the Puritans, a government of saints, nor, like the Quakers, one of love and peace; they left such experiments behind them, and wrestled only with the hardest problems of frontier life. No wonder that foreign observers, and even the educated, well-to-do Americans of the sea-coast, could seldom see anything to admire in the ignorance and brutality of frontiersmen, and should declare that virtue and wisdom no longer guided the United States! What they saw was not encouraging. To a new society, ignorant and semi-barbarous, a mass of demagogues insisted on applying every stimulant that could inflame its worst appetites, while at the same instant taking away every influence that had hitherto helped to restrain its passions. Greed for wealth, lust for power, yearning for the blank void of savage freedom such as Indians and wolves delighted in,—these were the fires that flamed under the caldron of American society, in which, as conservatives believed, the old, well-proven, conservative crust of religion, government, family, and even common respect for age, education, and experience was rapidly melting away, and was indeed already broken into fragments, swept about by the seething mass of scum ever rising in greater quantities to the surface.

Against this Federalist and conservative view of democratic tendencies, democrats protested in a thousand forms, but never in any mode of expression which satisfied them all, or explained their whole character. Probably Jefferson came nearest to the mark, for he represented the hopes of science as well as the prejudices of Virginia; but Jefferson's writings may be searched from beginning to end without revealing the whole measure of the man, far less of the movement. Here and there in his letters a suggestion was thrown out, as though by chance, revealing larger hopes,—as in 1815, at a moment of despondency, he wrote: "I fear from the experience of the last twenty-five years that morals do not of necessity advance hand in hand with the sciences." In 1800, in the flush of triumph, he believed that his task in the world was to establish a democratic republic, with the sciences for an intellectual field, and physical and moral advancement keeping pace with their advance. Without an excessive introduction of more recent ideas, he might be imagined to define democratic progress, in the somewhat affected precision of his French philosophy: "Progress is either physical or intellectual. If we can bring it about that men are on the average an inch taller in the next generation than in this; if they are an inch larger round the chest; if their brain is an ounce or two heavier, and their life a year or two longer,—that is progress. If fifty years hence the average man shall invariably argue from two ascertained premises where he now jumps to a conclusion from a single supposed revelation,—that is progress! I expect it to be made here, under our democratic stimulants, on a great scale, until every man is potentially an athlete in body and an Aristotle in mind." To this doctrine the New Englander replied, "What will you do for moral progress?" Every possible answer to this question opened a chasm. No doubt Jefferson held the faith that men would improve morally with their physical and intellectual growth; but he had no idea of any moral improvement other than that which came by nature. He could not tolerate a priesthood, a state church, or revealed religion. Conservatives, who could tolerate no society without such pillars of order, were, from their point of view, right in answering, "Give us rather the worst despotism of Europe, —there our souls at least may have a chance of salvation!" To their minds vice and virtue were not relative, but fixed terms. The Church was a divine institution. How could a ship hope to reach port when the crew threw overboard sails, spars, and compass, unshipped their rudder, and all the long day thought only of eating and drinking. Nay, even should the new experiment succeed in a worldly sense, what was a man profited if he gained the whole world, and lost his own soul? The Lord God was a jealous God, and visited the sins of the parents upon the children; but what worse sin could be conceived than for a whole nation to join their chief in chanting the strange hymn with which Jefferson, a new false prophet, was deceiving and betraying his people: "It does me no injury for my neighbor to say there are twenty Gods or no God!"

On this ground conservatism took its stand, as it had hitherto done with success in every similar emergency in the world's history, and fixing its eyes on moral standards of its own, refused to deal with the subject as further open to argument. The two parties stood facing opposite ways, and could see no common ground of contact.

Yet even then one part of the American social system was proving itself to be rich in results. The average American was more intelligent than the average European, and was becoming every year still more active-minded as the new movement of society caught him up and swept him through a life of more varied experiences. On all sides the national mind responded to its stimulants. Deficient as the American was in the machinery of higher instruction; remote, poor; unable by any exertion to acquire the training, the capital, or even the elementary textbooks he needed for a fair development of his natural powers,—his native energy and ambition already responded to the spur applied to them. Some of his triumphs were famous throughout the world; for Benjamin Franklin had raised high the reputation of American printers, and the actual President of the United States, who signed with Franklin the treaty of peace with Great Britain, was the son of a small farmer, and had himself kept a school in his youth. In both these cases social recognition followed success; but the later triumphs of the American mind were becoming more and more popular. John Fitch was not only one of the poorest, but one of the least-educated Yankees who ever made a name; he could never spell with tolerable correctness, and his life ended as it began,—in the lowest social obscurity. Eli Whitney was better educated than Fitch, but had neither wealth, social influence, nor patron to back his ingenuity. In the year 1800 Eli Terry, another Connecticut Yankee of the same class, took into his employ two young men to help him make wooden clocks, and this was the capital on which the greatest clock-manufactory in the world began its operations. In 1797 Asa Whittemore, a Massachusetts Yankee, invented a machine to make cards for carding wool, which "operated as if it had a soul," and became the foundation for a hundred subsequent patents. In 1790 Jacob Perkins, of Newburyport, invented a machine capable of cutting and turning out two hundred thousand nails a day; and then invented a process for transferring engraving from a very small steel cylinder to copper, which revolutionized cotton-printing. The British traveller Weld, passing through Wilmington, stopped, as Liancourt had done before him, to see the great flour-mills on the Brandywine. "The improvements," he said, "which have been made in the machinery of the flour-mills in America are very great. The chief of these consist in a new application of the screw, and the introduction of what are called elevators, the idea of which was evidently borrowed from the chain-pump." This was the invention of Oliver Evans, a native of Delaware, whose parents were in very humble life, but who was himself, in spite of every disadvantage, an inventive genius of the first order. Robert Fulton, who in 1800 was in Paris with Joel Barlow, sprang from the same source in Pennsylvania. John Stevens, a native of New York, belonged to a more favored class, but followed the same impulses. All these men were the outcome of typical American society, and all their inventions transmuted the democratic instinct into a practical and tangible shape. Who would undertake to say that there was a limit to the fecundity of this teeming source? Who that saw only the narrow, practical, money-getting nature of these devices could venture to assert that as they wrought their end and raised the standard of millions, they would not also raise the creative power of those millions to a higher plane? If the priests and barons who set their names to Magna Charta had been told that in a few centuries every swine-herd and cobbler's apprentice would write and read with an ease such as few kings could then command, and reason with better logic than any university could then practise, the priest and baron would have been more incredulous than any man who was told in 1800 that within another five centuries the ploughboy would go a-field whistling a sonata of Beethoven, and figure out in quaternions the relation of his furrows. The American democrat knew so little of art that among his popular illusions he could not then nourish artistic ambition; but leaders like Jefferson, Gallatin, and Barlow might without extravagance count upon a coming time when diffused ease and education should bring the masses into familiar contact with higher forms of human achievement, and their vast creative power, turned toward a nobler culture, might rise to the level of that democratic genius which found expression in the Parthenon; might revel in the delights of a new Buonarotti and a richer Titian; might create for five hundred million people the America of thought and art which alone could satisfy their omnivorous ambition.

Whether the illusions, so often affirmed and so often denied to the American people, took such forms or not, these were in effect the problems that lay before American society: Could it transmute its social power into the higher forms of thought? Could it provide for the moral and intellectual needs of mankind? Could it take permanent political shape? Could it give new life to religion and art? Could it create and maintain in the mass of mankind those habits of mind which had hitherto belonged to men of science alone? Could it physically develop the convolutions of the human brain? Could it produce, or was it compatible with, the differentiation of a higher variety of the human race? Nothing less than this was necessary for its complete success.

For Further Reading

While Henry Adams' multi-volume *History of the United States of America During the Administrations of Jefferson and Madison* remains the most thorough and most lucid account of American history from 1801 to 1817, more modern studies have in some instances supplanted Adams' accounts of specific aspects and events. Better on the diplomacy of the period are three volumes by Bradford Perkins: *The First Rapprochement: England and the United States, 1795–1805* (1955); *Prologue to War: England and the United States, 1805–1812* (1961), and *Castlereagh and Adams: England and the United States, 1812–1823* (1964). Relations with France are dealt with in J. K. Hosmer, *History of the Louisiana Purchase* (1902). On the coming of the War of 1812, see—in addition to the second volume of the Perkins trilogy (cited above) —A. L. Burt, *The United States, Canada and Great Brit-*

ain . . . (1940), and Reginald Horseman, *The Causes of the War of 1812* (1962). The war itself is treated briefly in two books entitled *The War of 1812,* one by Harry L. Coles (1965), the other by Reginald Horseman (1969). The war is covered at greater length and with more color by Glenn Tucker, *Poltroons and Patriots* (2 vols., 1954). On the Treaty of Ghent, see F. L. Engleman, *The Peace of Christmas Eve* (1962).

Although war and diplomacy have captured major attention from historians, many less dramatic events of the period are now seen to have had far-reaching importance. On political developments the best recent works are Noble E. Cunningham, Jr., *The Jeffersonian Republicans in Power* (1963); David Hackett Fisher, *The Revolution of American Conservatism: The Federalist Party in the Era of Jeffersonian Democracy* (1965); Leonard White, *The Jeffersonians: A Study in Administrative History, 1801–1829;* James S. Young, *The Washington Community, 1800–1828* (1966); and Richard Hofstadter, *The Idea of a Party System* (1969). Also excellent on their subjects are Thomas P. Abernathy, *The Burr Conspiracy* (1954), and William H. Goetzmann, *Exploration and Empire* (1966). In addition to the fourth volume of Dumas Malone's *Jefferson* (1970), significant studies of major figures of the period are Irving Brant, *James Madison* (6 vols., 1948–1961), Raymond Walters, Jr., *Albert Gallatin* (1957), and Samuel E. Morison, *The Urbane Federalist: Harrison Gray Otis* (1969). The best modern synthesis of the entire Jefferson-Madison era is Marshall Smelser, *The Democratic Republic, 1801–1815* (1968).

Cultural and social aspects of the period—which Henry Adams did so much to make meaningful and readable for later generations—are skillfully handled in Russell B. Nye, *The Cultural Life of the New Nation, 1776–1830* (1960), Harvey Wish, *Society and Thought in Early America* (1950), and John A. Krout and Dixon Ryan Fox, *The Completion of Independence* (1944).

Bank, Constitution, and Economic Development, 1816–1822

Bray Hammond

Alexander Hamilton's 1791 economic program to "restore the public credit" included measures that funded the national debt, "assumed" in the name of the central government the states' revolutionary war debts, imposed new taxes, and created a central, national bank with the power to issue currency. Although each proposal brought in its train bitter political debate, the last lingered as a key issue for the next fifty years. Indeed, the initial struggle over the bank helped crystallize opposing attitudes and led to the formation of political parties.

Hamilton had seen the bank and the funding proposals as the means by which the support of the wealthy and propertied class could be assured for the fledgling nation and indirectly for the Federalist Party. Jefferson as President also saw political advantages in the banking

Source: Bray Hammond, *Banks and Politics in America, from the Revolution to the Civil War* (Princeton, N.J.: Princeton University Press, 1957), pp. 251–285. Reprinted by permission of Princeton University Press.

system; he told his Secretary of the Treasury, Albert Gallatin, in 1803: "I am decidedly in favor of making all the banks Republican. . . . It is material to the safety of Republicanism to detach the mercantile interests from its enemies and incorporate them into the body of its friends. A merchant is naturally a Republican, and can be otherwise only from a vitiated state of things." Some three decades later another President, Andrew Jackson, would follow such a course with precision.

Jefferson, nonetheless, never did fully accept the idea of a central bank. In 1814, writing to John Adams, Jefferson declared: "I have ever been the enemy of banks. . . . My zeal against those institutions was so warm and open at the establishment of the bank of the U.S. that I was derided as a Maniac by the tribe of bank-mongers, who were seeking to filch from the public their swindling, and barren gains." His animosity was shared by many in the early republic, to whom banks connoted privilege, power, and financial corruption. Visionaries of a democratic republic peopled by yeoman farmers distrusted commercial institutions generally and banks particularly.

From the vantage point of mid-twentieth-century America it is tempting to label the bank's critics as irrational opponents of progress. Hamilton's 1791 measures brought rationalization of the credit structure and provided an easy but stable circulating medium. Yet the perceptions of early bank critics like Jefferson and John Taylor of Caroline were accurate appraisals of the significance of note-issuing banks as harbingers of a coming industrial-capitalist order. To them the portending change hardly seemed like progress. This is not to say that Jefferson and others distrusted *all* banks. Those that merely discounted notes for cash—as opposed to those that issued their own notes—were acceptable institutions.

Although Jefferson and Hamilton differed on whether Federalists or Republicans should control the banking system, they did agree on governmental promotion of economic development. That the Bank of the United States did just that is certain. It provided a stable national currency, helping the interregional flow of goods. Internationally, it enhanced American chances to attract investment funds from such areas as Great Britain and France. The Bank thus stands as a prime example of governmental "interference" in the economy, belying a long-lived myth about laissez-faire policies during the nineteenth century.

Bray Hammond, a former Federal Reserve Bank official, has written a fascinating account of American political history, viewing it from the vantage point of national banking policies from the Revolution through the Civil War. In the selection that follows, Hammond deals with the reestablishment of the national bank in 1816, after a lapse of five years.

The year 1817 was a year of false promise. The Bank of the United States was established anew, and its constitutionality was little questioned. Prominent political leaders who had formerly opposed it were now its friends. The private banks had recognized its place in the economy, and the Treasury relied on its special services. The general suspension had been ended, nominally at least. The same year the first permanent bank in Canada had been established—the Bank of Montreal—and being patterned after Alexander Hamilton's proposals, it seemed to confirm the correctness of the American precedent. The champions of the Bank of the United States had been justified by the miserable experience consequent on the dissolution of 1811. With the restraints of the old Bank out of the way, private banks had rushed into business, extended too much credit, and suspended *en masse* when trouble came. Continuance of the Bank would not have prevented the suspension, perhaps; but the suspension made the Bank's discontinuance harder to defend. Its opponents were chastened, and many had been converted.

Yet a new peril threatened the federal Bank in the grip on it that speculators and politicians got while it was still in the process of organization. Captain William Jones, an unfortunate Philadelphia merchant and politician, was made president of the Bank, though he had recently gone through bankruptcy. Neither that interesting circumstance nor his recently having been Secretary of the Navy and acting Secretary of the Treasury in Mr. Madison's cabinet would seem to have qualified him for so important a responsibility. According to Prime, Ward, and King, correspondents of the Barings and New York's leading merchant bankers, Congress, in setting up the Bank, "levied a tax which by our monied men was thought too oppressive, and a considerable proportion of the stock, with the power of governing the institution, fell into the hands of speculators." Stephen Girard tried to stop this development but failed. Of the meeting of stockholders in Philadelphia, 28 October 1816, he wrote that "Intrigue and corruption had formed a ticket for twenty directors of the Bank of the United States who I am sorry to say appear to have been selected for the purpose of securing the presidency for Mr Jones. . . . Although Mr Jacob Astor of New York and I have obtained . . . that the names of Thomas M. Willing of this city and Mr James Lloyd of Boston should be inserted in the ticket of directors now elected, yet there are still several persons whose occupations, moral characters, or pecuniary situation will not inspire that indispensable confidence which is absolutely necessary to establish and consolidate the credit of that institution." The day the Bank opened for business, 7 January 1817, Mr Girard wrote: "If I live twelve months more I intend to use all my activity, means, and influence to change and replace the majority of directors with honest and independent men. . . ." But his activity, means, and influence taken alone were inadequate.

This is not what might be supposed would happen. Girard had promoted the Bank earnestly, he was the largest and most prominent stockholder, his friends and associates were wealthy, he was one of the commissioners appointed by the President of the United States to supervise subscriptions, he was a government director, his banking offices had been the headquarters at which elections and organization had been determined, and his bank had been the agent in subscription payments and other preliminary transactions. He was astute and powerful. He might have been expected to wrap the Bank around his little finger. On the contrary, he was frozen out from the first, and his wishes were realized only after his participation had relaxed and the force of circumstances had taken over. The explanation, I think, is that he belonged to the 18th century, and his conservatism was uncongenial to the new and democratic enterprisers who were filling the business world with such numbers, such diversity, such commotion, such free-for-all aggressiveness, such sanguine irresponsibility, such readiness for sleights-of-hand, and such contempt for established codes and old-fashioned honesty, that though his money might be useful, his example was too slow and unambitious. In the past it had meant something that ships of his had been named for French philosophers—the *Voltaire,* the *Helvétius,* the *Montesquieu*—but he was left now among a generation who knew only enough of philosophers to distinguish one from a stock-jobber. The sober pace of 18th century business was giving way, on the wave of *laissez faire* and the Industrial Revolution, to a democratic passion to get rich quick—an ambition which America seemed designed by Providence to promote. And it was men imbued with this passion and the unscrupulousness appropriate to it who had snatched control of the Bank of the United States.

Captain Jones and his crew struck out at once on their new courses. He wrote Secretary Crawford in July 1817 that he was "not at all disposed to take the late Bank of the United States as an exemplar in practice; because I think its operations were circumscribed by a policy less enlarged, liberal, and useful than its powers and resources would have justified." And about the same time, February 1817, James W. McCulloch, cashier of the Baltimore office, who nearly ruined it a little later, wrote of the old Bank to the Secretary that, "Instead of extending its operations so as to embrace every real demand of commerce; instead of expanding its views as the country and its trade grew, it pursued a timid and faltering course." He and his associates meant to do otherwise.

Even before the federal Bank was opened, the management had made a revealing decision in the basic matter of payment on subscriptions to the Bank's capital. The charter authorized payment of one-fourth in specie, and three-fourths in government securities or specie, the expectation being that no one would pay more than the fourth in specie. But several conditions combined to upset this expectation. One was a premium of 8 per cent on specie, which meant of course—values being expressed in terms of state bank paper, notes or checks—that it took $108 worth of bank credit to obtain $100 in coin. Naturally, for the subscribers this was tantamount to a requirement that on one-fourth of their subscription they pay $108 for each $100 subscribed. At the same time, the credit of the government had so much improved that government stock was also at a premium. The result of these two conditions was that the stockholders found it harder to pay their subscription than they had expected. They turned to the Bank itself for help, and the Bank was indulgent. It accepted their promissory notes in payment, secured by the Bank's own stock valued at a premium of 25 per cent.

Legally it could not do this, and directly it did not. Instead, it "lent" its notes and these were "accepted" as specie on the principle that the notes of a bank that redeemed its obligations in specie were the equivalent of specie. This was another convenient consequence of Alexander Hamilton's having established the principle in 1790 that the notes of specie-paying banks were the equivalent of specie. For Hamilton's purposes —the payment of sums due the government—and for current monetary settlements the principle was a reasonable and useful one. But here it was different, for it evaded the basic need of putting silver and gold in the Bank's coffers. Its consequence, in fact, was that the Bank got neither the specie it should nor the government stock it should; for if specie notes were "specie," it was easier to pay the whole subscription in them than in either the precious metals or government stock. So the Bank did not begin operations in the intrinsically strong position its responsibilities required. It should have received from its private stockholders $7,000,000 in coin at least and $21,000,000 in government securities at most. According to Professor Dewey it received $2,000,000 in specie from them, $14,000,000 in government securities, and $12,000,000 in personal notes. The calculation is uncertain, however, because the capital was not paid all in one operation or before the Bank opened. Instead the subscribers paid in three installments, six months apart, and the Bank began operations when the first installment was made. Since the Bank's specie and government portfolio began to turn over in the course of operations, and since much "specie" was fictitious, I do not see how the exact amounts received from stockholders could be distinguished even nominally, much less in fact. This was the Bank's own view.

The Bank did acquire more specie, however, through its own efforts. In December 1816 it sent John Sergeant, a prominent Philadelphia attorney, to Europe to negotiate for as much as $5,000,000. Although it was folly to advertise the quest and so increase its hazards, the Bank's management with its characteristic pretentiousness must have told the newspapers, because they reported how the Bank was going to get specie and had already been offered $10,000,000 from London some weeks before John Sergeant's departure. Sergeant's arrival abroad was advertised in London also. This fanfare contrasted grimly with the difficulties actually encountered. The Barings rejected the business promptly, and other firms demanded too much for undertaking it. But in time Mr. Sergeant got an offer which he could accept, though he still demurred for better terms. It was a contract with Baring Brothers, and Reid, Irving, and Company for $3,195,000 in silver to be paid for within some twenty months, the loan to bear 5 per cent interest. Immediately the price of the metal rose in the European markets, and the firms were hard put to meet their obligations. The Barings eventually did, but the other firm seems to have done nothing. The newspapers in the States, however, published vague, inspiring reports of "specie pouring in from all quarters." From the summer of 1817 to the end of 1818 the Bank imported $7,300,000, of which $675,000 was gold from Lisbon and London, and the rest was silver from France and Jamaica mainly.

Since the $7,300,000 was more than the amount due from the private shareholders under the law, the Bank may be said to have done in effect what was required of it. A requirement that capital be *paid* in specie did not require a bank to retain the specie, and in practice a relatively small amount of specie going in and out in enough successive transactions in the course of enough time could amount to any sum conceivable. So a literal compliance with the law, which in this respect was the same as state laws, could be achieved easily. On the other hand, it was impossible in any practical sense for $7,000,000 of specie to be amassed in any one spot in America in 1817. What the law said, therefore, cannot be taken as a dependable register of what a bank could do. In getting the Bank of the United States organized with an adequate stock of specie, the shareholders and managers of the Bank did nothing to strike posterity with admiration, but neither did they do anything so much worse than posterity would do that their clumsiness and evasion can be reprobated.

Meanwhile, branch offices were being set up. Their organization had been undertaken early, and by the end of 1817 there were eighteen of them, after which the Bank established no more till 1826. In the next four years it established seven. Two were discontinued, and the maximum number at one time, 1830, was twenty-five. The offices, including Philadelphia, were established as follows:

- 1817 Philadelphia, Pennsylvania
- 1817 Augusta, Georgia (discontinued 1817)
- 1817 Baltimore, Maryland
- 1817 Boston, Massachusetts
- 1817 Charleston, South Carolina
- 1817 Chillicothe, Ohio (discontinued 1825)
- 1817 Cincinnati, Ohio (discontinued 1820; re-established 1825)
- 1817 Fayetteville, North Carolina
- 1817 Hartford, Connecticut (opened at Middletown but moved to Hartford, 1824)
- 1817 Lexington, Kentucky
- 1817 Louisville, Kentucky
- 1817 New Orleans, Louisiana
- 1817 New York, New York
- 1817 Norfolk, Virginia
- 1817 Pittsburgh, Pennsylvania
- 1817 Portsmouth, New Hampshire
- 1817 Providence, Rhode Island
- 1817 Richmond, Virginia
- 1817 Savannah, Georgia
- 1817 Washington, District of Columbia
- 1826 Mobile, Alabama
- 1827 Nashville, Tennessee
- 1828 Portland, Maine
- 1829 Buffalo, New York
- 1829 St. Louis, Missouri
- 1830 Burlington, Vermont
- 1830 Utica, New York
- 1830 Natchez, Mississippi

Contemporarily, the branches were known and designated as "offices of discount and deposit," which was what they were called in the law. They were in twenty states and the District of Columbia. The old charter had merely permitted the Bank to have branches at the directors' discretion. The new charter plainly presupposed their establishment and in some conditions made it obligatory, doubtless because of the reluctance of the old Bank on occasion to establish branches as the government wished. From the point of view of a responsible management, branches were a hazard, for it was impossible to maintain close control over them. Local and regional interests were apt to take things in their own hands and commit the Bank seriously before the headquarters in Philadelphia, in the absence of modern communication, knew what was happening or could make their will known and effective. But on top of that the branches seem to have been under no individual limitation during the first two years or so; each was allowed to lend as if it were the whole institution and not a fraction thereof only.

The Bank began business in the midst of temptations on every hand to over-extend itself. Trade was active and prices were high in its first two years, 1817 and 1818. Economic recovery after the war was intensified by the diversion of enterprise from foreign trade to the domestic field, by the exploitation of new territory, and by the Industrial Revolution, which with machines was multiplying the efficiency of human effort miraculously. In the vast business parade that was forming, banks had a prominent place. They provided money, quintessential in what was being undertaken, and offered little resistance to the pressure upon them to lend. Very few men specialized in banking sufficiently to make it a conservative force in the general play of enterprise. Bankers were themselves imbued with the prevailing enthusiasm.

In such a situation the restraining powers of a central bank were spurned. All that was wanted was more steam. The Bank yielded. It yielded first to its own greedy stockholders, by helping them get their stock the easiest way possible. It yielded to borrowers in general, living up to the open-handed philosophy which its president and its Baltimore manager expressed in the passages already quoted from them; though by doing so it enlarged its liabilities and exposed its specie to withdrawal. It yielded to the state banks, which sought to frustrate its pressure upon them for the current redemption of their notes. Unreasonable and preposterous though the private banks' position was, the federal Bank itself, in this period, was scarcely better.

Stephen Girard resigned as a government director, 31 December 1817, when the Bank had been working not quite a year. He was still the largest single stockholder, but that gave him no direct weight, since the charter allowed no stockholder more than thirty votes, no matter how much stock he had. The insiders against whom he and his minority were ranged had got around this restriction by spreading a given ownership over many names. The extreme case was in Baltimore, where George Williams, a director of the Bank, owned 1,172 shares but registered them under 1,172 different names with himself as attorney for all. So he had thirty-nine times the maximum number of votes the charter allowed any one stockholder. Mr. Girard, dissatisfied with such things, aroused other stockholders, especially those in Charleston. "Although I would strongly recommend that the stockholders endeavor to effect a total change of its direction at the next election," he said, "I do not think they will accomplish it, but it may help to obtain competent men in 1820." The Charleston stockholders made opposition open by nominating Langdon Cheves of South Carolina for president of the Bank and by appointing a committee of correspondence to communicate with stockholders elsewhere in furtherance of a change in management.

The changes purposed by the minority were expedited by a panic and recession which swept the country in 1818 and shook the Bank severely. In July with demand liabilities outstanding in excess of $22,370,000, it had specie of only $2,360,000; this was a ratio of a little more than one to ten, whereas the statute presupposed a ratio of one to five. Its situation was still much the same in October when the Treasury called for $2,000,000 in specie to pay off obligations incurred by the purchase of the Louisiana territory. This was nearly all the specie the Bank had, and it settled for drafts on London instead.

Meanwhile the directors had begun tardily to give their duties serious heed. They initiated curtailments of credit and imports of specie, but just at the time that the Bank's slow-earning assets were least collectible and specie hardest to get. The Bank was forced in self-preservation to do exactly the opposite of what a central bank should do: it should check expansion and ease contraction. As lender of last resort and keeper of ultimate reserves, it should have those reserves in readiness before trouble comes, and not be driven to scurry for them vainly when the need for them is already at hand. Instead, the Bank had stimulated the expansion and now must intensify the contraction, having by its first course committed itself to the second.

In October 1818 a House committee under the chairmanship of John C. Spencer of New York was instructed to investigate the Bank; in January 1819 it reported that the charter had been violated in several particulars, but it recommended no drastic action to be taken, because "the Secretary of the Treasury has full power to apply a prompt and adequate remedy"—meaning evidently the power to remove the government deposits from the Bank. There were active demands, meanwhile, that the charter be repealed, but Congress took the judicious view that the conduct of the Bank though bad was not incorrigible. The first correction was effected when William Jones resigned, only a fortnight after his reelection; his resignation was followed immediately by an advance in the price of the Bank stock, which had been offered at 93 but after he resigned could not be bought at 98 and in a matter of days was selling at 101 and kept on rising. The second correction occurred when Langdon Cheves was chosen president.

It was moot whether the Bank was still worth saving, but the more responsible stockholders decided that it should be saved, and that was the conclusion in Congress; for the House, by heavy majorities, in February 1819, rejected proposals to repeal the charter. The Bank had, of course, as great potential usefulness as ever, if it were able to recover public confidence. That, as things turned out, it was unable fully to do. A popular hatred of it based on the grim efforts made to collect or secure what was receivable, subsided but was never extinguished. "The Bank was saved," wrote William Gouge, "and the people were ruined." Its violent efforts at recovery created a popular conviction of its power, when in fact they were impelled by a convulsive weakness. Twelve years later, Senator Thomas Hart Benton of Missouri dilated on the consequences of those efforts. "All the flourishing cities of the West," he exclaimed with oratorical fancy, "are mortgaged to this money power. They may be devoured by it at any moment. They are in the jaws of the monster! A lump of butter in the mouth of a dog! One gulp, one swallow, and all is gone!" In these chilling words he pictured the Bank, like the dog, in absolute control of the situation. On the contrary, in 1820, when the mortgages were taken, the Bank was as nearly gone as the butter. Its survival damned it worse than failure would have done. John Quincy Adams thought, as others did, that "the government is the party most interested in the continuance of the Bank and that the interest of the stockholders would be to surrender their charter." But at the moment, as usual in such crises, salvage seemed to the persons concerned an imperative duty, to be achieved at any cost.

But behind these embarrassments, something still worse had been hatching in Baltimore, where James A. Buchanan was president of the branch and James W. McCulloch was cashier. Baltimore had sought to be headquarters of the Bank, and perhaps the same ambition led the officers there to make it the biggest office if not the dominant one. From the outset the volume of its business expanded excessively. Baltimore was the newest of the important commercial cities, an active export center, and also an active distributor of northern products. "There is not a city in the Union," John Quincy Adams wrote, "which has had so much apparent prosperity or within which there has been such complication of profligacy." Taking advantage of the demand of its merchants for funds to remit to their suppliers, the Baltimore office discounted profusely and furnished drafts on the Boston, New York, and Philadelphia offices of the Bank. The Baltimore office, had it been an independent bank, would have had to send the other branches funds in some form to enable them to pay the drafts, and even as a branch it should have recognized a corresponding duty. But the Philadelphia directors, at the instance of William Jones, the president, who was under the thumb of the Baltimore people, carried to an extreme the meritorious principle that the Bank with its branches constituted one integral and universal organization, each part of which must honor the obligations of every other part. So, for example, notes issued by the office in Charleston could turn up in Portsmouth or Chillicothe and pass current there because the Portsmouth and Chillicothe offices were expected to redeem them in coin if asked to. This was admirable as an ideal, but it assumed that every office was able in fact to honor the notes or other obligations of every other office. That ability depended on the possession of the necessary means, and the possession of the necessary means depended basically on the exchange of commodities. If Baltimore sent just as many dollars' worth of tobacco to New York as New York sent her in dry goods and if trade otherwise kept each city's bank supplied with currency, then the federal Bank's branches in each city would be able to honor one another's obligations readily. In fact, however, such perfect balances of trade and balances of payments between centers, regions, and countries are never found. There is always some disparity, and in consequence it is always harder to maintain the flow of cash payments in some directions than in others. The United States has become so nearly homogeneous now in the middle of the 20th century—partly from general productivity, partly from means of transport and communication, partly from banking operations, partly from large scale corporate enterprise, and partly from the maintenance of wide-spread governmental activities—that the flow of payments is practically equalized. In 1820 the homogeneity was far less than it is now; inter-regional payments were constantly and irregularly out of balance. Hence the Bank was operating on a basis of inter-regional parity that did not exist. Yet Baltimore, and other southern and western offices to a less extent, drew persistently on the offices in the North and East without the means to pay, and the headquarters in Philadelphia tolerated their action in the name of unity.

As I said, it was a Baltimore director, George Williams, who registered 1,172 shares of stock in 1,172 different names, with himself as attorney voting them all; and his example, though extreme, was not unique. The Baltimore people borrowed from the Bank to buy stock and systematically engrossed voting power. They made loans on the Bank's stock without informing the directors and then made more with no collateral at all. They made these loans mostly to themselves, they overdrew their accounts, and they deceived associates not in their own circle. Their chicane, said Nicholas Biddle, "created that solecism—a monied institution governed by those who had no money; it reduced the Bank at Philadelphia to a mere colony of the Baltimore adventurers."

George Williams was a director both at Baltimore and at Philadelphia. James Buchanan, the president of the Baltimore office, was a partner of Samuel Smith, now a member of the House of Representatives but a Senator in 1811 when he opposed Albert Gallatin and renewal of the 1791 charter. The house of Smith and Buchanan had been for the past thirty years, according to John Quincy Adams, "one of the greatest commercial establishments in the United States" and notably an "exporter of specie to India by the half million at a time." All of Buchanan's transactions with the Bank were in the firm name, S. Smith and Buchanan. James McCulloch, the Baltimore cashier, had no means of his own, but he lent himself more than a half million dollars. The three, Buchanan, Williams, and McCulloch, composed a company for their carryings-on and paralleled Williams's device by holding 1,000 shares of the Bank's stock in 1,000 different names. Their dealings began as speculations, grew into frauds, and involved about $3,000,000 when the affair burst open. The net loss in the end exceeded $1,500,000. The straits the Bank was in on other scores had generated a vigilance which the conspirators could not elude, especially since their own difficulties were magnified by the recession. In January William Jones had resigned, in March and April they disclosed their dealings. It was one of the first things to confront Langdon Cheves when he became the Bank's president.

James McCulloch was removed from his cashiership, and "for a day or two there was great blustering in the Baltimore newspapers, as if the grossest injustice had been done" him; "but the mine was blown up." At the moment, however, the most striking aspect of the affair seems to have been the failure of S. Smith and Buchanan. The house broke, John Quincy Adams said, "with a crash which staggered the whole city of Baltimore." It well might. "The moral, political, and commercial character of this city of Baltimore has for twenty-five years been formed, controlled, and modified almost entirely by this house of Smith and Buchanan, their connections and dependents." Samuel Smith was rich, and active in public life. He had the rank of general from a military career; he had been a prominent and influential member of the Congress for twenty-six years; he was a generous public benefactor, a person of distinguished mien, and husband of an aunt, by a marriage since annulled, to the younger brother of the *ci-devant* Emperor Napoleon Bonaparte. Yet he was but mortal. "General Smith," wrote Mr Adams, "is reported to have gone distracted and to be confined dangerously ill in bed."

Langdon Cheves (whose name was pronounced Chivis) was a South Carolina attorney who had been a Republican member of Congress and Speaker of the House. He took the presidency of the Bank with some reluctance, for he might instead have been appointed by President Monroe to the Supreme Court—he had five years before refused the secretaryship of the Treasury relinquished by Albert Gallatin. When he went to Philadelphia he was already "satisfied that there was a great want of financial talent" in the Bank's management. "But I had not the faintest idea that its power had been so completely prostrated or that it had been thus unfortunately managed or grossly defrauded. I never imagined that when it had at so much expense and loss imported so many millions of specie, they had been entirely exhausted and were not yet paid for; nor that the Bank was on the point of stopping payment."

He began his administration March 1819 with a thousand things to be done at once, though the directors had already undertaken the changes required by the Bank's condition. He made drastic retrenchments in salaries and other expenses. He initiated investigations, dismissals, and prosecutions; for there were defaulters, though more modest ones, elsewhere than in Baltimore. He procured the appointment of new officers and directors and made the conservative minority dominant. His changes in policy began with curtailment of business at the southern and western offices. The government was persuaded to be accommodating and allow the Bank time to arrange transfers of public funds. A loan of $2,000,000 obtained from Baring Brothers and Hope and Company was taken largely in specie. The funds of the Bank were shifted into government securities. Definite limitations were put on the business of the various offices by allocation of capital to them. No branch was to draw on any other branch without having the funds to draw against.

These measures took time; and meanwhile there were difficulties with the state governments and the state banks. Here too Maryland was a seat of trouble, for in February 1818 the Assembly had passed a law which imposed a tax of $15,000 a year on all banks or branches thereof in the state of Maryland not chartered by the legislature. The Baltimore office of the Bank of the United States refused to pay and was sued in the name of J. W. McCulloch, the Baltimore cashier, for the amount claimed by the state. This was some months before McCulloch's speculations became known. The Bank lost in the state courts and appealed to the federal Supreme Court.

The case, *McCulloch* v. *Maryland,* was of recognized importance, for other states besides Maryland—Tennessee, Georgia, North Carolina, Kentucky, and Ohio—were adopting practically annihilatory taxes on the Bank, and still others were considering it. When the former Bank, some ten years before, had appealed to the Supreme Court against similar action by Georgia, the question became one of jurisdiction and the Bank lost without any decision on the constitutional issue. This was *Bank of the United States* v. *Deveaux,* February 1809. But now the constitutional issue was foremost. If the Maryland law stood, the individual states had it in their power to put the federal Bank out of business forthwith, and the federal government had not the power to form corporations or go in other directions beyond the letter of the Constitution.

The Bank's position was one of irony. It came before the Supreme Court suing for its legality when its solvency was in doubt. It was a half-sunk creditor, harassed and harassing. Its position was even more desperate than was known, for while its plea was being made to the Court in the name of James W. McCulloch, he was helping himself, with his two colleagues, to its funds. It had barely got rid of Captain Jones, and Langdon Cheves had not taken charge. According to some people, it would be best for the stockholders if the charter were surrendered and the Bank liquidated; according to many more, the public interest demanded that this be done. In Congress efforts to that end were making.

The chief counsel for Maryland before the Supreme Court was Luther Martin, Attorney General of the state, who thirty years before had been one of the most outspoken and active opponents of the federal Constitution. Counsel for the Bank were William Wirt, Attorney General of the United States, William Pinkney, and Daniel Webster. These were all among the greatest lawyers in the land. In preparation for the hearing, which opened 22 February 1819, Chief Justice Marshall sold the seventeen shares of federal Bank stock standing in his name; and he never afterward owned stock in the Bank. The hearing occupied nine days; its height was reached in the argument of William Pinkney, who spoke for three days.

Mr. Pinkney's argument was Hamiltonian: a government could not be effective unless it possessed the powers it needed for the performance of its functions. Federal responsibilities under the Constitution are large and federal powers are correspondingly so. Yet now it is being doubted, he said, "whether a government invested with such immense powers has authority to erect a corporation within the sphere of its general objects and in order to accomplish some of these objects." From this protasis of federal power, the apodosis was that Maryland had no countervailing power. It was absurd to suppose that if the union of states needed the Bank, an individual state could deny it the Bank. "There is a manifest repugnancy," Mr. Pinkney averred, "between the power of Maryland to tax, and the power of Congress to preserve, this institution. A power to build up what another may pull down at pleasure is a power which may provoke a smile but can do nothing else."

The court's decision, which was unanimous, was delivered by Chief Justice Marshall, 7 March 1819, the day after Langdon Cheves took office. It pursued William Pinkney's argument but derived more explicitly from that submitted by Alexander Hamilton to President Washington in 1791 in support of the Bank's constitutionality. It affirmed that Congress had power to incorporate and control a bank, and that the states had no power to interfere by taxation or otherwise. The import of the decision, as expected, went far beyond the status of the Bank itself and broadened the base of federal authority, confirming thereby the general identification of the Bank with strengthened federal powers. "Let the end be legitimate, let it be within the scope of the Constitution, and all means which are appropriate, which are plainly adapted to that end, which are not prohibited but consist with the letter and spirit of the Constitution, are constitutional." The court took no account of the Bank as a monetary agency, but it may have omitted purposely to do so, recognizing that to establish the Bank's constitutionality on narrow, specific grounds would fail to give the sweeping affirmation of federal powers from which the decision derived its importance. The federal government, the Court declared in effect, did not have to look closely in the Constitution for language which exactly or even approximately foreshadowed any particular means it wished to employ; it was assured by the Court that whatever its purpose, if constitutional, it had command of the means appropriate to that purpose. A further consideration is that since the Bank in 1818 or 1819 had signally failed in its monetary duties, a justification of the Bank on the ground of those duties would have been morally weak. As it was, the decision had far greater significance for the development of federal powers in general than for the development of federal powers with respect to money and banking.

The partisans of the federal government and of the Bank were comforted by the Supreme Court's decision; the partisans of states' rights, the private banks, and the enemies of the Bank were angered and alarmed. The state banks had to pay state taxes; the federal Bank, though conducting its business within the states, did not. The federal government was "invading" the states. If it could "create a monied institution in the very bosom of the states, paramount to their laws, then indeed is state sovereignty a mere name." In the South and in the West, where states' rights were most cherished, the decision was attacked and efforts were made to defend the state authority from it. It was a sardonic coincidence, giving the unpopular decision a still worse flavor, that the Baltimore officer in whose name the Bank had sued, was disclosed a week later to have been an embezzler beyond the dreams of most contemporaries' avarice.

Feeling was especially bitter in Ohio, where the Bank's earlier extensions of credit had been excessive and where it had now a host of debtors reviling it. Much Ohio real estate, especially in the city of Cincinnati, was coming into the Bank's hands on foreclosure. In the setting created by this condition, the Ohio legislature, 8 February 1819, had imposed a tax of $50,000 on each branch of the Bank in the state—there was then one in Chillicothe and one in Cincinnati—doing so on the rather remarkable legal grounds that since the Bank was transacting business at these two offices "in violation of the laws of this state," it was "just and necessary that such unlawful banking while continued should be subject to the payment of a tax for the support of the government." The statute also authorized the state Auditor in collecting the tax to enter every room, vault, and other place in the branch office and open every chest and receptacle. This was just a month before the Supreme Court heard *McCulloch* v. *Maryland.* When the decision in that case was announced, the Ohio officials were reluctant to undertake collection of the tax, but public and legislative opinion was for action. And especially, when the goings-on in the Baltimore office came out a week later, it was contended that the *McCulloch* case was factitious, that it had been arranged in order to bolster up the federal Bank when it was about to collapse from internal vices, that it had been heard as a test case by agreement between Maryland and the Bank, and that Ohio should not be bound by the collusive action of others. The state Auditor, Ralph Osborn, concluded that he had no choice but carry out the state law. Anticipating what was going to be done, the Bank sought protection from a federal court, but the court's orders were construed not to have the force of an injunction, and in September 1819 Osborn bade his deputy collect the amount due from the Chillicothe office. The cashier of the office reported to the Secretary of the Treasury, 17 September 1819, that the warrant of the state Auditor was executed at noon that day "by John L. Harper (late of Philadelphia, deputed for the purpose), accompanied by two others, who without any previous notice whatever suddenly entered the office, and in a ruffian-like manner jumped over the counter, took and held forcible possession of the vault, while the said Harper in like manner intruded himself behind the counter, and as I was proceeding to turn the others from the vault demanded to know if I was prepared to pay the said tax; to which I answered in the negative and made an ineffectual exertion to obtain possession of the vault, when they were repeatedly forewarned against touching any part of the property, and admonished in the presence of several citizens of said injunction, which was shown and read to them but for which he declared his disregard; and, after another fruitless effort on my part to dispossess them of the vault, proceeded to remove therefrom and from the drawer, a quantity of specie and bank notes, amounting to $120,425, including $7,930 in Muskingum Bank notes, the special deposit on account of the Treasury; all which were taken to and received by the cashier of the Bank of Chillicothe." Harper, however, withheld $2,000 as his fee.

The Bank obtained an order from the federal Circuit Court requiring the state Treasurer to restore the money. The Treasurer refused to obey the order and was lodged in prison. Federal commissioners appointed by the Court seized his keys and got the money, or what they could find of it, from the state Treasury themselves. The Ohio officials then appealed to the Supreme Court, a step which the radicals deplored, for they were unwilling to acknowledge the Court's jurisdiction. The state, they contended, was sovereign. They pictured the affair as an encroachment by the federal government, particularly by the federal Court. "Ohio has to complain of the imprisonment of the treasurer, the taking from his pockets the keys of the treasury whilst so imprisoned, and the entry into the treasury and violent seizure of monies therein contained, the property of the state!!!" This view was shared by the legislature. A committee recommended in January 1821 that the Bank of the United States be outlawed in the state courts and left "exclusively to the protection of the federal government." This action was not taken, but the Ohio Assembly did resolve in respect to the relative powers of the states and the Union to "recognize and approve" the Virginia and Kentucky Resolutions of 1798 and 1799, which, it will be recalled, had been inspired largely by the constitutional implications first raised by Alexander Hamilton's proposal in 1790 that the federal Bank be established.

The furor, though intense, was brief. The Supreme Court's decision in *McCulloch* v. *Maryland* stood, and no change in its position was to be expected. By the time the Ohio case was heard in 1824, the Bank's affairs were in better condition and emotions had subsided. The decision, *Osborn* v. *Bank of the United States,* reaffirmed the principles and conclusions pronounced in *McCulloch* v. *Maryland.* Whatever course the enemies of the Bank might take against it in future would have to be legislative or executive rather than judicial.

Concurrently, in the Maryland courts, the cases of the Baltimore speculators—Buchanan, McCulloch, and Williams—had been working their way through the anfractuosities of the law. So open was the misbehavior of the culprits, in old legal language called the Traversers, that little formality would seem required to have opened the jail door and thrust them in. It proved otherwise. New business and financial procedures attending the transformation of the country from an agrarian to a free enterprise economy made novel misdeeds possible for which the laws were unprepared. The simpler forms of cheating and stealing were well enough known but the more complicated dishonesty of distinguished-looking persons who sat at their desks month after month in plain view while appropriating other people's funds to their own use through bookkeeping entries, false reports or no reports, substitutions, and euphemisms—all this was beyond the simplicities of the common law and was something with which legislators had still to cope. So from the first it had been doubted whether criminal indictments could be sustained, and the cases were prosecuted in the hope that if the mischief-makers could not be punished, the legislators would at least learn how the defect in the laws might be remedied.

In other words, embezzlement, which involves misappropriating something entrusted to one and is now a familiar statutory crime, was not a crime to the common law, as larceny was. The theft of something *not* in the thief's possession occurred every day; but the theft of something already in his possession was rare in simpler times than ours and incongruous with the rule that possession was evidence of ownership. The novelty is clearly implied in the following statute of 1799 making embezzlement a crime in the United Kingdom:

"Whereas bankers, merchants, and others are in the course of their dealings and transactions frequently obliged to entrust their servants, clerks, and persons employed by them in like capacity with receiving, paying, negotiating, exchanging, or transferring money, goods, bonds, bills, notes, bankers' drafts, and other valuable effects and securities:

"And whereas doubts have been entertained whether the embezzling of the same by such servants, clerks, and others . . . amounts to felony by the law of England, and it is expedient that such offences should be punished in the same manner in both parts of the United Kingdom;

"Be it enacted and declared by the King's Most Excellent Majesty . . . that if any servant or clerk or any person employed . . . shall, by virtue of such employment, receive or take into his possession any money, goods, bond, bill, note, banker's draft, or other valuable security or effects for or in the name or on the account of his . . . employer . . . and shall fraudulently embezzle, secret, or make way with the same, . . . every such offender shall be deemed to have feloniously stolen the same. . . ."

Maryland as yet had no such law. In its absence the charge was "conspiracy," a vague but ancient and fairly comprehensive tort. The Traversers made no denial of their deeds but only the excuse that they had intended no wrong and were sufferers for what others had done. "The conduct of the Traversers was indiscreet," their counsel granted; "they relied too strongly upon the hopes and calculations in which the whole community indulged; but the failure of their stock speculations was rather to be pitied as a misfortune than condemned as a crime." In fact, counsel averred, the fault was really that of France; for France at quite the wrong time for the defendants had borrowed money from England which would otherwise have been invested in the Bank's stock but going to France instead had left the stock "a drug on the market." The Traversers were the victims of this miscarriage. Moreover, the Bank itself was to blame because it was badly managed. "Its strange administration was an *incubus* upon it," and depreciated its stock. By this depreciation the Traversers' speculations were ruined; "so that in fact the Bank itself occasioned the losses" upon which the charges rested. But for its clumsiness, prices presumably might have advanced forever. And if the stock could have risen instead of falling, then the Traversers "would have been looked upon as nobles, as the architects of their fortunes, by the very men who now prosecuted them, and lauded to the skies as possessing spirits fraught with enterprise."

The court was impressed with this persiflage and took the same indulgent view. In the words of one of the three judges, the Traversers "had charged themselves with the loans in the books of the Bank," they had at the time a prospect of repaying them, and "it appeared that they did then intend to repay" them. "Their subsequent disappointment by the failure of their speculation and their consequent ruin could not convert that into a crime which was not one at the time of doing it"; and the later measures to which they resorted for concealment "could make no difference in the case, since the act was to be judged of by the views and intentions with which it was done and not by anything which subsequently took place." The court's decision was accordingly "not guilty in law or in fact."

But at another point, whose relation to the first is confused in the record, the court stated that the question before it was "simply, whether or not the acts charged amount to an indictable conspiracy at common law." It held that the principles upon which the indictments rested were "not sufficiently intelligible" and that its duty was to protect the people of Maryland "from punishment for any act which it is not *perfectly satisfied* is forbidden by the laws." The Traversers had also demurred that the state court had no jurisdiction, since the Bank was a federal corporation; but this the decision dismissed on the prior ground that the offense alleged was not indictable.

The case had been heard first in 1820 before the Harford County Court, Bel Air, Maryland, whither it had been transferred lest "a fair and impartial trial could not be had" in Baltimore. The case then came before the Maryland Court of Appeals, in the December term 1821, where counsel for the state was joined by William Wirt, Attorney General of the United States, and counsel for the Traversers by William Pinkney. The Appeals Court unanimously reversed the lower court's judgment and remanded the cases for retrial "on the facts." Yet upon retrial at Bel Air in March and April 1823, the original judgment was reaffirmed, two judges concurring and the third dissenting as before. To the dissident the case still presented this simple aspect: "The Traversers, in violation of a sacred trust and under false representations calculated to deceive those who were interested in the due execution of the trust, have taken from the funds of the office a large sum of money, which they converted to their own use, and have failed to return to the Bank a cent of their spoil." But this was not the view that prevailed.

Though the Maryland laws were evidently wanting, it is probable that the court would have found the defendants guilty had the injured party not been the federal Bank. It joined instead the popular clamor and found the Bank guilty. The Bank was an alien in Maryland, unworthy to have its privileges sustained by the Free State against her erring, over-sanguine citizens—the Supreme Court of the United States in *McCulloch* v. *Maryland* to the contrary notwithstanding.

Meanwhile, the federal Bank was being watchfully flouted and resisted by a large portion of the state banks. As depository of the United States Treasury, it received their notes from the public in payment of taxes, and it credited the notes to the Treasury's balance, giving the Treasury immediate use of its funds. The natural expectation would be that the state banks would promptly redeem their notes and reimburse the government Bank. Some did, and some did not. In 1818 the Pittsburgh office asked payment of $10,920 of notes issued by the Commercial Bank of Lake Erie, in Cleveland, Ohio, and the latter in seeming compliancc took the notes and boxed up the specie to redeem them; but when the wagons drew up to get the boxes, the bank's president refused either to deliver the specie or to return the notes. He offered instead a post-note due in twenty days and the Bank could take "that or nothing." He explained publicly that he considered the federal Treasury and the federal Bank "the same thing; that the Bank of the United States had converted their offices into broker's shops; and that he considered it a duty that he owed to society to resist their encroachments; that he would publish to the world the reasons for his refusal to pay and call on the other banks to act in the same manner and to form a coalition against the Bank of the United States."

The Planters Bank and the Bank of the State of Georgia,

both in Savannah, went still further. Instead of paying their debit balances promptly, they temporized, and the Bank had to allow its holdings of their notes to accumulate. In 1820 their indebtedness to it ran as high as $500,000, on which they paid no interest. The Bank offered to carry them for $100,000, without interest, but required that notes in excess of this amount be redeemed punctually. The state banks declared this preposterous. Their committee said: "The requisition by the office of the United States Bank for a *daily cash settlement* from the local banks has been resisted, not only as unnecessary and totally without example in the intercourse of the banks in this quarter of the Union, who have always acted towards each other with unlimited and distinguished confidence, but as otherwise objectionable." The Bank yielded to the extent of weekly settlements instead of daily, interest to be paid at 6 per cent on balances due it in excess of $100,000, and agreed to accept drafts on northern banks in place of specie. The local banks haltingly acquiesced in this arrangement but stuck to it less than six months. It interfered with their lending what they wished. So the Planters Bank, seconded by the Bank of the State of Georgia, annulled the agreement and advised the federal Bank not to accept any of its notes because it would not pay them: "we wish you to refuse our paper hereafter," the Planters president stated, "and I am instructed to request that . . . it may not be received at your office in any shape"; for the Planters was resolved "on refusing to pay its bills accumulated by the Bank of the United States unless their intercourse can be conducted on the liberal and friendly footing which prevails among the state institutions."

Thus spoke men, in Savannah as in Baltimore and in Cleveland, "possessing spirits fraught with enterprise." One is uncertain which to admire the more, their effrontery or their enthusiasm. They believed in America as a place to get rich, and they recognized the magic possibilities of inflating the supply of money by avoiding cash settlements. Let every one honor every one else's promises, nor threaten the beautiful structure of unlimited credit by deflationary demands that the promises be redeemed. Let the economy float off the ground in a trance of mutual confidence. It was a monetary burlesque of Pauline theology, faith taking the place of works. The menace to this speculators' paradise was the federal Bank's insistence that it be paid promptly what was owing it; for in paying it the lending banks had to reduce their specie reserves and thereby inhibit their ability to lend. So contrary to the money-making interest were the Bank's restraints felt to be that resistance to them of any sort seemed warranted; and when the Bank sued the Georgia banks for payment, they fought it all the way to the Supreme Court, where in March 1824 they lost.

In these court actions that I have been describing—*McCulloch* v. *Maryland,* 1819; the *Baltimore Conspiracy Cases,* 1819–1823; *Osborn* v. *the Bank of the United States,* 1824; and *The Bank of the United States* v. *Planters Bank,* 1824—there was a mesh of moral, economic, and constitutional problems which were profoundly disturbing to the American people. They arose from basic changes produced in the economy by the Industrial Revolution, the attendant diversification of economic effort, the expanding utilization of credit, and the spread of the spirit of enterprise. These were shaking to pieces the simpler economy of 18th century America and undercutting the moralities that had subsisted among a people who were mostly agrarian and whose minor commercial pursuits, by comparison with the free-for-all of 19th century democratic enterprise, were a cult as much as a business. The business world in a mere two or three decades had expanded enormously, absorbing thousands who had never known the traditionary discipline of 18th century commerce; and now, transactors in a new *milieu,* they were scheming, promoting, inventing, stock-jobbing, and scrambling on a scale and in fashions wholly novel to most of them. Speculators were replacing conservative merchants, and embezzlement had made mere cheating and larceny contemptible. In the business world were a minority, the most successful as well as the most honest, who maintained as fine a morality as tradition had inculcated: Stephen Girard, Prime, Ward and King, and Alexander Brown were leaders among them. But the majority were green, brash, and irresponsible. They were cunning rather than sagacious, and ignorance more than turpitude made a large proportion of them corrupt.

For enterprise had placed such subtle instrumentalities as credit, accounting, and the corporate forms of organization at the disposal of people unaccustomed to such things. The conventions of a monetary economy were coming swiftly into use and sweeping the unsophisticated off their feet. An economy in which barter had been important and financial transactions had been wholly subordinate to the exchange of goods was giving way to an economy concerned more and more with obligations, contracts, negotiable instruments, equities, and such invisible abstractions. Money *per se* was giving way to promises to pay money, most of which were never performed, in a primitive sense, but were canceled by bookkeepers in the increasingly frequent offset of liabilities; and specie was dissolving into obligations to pay specie in a volume greatly exceeding the total that existed. These devices yielded fortunes and so had validity, but they were as unsettling to society as were in their way the Newtonian physics, the sentiments of the French Revolution, romanticism, or machinery driven by steam. In the absence of enough experience, the point at which the proper use of a convention became an abuse was unperceived. If a promise was as good as a deed in some instances, it was unapparent why everything might not be left to promise. If things were worth what people thought they were worth, why was deception not preferable to reality? It was a principle stated by Adam Smith and other respected economists that a bank could virtuously put into circulation promises to pay equal in amount to five times the gold and silver it had to pay them with; to John Adams, as honest and intelligent a man as there was in the States, such a thing seemed a monstrous cheat. To Thomas Jefferson it was a swindle. So it continued to seem to perhaps the majority of Americans, though many of them, seeing how well it worked, calmed their consciences and made what they could of it. I doubt if one banker in four clearly understood what he was doing and what made it sound and proper. The others could not intelligently explain what they were doing and therefore could not intelligently justify it. To a certain extent, therefore, they literally could not tell the difference between right and wrong; for if they could owe five times what they could pay, why not a hundred? Or why not slip along with no means at all? If insolvency could be concealed, why not be insolvent?

Another novelty, inexplicable but momentous, was that by forming a corporation men could escape the obligation to pay their debts. Or so it seemed. And probably the majority who profited from the arrangement did not understand it and could not justify themselves. Nor could they convincingly deny the harsh judgment that as a corporate group men would do things that shame would keep them from doing individually. But incorporation was a form of collective effort that greatly augmented the efficiency of capital, and it throve in spite of moral misgivings.

So sudden and wide-spread was the recruitment into enterprise of men unprepared for its responsibilities that a lowering of moral standards was bound to occur. The more conservative, whether commercial or agrarian, were appalled by it. In that they were alike. But the agrarian majority were not very discriminating; they inclined instead to decry all business and enterprise. They were unaware of the difference between a Langdon Cheves and a William Jones. They longed for the sturdy virtues of colonial and revolutionary times. In the austere light of their native ideals, corruption and business were one and the same thing. John Quincy Adams, who was not agrarian and who saw things very differently from his father, noted "the wide-spread corruption of the numberless state banks." A hundred honest bankers made less impression on these staunch moralists than one Andrew Dexter wrecking his bank in Glocester, or the three pickers and stealers in the Baltimore office of the Bank of the United States, with a number of smaller fry defaulting and embezzling here and there between.

Moreover it was futile to consider the problem merely a moral one, as if a whole generation of men had all at once been born dishonest. The problem was the practical one that old disciplines had broken down in new circumstances. The bankers in particular were like boys with racing cars—the first ever built. What they needed was precisely what they would not have—an operating restraint such as the Bank of the United States automatically imposed, being so constituted, as Isaac Bronson said years later, that its own existence depended on its exercise of a controlling influence over the state banks. That restraint remained, so long as the Bank continued to have the deposit account of the largest transactor in the economy. But it was a restraint which the Bank in its current condition could not modify and direct with wisdom, as a central bank should.

It was not long before the Bank's successes in the Supreme Court were paralleled by its improved operating condition. Langdon Cheves, with the indispensable support of the Bank's more responsible stockholders and directors, Stephen Girard, Nicholas Biddle, Alexander Brown, and others, had saved it. His achievement was the sort that gains a man no popularity; even many of his stockholders, whose investment he had preserved, were disgruntled because he was niggardly with dividends. There would be a decided opposition to him, Secretary Crawford wrote to Mr. Gallatin in May 1822. In July Mr. Cheves informed the stockholders that he would resign at the end of the year. "It was my desire to have done so," he said, "very soon after I entered upon the duties of the office." Albert

Gallatin in October was asked to succeed him but refused. Late in November delegates representing stockholders in several seaboard states met to select a candidate and agreed upon Nicholas Biddle. "This gentleman is highly commended by some and much objected to by others," Niles' *Register* reported; but he was elected president of the Bank, 6 January 1823, without marked dissent.

Mr. Gallatin would have been a better choice, ideally. He was experienced, firm, sagacious; and no one else in public life equaled him in character and intellect. He was also quite without fancy or egotism. Neither he nor Langdon Cheves would have let himself be demoralized by the Jacksonians. They would have withdrawn in dignity, and let Andrew Jackson have his blundering way. But, as things were, I doubt if either would have managed the central bank better than Nicholas Biddle did before the Jacksonian attack. Mr. Gallatin and Mr. Cheves were both too conservative to last. In an expanding economy, with a powerful demand for credit, the central banker is called on mostly to be negative. He must resist and say no. He must endure the revilings of the optimistic, the speculative, and the enterprising, who will denounce him for holding back progress and enslaving mankind to the monetary system. Both Albert Gallatin and Langdon Cheves were contemptuous of such cant and would scarcely have survived the first collision. Nicholas Biddle also had the brains to see through it, but he had the resilience to maintain control. So long as the problem was mainly economic rather than political he made the central bank work as it should. It was his success that made the issue political. When it became political, he failed. The others would have failed too but sooner and less painfully.

Though Mr. Cheves may have wished sincerely to resign, it is evident that he resented the readiness of the Bank to let him do so. He blamed Mr. Biddle for what happened, and it seems likely that with the latter's support he might have stayed, the dissatisfied stockholders notwithstanding. For Mr.

Biddle put off increasing the dividends and in that respect pleased the stockholders no better. Both remained very reticent about their differences. They met and corresponded on rare occasions, but their courtesy to one another was punctilious and cool—Cheves because he would have it so, Biddle because he could not be friends alone. Mr. Cheves, proud, sensitive, and conscious of having been given the really dirty work to do and then let go, was aggrieved. So would any one have been, though few would have been so gentlemanly about it. But a quite objective decision as to policy had to be made and that, not personalities, was the ground of differences.

Fifteen years later, in 1837, when the charter of the Bank had expired and Mr. Cheves was sixty-one years old, his fellow Carolinian, Dr. Thomas Cooper, mildly criticized "the very harsh but really salutary exercise of his arduous office" and highly praised Nicholas Biddle. This stung Mr. Cheves to an interesting and moving *apologia:* he described the scandalous situation of the Bank in 1819, the ordeal of making its debtors pay, and the snobbish resentment of Philadelphians at having a stranger running the Bank. "The office was one for which I had no particular predilection, independent of the peculiar difficulties which attended it, of which I had scarcely any idea when I agreed to accept it. . . . I know no earthly misery greater than to live in perpetual strife, and seeing this to be my probable fate, I determined in a few weeks after I entered the Bank to leave it" as soon as the task was finished. "I have . . . almost as little ambition to be considered an eminently skilful banker as an eminently skilful physician. . . ." Of his successor he said: "I have always borne testimony to Mr. Biddle's talents and general fitness for his station. Our fate was to encounter very different circumstances. . . . I am very sure, however, that he has made larger profits for the stockholders than I should have done. . . . I have always been of opinion that a Bank of the United States neither ought, nor ought to be permitted, to conduct its business with a view to the largest possible profits, and therefore I should probably have done a more limited business. . . . If in the struggles of the Bank to be rechartered, my opinion was against it (as in fact it was), I nevertheless was silent. The relations in which I had stood to it forbade me to manifest opposition to it, in any way or in any degree. It is now no more, and I am free to declare that I am opposed to a national bank in any shape. I always believed it to be unconstitutional, and my experience and observation have satisfied me that it is inexpedient, unnecessary, and dangerous."

This final and surprising declaration, which is unsupported by Mr. Cheves' earlier record, if not indeed contradicted by it, seems to reflect the extreme position to which he advanced toward the end of his life in assertion of states' rights and limited federal powers. But there is no reason to doubt that he was correct in thinking that he would have managed the Bank more conservatively than Mr. Biddle. He would probably have managed it too conservatively and roused even more quickly than Mr. Biddle did the outcry of "oppression" against it.

For the Bank by nature and purpose conflicted with the dominant wishes of Americans. They wanted to exploit their resources, and to do that they wanted all the money they could get. An institution designed to curb the supply of credit could scarcely perform what Mr. Gallatin called its "unpopular duty" without becoming not merely unpopular but intolerable —and the more conservative it was the more intolerable. The business world since the days of Thomas Paine's and Alexander Hamilton's identification of business enterprise with free government had been hurrying on with every encouragement, practical and philosophic, to the logical extremes of *laissez faire* and would brook no restraints upon its liberty to borrow.

Although the hostility most responsible in the end for destruction of the Bank of the United States was that of the state banks and of allied business interests requiring credit—

and more particularly of those in New York—the chief hostility in the beginning had been agrarian and strongest in the Ohio valley. In the conventional accounts, this agrarian hostility still remains the real force that destroyed the Bank. One gets a picture of the Bank as a Shylock lending to distressed farmers, then exacting its pound of flesh from them, but in the end having its exactions frustrated by Andrew Jackson. The picture is fanciful. The Bank did not wish to lend to farmers, and farmers did not wish to borrow from it. It lent chiefly to merchants and other business men, most of whom owned some land—as everyone did who owned anything—and when in a period of depression it had to take possession of its debtors' property, it found itself in possession of land. This did not make its debtors agrarians. The Bank acquired, for example, a large part of the city of Cincinnati; but no one supposes that Cincinnati property was farm property.

The farmers of the Ohio valley, however, as of most frontiers, had been in debt and in distress, though not to the Bank of the United States. They had been in debt to those from whom they had purchased their land; their principal single creditor was the government of the United States. The basic cause of their distress was the universal tendency to under-estimate the cost of bringing undeveloped land into profitable cultivation. That cost had always been high in terms of labor, but now it had become high in terms of cash, largely because land alone had lost in economic adequacy but must be supplemented more and more by stock and equipment. In the 17th and 18th centuries a farmer's needs had been supplied almost wholly from his labor and his land, for with these and with a few tools and weapons he could shelter, clothe, and feed his family. He had timber for fuel and shelter, and from hunting, fishing, and tillage he had food and apparel. There was little relatively that he needed to buy. But with increased settlement, the game disappeared, tillage became more important, equipment and live stock were needed in larger amounts. With these changes, the relative importance of land shrank, that of equipment and stock increased, and so did that of cash; till now in the 20th century, land is but a fraction of the farmer's total investment, its former relation to stock and equipment having become reversed. The turn came early in the 19th century, coincidentally with the Industrial Revolution, which indeed was largely responsible for it. For the Industrial Revolution provided new occupations alternative to farming, it provided implements and supplies which were indispensable but cost money, and it stimulated farm production, though at the same time subjecting it to the rough pressure of change.

The fact and the import of these changes were seldom recognized. Men continued thinking and trying to farm as if they were still in 18th century America, and they emigrated in their thousands across the Appalachians to the valley of the Ohio, where land was accounted rich, abundant, and cheap, in the supposition that with the acquisition of such land their economic difficulties would disappear. But the conditions long taken for granted no longer held, and this land though rich and abundant was not cheap, though it appeared so. The settler, to make his initial payments, transport his family, provide himself with the necessary housing, tools, and animals, sustain his family while awaiting returns from the soil, and survive his errors and misfortunes, required capital in amounts of which he mostly never even dreamed. Wanting such capital, many and probably most immigrants contributed their labor gratuitously to the clearing of land, to its rudimentary improvement, and to the testing of its adaptabilities; and they got nothing but bare subsistence in return. All the gains were realized by their successors.

Later generations that contemplate an America which is miraculously productive in a myriad of ways, from sea to sea, can understand only with an effort the terrible cost to their progenitors of settling and improving it. Amos Kendall, who arrived in Kentucky in 1814 from New England and who became fifteen years later one of Andrew Jackson's closest advisers, describes in his autobiography the situation in which in 1809 he had found his older brother and sister, who were pioneering in northern Vermont, where they had purchased tracts of wild land on credit, built small log cabins, and made clearings. Kendall was satisfied "that they could never meet the payments for their land and were making improvements upon it for the benefit of others." So it turned out. "In the winter of 1813, his brother Zebedee abandoned his place, giving up all his improvements, and returned to his father's with little else than a wife and five children. In August of the same year his sister, having also five children, arrived at her father's. . . . Her husband, finding himself in painful pecuniary straits, had enlisted in the army of the United States and left her." The cost of pioneering was borne by all generations. My great-grandfather, leaving the Eastern Shore of Maryland about 1800, was one of the thousands crossing into Kentucky, where about fifteen years later he was one of the thousands who moved on into Indiana, whence his son moved on to Iowa, whence in turn his grandson, some eighty years after the removal from the Eastern Shore, went on to California. There this grandson, my father, cultivating oranges on land which hitherto had produced only sage brush, helped to determine the important fact that the land he had purchased was not good for oranges. He lost, in this bit of economic exploration, all he had accumulated. Since then, race horses have been bred there, but with no advantage to him, or me.

On all frontiers the cost of pioneering—in effort, in spirit, and in cash—tended to exceed expectations tragically, though the situation was different in the South where the large scale production of cash crops prevailed and where slave labor had made a large capital investment other than in land long customary. The dearth of capital was worst where the illusion of cheap land prevailed; it made relief for agrarian distress a dominant issue for years in the politics of Ohio, Kentucky, Tennessee, and other parts of the West in the early decades of the 19th century. Settlers on land eventually rich found themselves unable to complete their payments, and abandoning what they had held and labored over, tried their dismal luck further on in still greater primitivity. Some, unable or unwilling to move, sought by political action to halt the surrender of their property to their creditors, and laws were passed staying executions and otherwise protecting the equity of debtors. This threw the burden on creditors, who were mostly no better able to bear it than their debtors were, for they also were debtors themselves. These included banks, forty of which had been set up in Kentucky alone in 1818 and failed in 1819. So in 1820 that state tried a new institution, the Bank of the Commonwealth of Kentucky, which added still more bank credit to too much bank credit. The notes of the forty banks set up two years before were already "redeemable" in notes of the Bank of Kentucky, established in 1806; and now there were also the notes of the new Bank of the Commonwealth of Kentucky, a corporation without real capital and merely a pathetic aspect of the state of Kentucky, which elected its directors and paid the salaries of its staff but could provide it no real substance.

Banking had been defined for George Washington by Alexander Hamilton as a means of supplying a large circulating medium on a relatively small base of specie: Hamilton had considered a ratio between specie and circulation of as much as one to five. Kentucky was stretching it toward a ratio of nothing to infinity. And this was being done by an agrarian community. After virtuously eschewing credit while the commercial world was thriving on it and while its own lot was retrogressing, these Kentucky agrarians had turned at length, desperately and emulously, to grasp the heady elixir, and had carried to ruinous absurdity the very power wherein Thomas Jefferson had discerned the danger of banking lay. They were resorting deliberately and officially to measures whose consequences were the same as those that agrarians had denounced for generations in John Law's projects, in the South Sea Bubble, and latterly in Andrew Dexter and his Farmers Exchange Bank of Glocester.

The confusion of the agrarian community was painful. It had sought to relieve its distress by legislation, it had disobeyed its traditions in the process, its distress was worse than before. But in this snarl of principles, possibilities, realities, and exigencies, psychological escape was found in blaming the federal government and the federal Bank for everything. The solution, for which the state banks and the politicians were responsible, was a perfect one: it gave the suffering farmers sympathy and it gave the politicians fresh ground to stand on. In 1825 Governor Desha of Kentucky, a veteran enemy of the federal Bank, deplored "the insecurity now felt by numberless cultivators of our soil," which he considered "the chief cause of that extensive emigration which is now thinning the population of some of the finest sections of our state. . . ." "At every term of the federal court," said the Governor, "numerous judgments and decrees are obtained against our peaceful citizens for the lands and houses which they have honestly purchased, built, and improved, and orders given for their execution contrary to our laws. . . . And thus does this commonwealth suffer those who have improved, supported, and defended her, to be stripped of the proceeds of their life's labor and made the unpitied victims of heartless speculation and assumed power."

The federal Bank preyed on the state banks, and the federal courts defended it. It received the notes of the state banks and demanded redemption. It made the state banks pay, when what they wanted to do was lend. To the state bankers, most of whom were politicians themselves, this was oppression, and they readily convinced their fellow citizens that it was these measures of the federal Bank that drained wealth from the West and prevented them from being as generous as they wished. The Bank was an alien corporation which entered the individual states against their will and went about in them scot-free. When the states sought to oust the monstrosity from their soil, Chief Justice Marshall and his coterie of soulless old Federalists on the Supreme Court affirmed its inviolability, and the federal courts within the states truckled to him, upholding the usurpation and rendering the regional sovereignties impotent to deal with their paramount problems. "How," asked Amos Kendall, "shall the states resist the consolidating tendency of our national government, which the decisions of the federal courts are annually making more apparent?" The states found no political or legislative answer. Even their own people denounced laws which sacrificed creditors to debtors. To General Andrew Jackson, for example, a Tennessee relief measure was "wicked, and pernicious, . . . profligate, and unconstitutional, . . . a law that will disgrace the state, destroy all credit abroad, and all confidence at home."

So, bitter as was the western feeling, it did not become fatal to the Bank. The farm products of the western states—the most important being cotton—began to reach foreign markets with the extension of river haulage to New Orleans. The region grew economically more comfortable, the Bank's management improved, and the bitterness subsided. Later, when the assault arose that proved fatal to the Bank, it came from New York, and only its instrument was western. An advantage of the Bank in the West but its disadvantage in the East was that it engaged in the same type of lending and exchange dealings as the state banks. In the West this was advantageous because there was less good banking service there than the region required. In the East it was disadvantageous because the state banks felt that they were adequate and resented its competition. In the 20th century the central bank is not typically a competitor of the commercial banks. The Federal Reserve Banks are not, though many commercial bankers mistakenly think they are. But in the early 19th century no central bank anywhere in the world confined itself to central banking exclusively. The Bank of the United States was typical of the stage of central banking evolution so far achieved.

For Further Reading

A more detailed study of the formation and early career of the Second Bank can be found in Walter B. Smith, *The Second Bank of the United States* (1953), while the broader context of economic developments, of which the bank was but a part, are presented in Edward C. Kirkland, *A History of American Economic Life* (1932); Joseph Dorfman, *The Economic Mind in American Civilization, 1606–1865* (2 vols., 1946); Stuart Bruchey, *The Roots of American Economic Growth* (1965), and Douglass C. North, *The Economic Growth of the United States, 1790–1860* (1961). The emergence of new modes of transportation, an integral part of the economic boom of the early national period, is treated by George Rogers Taylor in *The Transportation Revolution, 1815–1860* (1951), while Robert G. Albion illustrates what a change in the transportation system did for one community in *The Rise of New York Port, 1815–1860* (1939).

The history of the Supreme Court under John Marshall is the subject of W. Melville Jones, ed., *Chief Justice John Marshall* (1956), a collection of interpretive essays. Marshall is also the subject of biographies by Albert J. Beveridge (4 vols., 1916–1919) and E. S. Corwin (1919). The standard authority on the history of the Court in Marshall's times and since is Charles Warren, *The Supreme Court in United States History* (2 vols., 1927). A thoughtful recent analysis of McCullough v. Maryland can be found in John A. Garraty, ed., *Quarrels that Shaped the Constitution* (1964).

Many of Marshall's contemporaries in the second decade of the nineteenth century may also be examined through biographical studies. Among the best are Samuel Flagg Bemis, *John Quincy Adams* (2 vols., 1949, 1956); Claude M. Fuess, *Daniel Webster* (2 vols., 1930); Glyndon Van Deusen, *The Life of Henry Clay* (1937); Charles M. Wiltse, *John C. Calhoun: Nationalist* (1944), and W. P. Cresson, *James Monroe* (1946).

Capstone to Independence

George Dangerfield

Curiously, the period in American history from 1801 to 1828 has attracted few scholars, although Henry Adams may be said to be worth more than a handful. The exciting first days of Jefferson's administration—the deadlocked election itself, the battle with Marshall and his Court, and the Burr conspiracy—of course have been well chronicled. Nonetheless historians generally have paid scant attention to domestic events.

Just as historians and political scientists focus their discussion on the cold war and foreign policy in treating Harry S Truman's presidency, so scholars have devoted their energies to analyzing and describing foreign policymaking during the period 1801 to 1828. Domestic matters seem less important during those years; embargo, war, and other external threats have overshadowed internal topics. This emphasis on foreign policy may indeed be proper—in those years long-lasting traditions were established and independence assured.

The Declaration of Independence, to be sure, did proclaim to the world that thirteen relatively weak and

Source: George Dangerfield, *The Era of Good Feelings* (New York: Harcourt, Brace & World, Inc., 1952), pp. 283–308.

loosely confederated states were no longer colonies. The public edict described both wish and actuality. Seven years later, at Paris, Great Britain formally acquiesced to that state of independence. But years were to pass before the new American nation could escape fully from its colonial status. The Anglo-American economy, a classic colonial relationship, had evolved over a century and a half; it could not be changed overnight. Accustomed to rule and born to mercantilism, British statesmen during the half century after 1776 often seemed to act as if the United States still belonged to the crown. Events in Europe placed British supremacy at stake; these pressures sometimes led English leaders to ignore niceties of international relations in respect to the United States. Furthermore, not convinced that the American experiment would or should succeed, most of the other European diplomats and rulers were not disposed to treat the United States seriously.

Just when America achieved real independence on the one hand, and international respect as a nation on the other, are still subjects for debate. One could argue, for example, that any of the following events mark either the first or second (or both) of these accomplishments: the Declaration of Independence, the Treaty of Paris (1783), the Jay Treaty (1794), the Commercial Conventions of 1815 or 1818 with Great Britain, the Treaty of Ghent (1815), the Florida Treaty (1819), or the Monroe Doctrine (1823). The question has merit, since it focuses attention on the obvious yet extremely significant fact that American independence was more than a single act; it was a process.

The diplomatic emphasis, moreover, reminds us that the question of the winning of American independence was but one of a connected series of events during a period of turbulence in the Western Atlantic community. Europe had its share of convulsions. During the period 1776–1815, to a greater or lesser extent, Spain, England, France, and Russia faced domestic upheaval or revolution. After the defeat of Napoleon and the Congress of Vienna, the great powers formed the Quadruple Alliance to preserve the postwar settlement. Preservation of this settlement meant preservation of the status quo of 1815 and this entailed the task of preventing revolution from once again disturbing the peace. Some of the more reactionary powers wished to go even further in turning back the clock by restoring Spain's lost empire in the Western Hemisphere. Beginning in 1808, and superbly led by such patriots as Simón Bolívar, José de San Martín, and Bernardo O'Higgins, one after another of the Spanish-American colonies had separated themselves from the motherland. By 1822, with the success of the national independence movement in Mexico, and the proclamation of Brazilian independence from Portugal, nearly all of Latin America had become independent. In retrospect, no chance of restoring Spanish sovereignty over its old colonies existed, particularly with Great Britain sternly opposed to all such proposals. To American statesmen, however, the threat seemed real enough in 1823, and President James Monroe determined to meet it. After consulting with his fellow Virginians and predecessors in the White House, Thomas Jefferson and James Madison, and relying on the expertise of his Secretary of State, John Quincy Adams, Monroe devoted a large section of his State of the Union message in 1823 to discussion of international affairs. He announced "that American continents by the free and independent conditions which they have assumed and maintain" would no longer be subject to European colonization; furthermore, the United States should consider any attempt of the European allies "to extend their system to any portion of this hemisphere as dangerous to our peace and safety." This, then, was the substance of the Monroe Doctrine, which has become one of the cornerstones of American foreign policy.

Partly as a result of the natural tendency of statesman and citizen alike to simplify historical events, it has become fashionable to scoff at the policy. After all, as critics point out quickly, the British fleet—not the

United States' might and majesty—kept European powers from interfering with the Spanish-American colonies' claims to independence in the 1820's. Nonetheless, despite their modest origins, Monroe's words have become part of American national subconsciousness. It is fitting that one of the finest accounts of the Monroe Doctrine has been penned by an English historian, George Dangerfield. His study of American life during the Monroe adminstrations (1817–1825), *The Era of Good Feelings,* has become a modern classic. Dangerfield, as is evident from the following selection, writes with a lively and often amusing style. Complex diplomatic maneuvering becomes clear at his hand; the shift from European to American politics is made effortlessly. Above all, although alert to details, Dangerfield never loses sight of the larger significance of his subject. The result is a superb re-creation of the history of the formulation of the Monroe Doctrine.

The Great Flirtation

When Mr. Canning began his battle with France and the Neo-Holy Allies, Great Britain was climbing out of her postwar depression. The fall in world prices, owing to a shortage of specie and an absence of an elastic credit system, did not hurt her industrial system with its exportable surplus. Her manufacturers were learning those technical refinements which reduce costs. As the collapse of the American cotton market had shown, raw materials were becoming cheap; and though wages are said not to have fallen as low as prices, the English industrial worker of those days was one of the most cruelly exploited people in the world. The British manufacturer, therefore, was able to quote prices that could attract even the misery of postwar Europe: but his chief single market was still the United States of America. As Lord Liverpool had told the House of Lords in 1820, whoever wished prosperity to England must wish prosperity to the United States. In 1822, 95 per cent of all its imports of woolen goods and 89 per cent of its imports of cotton goods were of British manufacture; in 1823, the percentages were 96 and 84. In 1822, 47 per cent of its total imports, and in 1823, 42 per cent were of the growth, produce, or manufacture of England and her colonies. From the British side, this meant that roughly one sixth of Britain's export was consumed by the United States. It was easy for the American merchant to avail himself of the banking and credit facilities open to British merchants and manufacturers; this fact and the basic Anglo-American exchange—raw cotton for textiles—gave the United States a somewhat colonial position in British economy. This exchange had not begun to worry American agrarians; but the manufacturers were growing restive. In 1823, however, they had not yet been able to do what Lord Liverpool so earnestly suggested that they should never do—and that was to persuade Congress to impose a protective tariff.

When the American Navigation Act of 1823, with the word "elsewhere" in its tail, was known in England, there was more surprise than pain. It was thought that an Order-in-Council, which took immediate retaliatory measures, would speedily bring the Americans to their senses. Their Act, in short, was regarded rather as a temporary aberration than as a deliberate policy. The Order-in-Council was, of course, exceedingly firm. It provided that the shipping of the United States, when entering the ports of British colonies in North America and the West Indies, should pay a duty of 4*s.* 3*d.* per ton and of ten per cent upon their cargoes. This Order, it was thought, would soon remove the American one dollar per ton and ten per cent on the cargo, levied upon British ships: it was simply tit for tat. The Americans now seemed anxious to settle matters with a convention; and George Canning, who did not know the precise nature of Mr. Rush's instructions, probably thought at the time that this would be as good a way as any to get everyone out of their difficulties.

His behavior towards Minister Rush was, indeed, extremely affable. In July, he asked Mr. Rush to send copies of his speech of April 16 against repeal of the Foreign Enlistment Act to Mr. Monroe and Mr. Adams. These copies were corrected in Canning's own hand. In the course of the speech, he had said: "If I wished for a guide in a system of neutrality, I should take that laid down by America in the presidency of Washington and the secretaryship of Jefferson."

Now it was quite well known that Mr. Canning did not care for Americans and that he had no love for republics. He had never, in all his private correspondence, shown any more disposition to understand or appreciate the United States than Sidney Smith had offered in his famous and bitter article in the *Edinburgh Review*. In society, American gentlemen and English gentlemen did not as a rule hit it off together: and there are few examples of misunderstanding more complete than the comments privately passed upon each other by Charles Greville and Washington Irving, or by Sir Walter Scott and James Fenimore Cooper. But in the summer of 1823, Mr. Canning's formal courtesy—which he had not always been too careful to maintain—became suffused with an extraordinary warmth. The rather snobbish and rather voluble Christopher Hughes, now *chargé d'affaires* at Stockholm, happened to be passing through Liverpool on his way to St. Petersburg with dispatches; and here he met the Foreign Secretary, who had come up to his old constituency to make a speech. Canning went out of his way to shower kindnesses upon the American, and at the Mayor's banquet, where Hughes was a guest, he said of the United States and Great Britain that "the force of blood again prevails, and the daughter and the mother stand together against the world." Mr. Hughes was enchanted: he was even more enchanted when Canning passed him on to the hospitality of the Duke of Buckingham, the Ph.D. When he arrived in St. Petersburg, the British Ambassador reported that he "was not yet recovered from his delight and astonishment."

Mr. Hughes, had he read these words, might have remarked that any American diplomat would be astonished and perhaps even delighted at being so cordially received in England: it was not the usual experience.

Canning now carried his "flirtation" with the United States —as he afterwards called it—one step further. On August 16 he had a conference with Richard Rush, in the course of which Mr. Rush asked him "transiently" for his opinion on the state of affairs in Europe, adding that he derived much consolation from the thought that England would never allow France to interfere with the emancipation of the Spanish colonies, nor would she remain passive if France attempted to acquire territory there by conquest or cession. Canning listened gravely, and then asked what the American government would say to going hand in hand with England in such a policy. He did not think that any concert of *action* would be necessary; the simple fact of the two countries being known to hold the same opinion would, by its moral effect, check the French government in any design upon Spanish America. To this astonishing proposal the American Minister replied that he could not say in what manner his government would look upon it, but that he would communicate it in the same informal manner in which it had been thrown out. He went on to remark, very shrewdly, that much depended upon the precise situation in which the British government then stood towards the Spanish-American colonies. Were they taking, or did they think of taking any step towards the recognition of those states? This was the point, said Mr. Rush, "in which we felt the chief interest." Canning was unable to give a direct answer. He said that Great Britain was contemplating a step, not final, but preparatory, which would leave her free to "recognize or not according to the position of events at a future period." To an American, whose country was already committed to the independence of Spanish America, this would not have seemed a candid reply. Mr. Rush's very cool report of this momentous conversation was dispatched from

London on August 19, and reached Washington on October 9.

On August 17, the Russian Ambassador, Count Lieven, had a long conference with Canning, in which he sought to impress upon the Foreign Secretary the foolishness of his attitude towards France. Could he not see that the French fortunes were not, after all, at a low ebb? That, on the contrary, their expedition in Spain had succeeded, and that the absolutist cause throughout Europe had received a corresponding impetus? Mr. Canning listened eagerly, and yet—it was very strange—he did not strike Lieven as being at all despondent. He replied that the time had come for him to take an active part in the new arrangements which would be made in Spain. Lieven hurried back to his wife with this news, and Madame de Lieven pondered over it, and pondered in vain. "Will his part be to arrange or to upset?" she wrote to Metternich. "We shall see."

She did not wait to see. The fact was that the plot against Canning, in which she had been so industriously engaged, had failed. Neither the secret letters of Metternich, nor her own representations with Wellington and the king, nor the persistent intrigues of Count Lieven and Prince Paul Esterhazy, the Austrian Ambassador, had succeeded in dividing the government against itself. Wellington, she declared, was "stupid," and the king, though his sympathies were entirely with the Holy Alliance, was incurably lazy. As for England, "her domestic prosperity justifies her behavior. . . . We do not like her foreign policy; but what does John Bull mind? He has his mug of beer. And what do the Ministers mind? They are at peace among themselves." Really ill with mortification, she went to Brighton and made plans to recruit her strength in the Italian sunshine.

Her eager, astute, and restless mind, so brilliantly at home in the Age of Castlereagh, was still imprisoned there. She understood the politics of reaction, but the politics of the middle class entirely eluded her. She was nothing if not aristocratic. She perceived that the Liverpool-Canning-Huskisson wing of the government was firmly in the saddle, but, for the life of her, she could not realize how it had come to get there. With all her cleverness, it never occurred to her that the power now so visibly departing from Windsor Castle and the Brighton Pavilion might perhaps one day be rediscovered in the Manchester Chamber of Commerce.

Mr. Canning, therefore, was well established at home. He had defeated a very foolish but very dangerous plot. At the same time, his diplomacy, there was no denying it, had suffered an obvious setback. In September, the French army was approaching Cadiz where Ferdinand VII, the prisoner of the Constitutionalists, lay idly meditating revenge and tribulation. On August 20 Mr. Canning wrote a note to Mr. Rush, in which he stated in "unofficial and confidential" terms that

1. We conceive the recovery of the Colonies by Spain to be hopeless.
2. We conceive the question of the Recognition of them, as Independent States, to be one of time and circumstance.
3. We are, however, by no means disposed to throw any impediment in the way of an arrangement between them and the mother country by amicable negotiations.
4. We aim not at the possession of any portion of them ourselves.
5. We could not see any portion of them transferred to any other Power with indifference.

"If these opinions and feelings are [he added], as I firmly believe them to be, common to your government with ours, why should we hesitate mutually to confide them with each other; and to declare them in the face of the world? . . . Do you conceive that under the power which you have recently received, you are authorized to enter into negotiation, and to sign any Convention upon this subject? . . . Nothing would be more gratifying to me than to join with you in such a work, and, I am persuaded, there has seldom, in the history of the world, occurred an opportunity, when so small an effort, of two friendly Governments, might produce so unequivocal a good and prevent such extensive calamities." The flirtation had become a courtship.

Mr. Rush replied, three days later, that his government fully agreed with the sentiments in Mr. Canning's note, but that the paramount consideration must be the reception of the Spanish-American states into the family of nations by the powers of Europe, "and especially, I may add, by Great Britain." His instructions, he said, did not permit him to commit his government in advance; and he contented himself with remarking that it would give him particular pleasure to bring Mr. Canning's views before the President as promptly as he could. Mr. Canning, however, had just received word that, as soon as the French campaign was over, a new European Congress would be called to deal especially with the affairs of Spanish America. "I need not point out," he said in a letter from Liverpool, which crossed Mr. Rush's in the mail, "all the complications to which this proposal, however dealt with by us, may lead." All he received by way of answer was the familiar hint that if the British government would fully acknowledge the independence of the Spanish-American states, "it would accelerate the steps of my government (and) it would also naturally place *me* in a new position in my further conferences with you, on this interesting subject."

If Rush had succeeded in forcing the British to recognize the Spanish Americans, he was then honestly prepared to go through with his part of the bargain—that is to say, "to make a declaration in the name of my government that it will not remain inactive under an attack upon the independence of those states by the Holy Alliance," and to make this declaration explicitly and avow it before the world. He was well aware that, in thus exceeding his instructions, he might be disavowed by his own government; but he was prepared to take all the blame upon himself, and to sweeten his disgrace with the thought that he had acted for the best. In these very anxious days, with no one to advise him, his actions were astonishingly cool and brave. Canning answered from Westmoreland that he could not bind himself and his colleagues—whose sentiments he had been expressing as well as his own—simply on the American Minister's word without the support of positive instructions from Washington: in other words, that the British government was not yet ready for an immediate recognition. Mr. Rush at first seemed to think that this unwillingness to negotiate on the basis of equivalents—recognition for co-operation—would bring the whole business to an end. But as day followed day without another word from Canning, who was due to return to London in the middle of September, he changed his mind; he thought that the Foreign Secretary would renew his conversations with all his former urgency; and, while preparing his mind for this encounter, he wrote a very strange letter to President Monroe.

He told the President that he deeply mistrusted the Tory government. It was true that they had lately become very liberal in their foreign-trade policy, and he believed that they would become more so. But he did not think that they had changed in their attitude towards political freedom, or that a change, if it took place, would be of a sort to invite the confidence and co-operation of the United States. Great Britain had fought the Napoleonic Wars, ostensibly in support of the freedom of other states, but actually against the people of France. She had aided the Holy Alliance, either positively or negatively, until the Alliance seemed to threaten her commercial interests in Spanish America and her political sway in both hemispheres. She would continue to act the part "which she acted in 1774 in America, which she has since acted in Europe, and is now acting in Ireland. . . . I shall therefore find it hard," he wrote, "to keep from my mind the suspicion that the approaches of her ministers to me at this portentous juncture for a concert of policy which they have not heretofore courted with the United States, are bottomed on their own calculations."

Mr. Rush knew as well as anyone that diplomatic approaches are rarely if ever "bottomed" on anything else. He hastened to add that he did not accuse the British Cabinet, "as it is now composed," of any sinister motives toward the United States. On the contrary, he believed that Lord Liverpool and Mr. Canning would advocate an even more intimate and friendly policy towards them, "no matter from what motives arising." He did not think that the Whigs or the Radicals would ever offer such good terms.

This letter, with its odd alternations of suspicion and speculation, is an admirable example of the effect of the new Liberal Toryism upon a shrewd observer. Mr. Rush was not, like Madame de Lieven, simply bewildered. He saw very clearly that a government might have no respect for civil liberties but still might show a high regard for commercial advantages. He perceived rather less clearly that a British foreign policy based on the conservation of wealth was gradually being superseded by a British foreign policy dedicated to the enlargement of opportunity. He did not believe that the friendly overtures of Mr. Canning were due entirely to a British anxiety for South American markets. He was not sure what other motives might lie behind these overtures, and he was evidently surprised that a Tory Cabinet should be making them—so surprised, indeed, that he could only suppose that a Whig or a Radical Cabinet would be "the decided opponents of such a policy." He did not realize that British statesmen were not their own masters; that all would follow, willingly or unwillingly, wherever the Industrial Revolution led them. In 1823, the Industrial Revolution was not a recognizable concept.

Mr. Rush never lost his head, but he grew more puzzled and suspicious. It is well to remember that he was to become a Protectionist Secretary of the Treasury under John

Quincy Adams, and that it was a Tory Prime Minister, Sir Robert Peel, who, years later, dealt the final blow for British Free Trade. There was a prophecy in Rush's letter to Monroe but, like most prophecies, it was indistinct.

At any rate, when George Canning reappeared in London he did fulfill one of Richard Rush's predictions. He renewed his overtures and he imparted to them a degree of warmth which still surprises us, coming as they did from a man who disliked republics only a little less than he despised republicans. He said that the United States were the first power established on the American continent, "and now confessedly the leading Power. Had not a new epoch arrived in the relative position of the United States toward Europe, which Europe must acknowledge? Were the great political and commercial interests which hung upon the destinies of the new continent, to be canvassed and adjusted in this hemisphere, without the co-operation or even knowledge of the United States? Were they to be canvassed and adjusted, he would even add, without some proper understanding between the United States and Great Britain, *as the two chief commercial and maritime states of both worlds?* He hoped not, he would wish to persuade himself not." These were seductive words, but the cautious Rush still hung back. He replied that if he were to take the risk of entangling the United States in the affairs of Europe, he must have some justification beyond any that had yet been laid before him. At this, Mr. Canning grew lyrical. "Why . . . should the United States, whose institutions always, and whose policy in this instance, approximated them so much more closely to Great Britain than to any other power in Europe, hesitate to act with her to promote a common object approved alike by both?" No British statesman, while in office, had hitherto been able to detect a close resemblance between the institutions of the United States and those of Great Britain. It only remained for Mr. Canning to declare that if he were invited to the European Congress, he would decline to appear unless the United States were invited also. He could go no further. But he received the same stubborn answer: if he would pledge his government to an immediate recognition of the South American states, Mr. Rush would sign a joint declaration on Spanish America. But the economic wing of the British government, strong as it was, was not yet strong enough to force the whole Cabinet into such an open break with the Powers of Europe; nor would it do so, in any case, as long as the Spanish Constitutionalists were in the field. Eight days after this remarkable interview, which took place on September 18, Canning made a last effort: he summoned Rush to Gloucester Lodge and asked him if "a promise by England of *future* acknowledgment" would satisfy his scruples; but the answer was the same as before. When they met again on October 8 and October 9, not a word was said about co-operation with regard to Spanish America: nor did they ever speak of it again.

The great courtship was ended, and for a very simple reason: there was no longer any time for dalliance. On September 30 Cadiz fell to the French, and the Revolution was over. This news did not reach London until October 10, but Canning had already taken steps to soften its consequences. He believed that the French contemplated a direct interference in Spanish America, certainly with ships and perhaps with soldiers. He did not think for a moment that they could succeed in this venture against the opposition of British sea power. But, as Foreign Secretary, he could not watch with complacence or without fear this resounding victory for the reactionaries of Europe. On October 3, he began a series of conversations with Prince Jules de Polignac, the French Ambassador, which resulted in the great Polignac Memorandum of October 9 to 12, 1823. In this Memorandum, the British government declared that they regarded the reduction of Spanish America to its ancient submission as hopeless; that they would not interfere in any practicable negotiation between Spain and the colonies; but that "the junction of any Foreign Power in an enterprise of Spain against the Colonies, would be viewed by them as constituting an entirely new question, and one upon which they must take such decision as the interests of Great Britain would require." To this exceedingly strong language there were added certain trade requirements of vital significance. The British government maintained that ever since 1810 the trade with the Spanish colonies had been open to British subjects, and that the ancient coast laws of Spain were "as regarded them at least, racially repealed." Great Britain did not ask for a separate right to this trade: the force of circumstances and the "irreversible progress of events" had already made it free to all the world; but if her claim were disputed she would immediately recognize the independence of the Spanish-American states. The Prince de Polignac replied that France, on her part, disclaimed any intention or desire to appropriate to herself any part of the Spanish possessions in America; that she asked for nothing more than the right to trade in Spanish America upon the same terms as Great Britain ("to rank, after the Mother Country, among the most favored nations"); and that she "abjured, in any case, any design of acting against the colonies by force of arms."

It is evident that here was at least as much of an agreement on trade rights as of a warning to France against aggression. None the less, its language was decisive. Nor would it be just to Canning to regard it as anything but a personal triumph for him. The details of those conversations are lost, but we can imagine that imperious manner and that persuasive voice as they laid before M. Polignac the young commands of the British middle class. Canning's belief that he had won a great victory is evident in the curious, the almost menacing exultation of a speech he made at Plymouth on October 28. He compared England's neutral quiescence to the sleep of a battleship:

> one of those stupendous masses now reposing on their shadows in perfect stillness—how soon, upon any call of patriotism, or of necessity, it would assume the likeness of an animated thing, instinct with life and motion—how soon it would ruffle, as it were, its swelling plumage—how quickly it would collect all its beauty and its bravery, collect its scattered elements of strength, and awaken its dormant thunder.

The Memorandum had not been made public; so that this imagery, however gratifying to the taste of naval Plymouth, must have been designed especially for M. Polignac and M. Villèle and the ministers and autocrats of the Holy Alliance.

Richard Rush maintained that Canning's first overture was a "fortuitous" one. In one sense, no doubt, it was. He seems to have consulted the Cabinet after and not before making it. But, in another sense, it was not fortuitous at all. It was the culmination of those friendly advances towards the United States which had been evident in the settlement of the Arbuthnot-Ambrister affair, and which had been intensified on the one hand by distress in the West Indies and on the other by the Spanish crisis and the optimistic reports of Mr. Stratford Canning.

The drama of the Rush-Canning conversations—for they *were* dramatic—lies in the interplay of the conscious and the unconscious motives in Canningite diplomacy. Consciously, no doubt, Canning wished above all to extract from the United States, in the course of the joint declaration, a pledge never to seize the island of Cuba. Then again, he thought that he could offset his diplomatic defeats in Europe by coming to a public understanding with America. He also feared that the French might revive their colonial empire and their old sea power; and he perceived in the purchasers of Louisiana the most eloquent opponents, with England, of such an ambition. He was concerned about the freedom of the South American trade and he knew that the United States, more than any other nation except France, shared this anxiety. And he was eager to "prevent the drawing of the line of demarcation which I most dread—America versus Europe."

All these were powerful reasons for an overture to the United States; all were unquestionably present in his mind; yet all together do not quite satisfy the conditions necessary for so urgent a plea to Rush. He had learned from Stratford Canning that the United States did not intend to seize Cuba, either then or in the near future. He could hardly have persuaded himself that the United States meant a great deal to the Powers of Europe. He was quite convinced that British sea power could sink any expedition, whether French or Holy, long before it reached Spanish America. As for the future of the South American market, how much better to stand forth as the single defender of Spanish America, not by an act of recognition, but by simply threatening the aggressors with the British navy! Nor could he have concealed from himself that a line of demarcation would be more easily drawn by tariffs than expunged by joint declarations. Every reason had a counterreason; but Mr. Canning pressed on.

The very essence of Lord Liverpool's government can be discovered in its instinctive response to the demands of industry; and this was strange, since Lord Liverpool's party was a party of landed proprietors, to whom the demands of industry meant less than nothing. The manner of this response was one of arid paternalism: Lord Liverpool's government led the way, it did not conceive itself as yielding to pressure. Its reforms were practical, common-sense reforms; and if they were tentative, that was because it was a pioneer and an experimenter, working against immense obstacles and in an economy not fully developed. Lord Liverpool had always to calm the Ultra Tory members of his own Cabinet. William Huskisson's assault upon the silk monopoly was conducted in spite of the best manufacturing opinion. And even Huskisson proposed no more than a modification of the Navigation Laws and the tariff schedules; even his free trade opinions, vigorous and transforming though they were, were only the leaven in a lump of mild protectionism. In one respect, moreover, all the leading reformers in this singular government—Liverpool, Canning, Huskisson, Robinson—were very Tory indeed: all were opponents of Parliamentary reform.

None the less, the instinct of an industrial economy, hovering upon the edge of an unparalleled expansion, is always to make friends with friendly, free, and subservient markets; and this instinct seized upon Lord Liverpool and his liberal colleagues, using them for its own mysterious ends. When the merchants of London, the Chamber of Commerce of Glasgow, the woolen manufacturers of Howick, and the manufacturers of Manchester and Birmingham appealed to Parliament in 1820 for a greater freedom of trade, Lord Liverpool replied with his blunt suggestion that the prosperity of England depended upon the prosperity of a tariff-free United States. He did not direct the foreign policy of George Canning, but he supported and encouraged it, in Parliament and out. And George Canning approached Richard Rush not only as the conscious diplomatist but also as the partly unconscious servant of the energies of British coal and iron, of British spindles and furnaces. Nor was his plea simply directed towards the safety of Cuba or the enlargement of South American trade: it was also, and more so, a wooing of the free North American market—a diplomatic extension, in a moment of crisis, of Lord Liverpool's 1820 speech. It was aimed, in brief, ultimately and instinctively at the agrarian mind of the United States; or at that portion of the agrarian mind which was contented with the exchange of staples for manufactures.

The Polignac Memorandum was known to France, Austria, Russia, and Prussia by the end of the third week in October; and it was circulated definitely to all the European Cabinets at the beginning of November. It was communicated to Mr. Rush, by word of mouth only, on November 24, and not circulated to him until December 13. It seems that Canning was still trying to effect in Washington, through his *chargé d'affaires,* the joint declaration he was unable to extract from Mr. Rush in London. But the answer he received was President Monroe's great Doctrine of December 2, 1823; and this Doctrine, whatever else it may have been, was not agrarian at all.

President Monroe's Message: December 2, 1823

August of 1823 found Washington City a steamy tribute to the isolation of America. Even Secretary Adams, impervious to the crises of Europe, had fled from the heat into Massachusetts. There he remained buried and oblivious while the Duc d'Angoulême took Cadiz and Ferdinand VII was let loose, to teach his people the meaning of amnesty; while the Holy Allies meditated a new Congress and Canning made his final appeals to the American Minister. Returning on October 11, he found awaiting him Mr. Rush's first two dispatches concerning the Canning overtures. The President gravely showed him these communications, asked for copies to be sent on to him, and left for his farm in Loudoun County.

Mr. Monroe had two anxious and affectionate mentors—Jefferson at Monticello, and Madison at Montpelier. The three venerable men drew closer together as the dusk gathered around the Virginia Dynasty. If Monroe's Administration seemed to be moving further and further away from early Republicanism, all three agreed to blame it upon judges and Congressmen. When the two ex-Presidents discussed Monroe, they did so on a strangely elegiac note. Now he turned for advice to them, sending copies of the Rush dispatches to Jefferson on October 17, with a request that Jefferson send them on to Madison. "Many important considerations are involved in this proposition," Monroe wrote in his covering letter.

> 1st Shall we entangle ourselves, at all, in European politicks, & wars, on the side of any power, against others, presuming that a concert, by agreement of the kind proposed, may lead to that result? 2d If a case can exist in which a sound maxim may, & ought to be departed from, is not the present instance, precisely that case? 3d Has not the epoch arriv'd when G Britain must take her stand, either on the side of the monarchs of Europe, or of the U States, & in consequence either in favor of Despotism or of liberty . . . My own impression is that we ought to meet the proposal of the British govt.

Jefferson's reply was exceedingly suggestive. "The question presented by the letters you have sent me," he wrote,

> is the most momentous which has ever been offered to my contemplation since that of Independence. That made us a nation, this sets our compass and points the course which we are to steer through the ocean of time opening on us. . . . While [Europe] is laboring to become the domicil of despotism, our endeavor should surely be, to make our hemisphere that of freedom. One nation, most of all, could disturb us in this pursuit; she now offers to lead, aid, and accompany us in it. By acceding to her proposition, we detach her from the bands, bring her mighty weight into the scale of free government, and emancipate a continent at one stroke, which might otherwise linger long in doubt and difficulty. Great Britain is the nation which can do us the most harm of any one, of all on earth; and with her on our side we need not fear the whole world.

After all, he argued, if the issue came to war it would be "not her war, but ours. . . . But I am clearly of Mr. Canning's opinion, that it will prevent instead of provoking war." He was prepared even to sacrifice his dearest wish—that of adding Cuba to the United States—if this would produce a similar self-denial on the part of England. Sooner or later Cuba would become independent and then—by something like Adams's "law of political gravitation"—it would attach itself to the northern republic. "I could honestly, therefore, join in the declaration proposed."

Mr. Madison was more cautious. He replied that the success of France against Spain "would be followed by an attempt of the Holy Allies to reduce the revolutionized colonies of the latter to their former dependence. . . . It is particularly fortunate that the policy of Great Britain, though guided by calculations different from ours, has presented a co-operation for an object the same with ours. With that co-operation we have nothing to fear from the rest of Europe. . . . There ought not, therefore, to be any backwardness, I think, in meeting her the way she has proposed." Unlike Jefferson, however, he did not think that Great Britain had undergone some miraculous conversion. She would prefer not to fight alone, he thought, because that would allow the United States, as a neutral, to extend its commerce and navigation at her expense. If he favored a joint declaration, it was because this was "due to ourselves and to the world." He thought that such a declaration should censure France for her interference in Spain and that it should come out strongly in favor of the revolutionary Greeks.

With these two letters in his pocket, Monroe returned to Washington on November 4. He was prepared to go all lengths with Great Britain.

The Cabinet that met on November 7, 1823, had temporarily lost one of its most influential members. William H. Crawford, Secretary of the Treasury, had been taken ill in September while on a visit to Virginia. The nature of his disease has never been determined: it was possibly erysipelas. The local physician administered a deadly nostrum—perhaps calomel, perhaps lobelia—which fettered the Secretary to his bed, half paralyzed and almost blind. A man of vast physique and invincible ambition, Crawford did not resign; he even made a partial recovery in 1824; but he was never the same man again.

Crawford was certainly Jefferson's choice for successor to Monroe; he was the favorite of the Old Republicans; and he had the support of a group of men who, though they rejected the pure Pierian of Old Republicanism, were prescribing for the electorate a somewhat less heady brew called Radicalism. Radicalism was compounded partly of a fondness for economy and partly of an aversion to Calhoun and Adams. Another Presidential aspirant, Smith Thompson of New York, had just decided that his chances were too slim and had left the Navy Department for the Supreme Court: his place had been taken by Samuel L. Southard of New Jersey. The potential successors to Monroe in Monroe's Cabinet, therefore, had now been reduced to Calhoun and Adams. It is to be remarked that, in the anxious days that followed Monroe's return, they forgot their differences and worked, each according to his lights, solely for the public good. Had Crawford been present, he would have done the same. (The facts in the Adams memoirs support this contention: his interpretations do not. He was convinced that Calhoun was a troublemaker.) It is significant that Southard, who was known to be a Calhoun supporter, invariably though silently followed Adams's lead in this critical time. William Wirt, the Attorney-General, philosophically opposed to strong executive action, and inclined to shift the responsibility to Congress, was more vocal than Southard; but his sunny disposition prevented him from sowing discord, and he, like his colleagues, was dominated by a common feeling of profound responsibility.

No set of men, detached from Europe by time and space, had more reason for anxiety and dejection than the Cabinet that met on November 7. Three weeks earlier, on October 16, Secretary Adams had received a note from the Baron de Tuyll, the Russian Minister, which announced that the Tsar positively would not receive any agents from the South American states, and that he congratulated the United States on their *neutral* position towards South America. This ominous communication, coinciding with the news of Canning's overtures, was enough to convince anyone that a new Holy plot, or an old one refurbished, was in the making against the South Americans.

The famous discussions which began on November 7 reached one significant conclusion, possibly the most significant, at the very outset. Calhoun suggested that Rush should be given a discretionary power to make a joint declaration with Canning, even if it pledged the United States never to acquire Cuba or Texas. He had not then been shown Jefferson's and Madison's letters. This suggestion was undoubtedly agreeable to Monroe, since he brought it up two weeks later, and since it was in line with the advice of the two ex-Presidents. Adams vehemently disagreed. He said that we had no designs upon Cuba or Texas, but that they might one day exercise their primitive rights and join the Union; moreover, and above all, he thought that we should not tie our hands by a joint declaration. Monroe, deeply impressed, remarked that he did not wish to take any course that might make the United States subordinate to Great Britain—thus abandoning the Jeffersonian position that Great Britain should take the lead. Adams went on to say that the communication from Tuyll gave the United States an opportunity to take a stand against the Holy Alliance and at the same time decline the overtures of Great Britain. It would be more candid, he said, as well as more dignified to avow American principles explicitly to France and Russia "than to come in as a cock-boat in the wake of the British man-of-war." Speculations are hazardous where there are no facts to support them; we know only that all agreed with him. We are left guessing at the amount of authority with which he made his formidable statement.

This was the first response in Cabinet—a response entirely

dictated by Adams—to the overtures of Canning. Though Monroe wavered towards the British thereafter, it was also the final one.

On November 13, word was received in Washington that Cadiz had fallen, and the President, alarmed beyond anything Adams conceived possible at the thought that the Holy Allies would immediately attack Spanish America, talked once again of a joint declaration with Great Britain. "He will recover from this in a few days," Adams wrote, "but I never saw more indecision in him." On November 15 the President at length showed his Secretary of State, as a final argument, his two letters from Jefferson and Madison; but Mr. Adams was unimpressed. The Cabinet met at one that afternoon, and Secretary Calhoun—"perfectly moon-struck at the surrender of Cadiz"—gave it as his opinion that the Holy Allies with ten thousand men could restore all Mexico and South America to Spanish dominion. He was all for plunging into war, with Great Britain's help or without it. "They will no more restore Spanish dominion on the American continent," said Adams, "than the Chimborazo will sink beneath the ocean." On November 16 Mr. Rush's dispatch arrived, announcing that George Canning had lost interest in a joint declaration; and the tension immediately lessened. On November 17 Baron de Tuyll called upon Adams to thank him for his amicable reply to the note of October 16, and to present him with two extracts from dispatches from Count Nesselrode. The second of these spluttered like a firecracker and concluded with a loud explosion. It contained an " 'Io triumphe' over the fallen cause of revolution," and a further panegyric upon the "liberation" of Naples, Piedmont, and Spain. It ended with the sinister remark—which concerned the Americas alone—that the Tsar wished to "guarantee the tranquillity of all the states of which the civilized world is composed." This might well have been one of those vague generalizations to which Alexander was so notoriously addicted. Or could it have meant that he hoped to return Spanish America, by force, to the rule of Ferdinand VII?

So Calhoun construed it. He was now confirmed, he said, in his views regarding the designs of the Holy Alliance. "It quite confirms me in *mine*," retorted Adams. He noted coldly that Monroe was extraordinarily dejected; "there must be something that affects him," he wrote, "besides the European news." On the next day but one, Monroe suggested again that Rush should be given discretionary powers to make a joint declaration with Great Britain; and once again Adams opposed him. When the Cabinet met on November 21, and the instructions for Rush were discussed, no further mention was made of such powers. The joint declaration was a dead issue. And no voice was raised against Adams's proposed reply to the Baron de Tuyll, Count Nesselrode, and the Tsar of Russia. He intended, he said, to announce in a moderate and conciliatory manner his government's dissent from the principles set forth in the second extract; to assert those upon which his government was founded; and, while disclaiming all intention to propagate these principles by force, and all interference with the political affairs of Europe, to declare "our expectation that European powers will equally abstain from any attempt to spread their principles in the American hemisphere or to subjugate by force any part of these continents to their will."

This ends the first phase of these renowned discussions. The original tension was undoubtedly created by Canning's offer of a quasi-alliance. It was increased by the incongruous menaces of that kindly and bustling gentleman, the Baron de Tuyll. Throughout, John Quincy Adams was the leader, imposing his will upon his overwrought and discouraged colleagues, partly by the force of a diplomatic experience none of them could equal, partly by the sheer weight of his dour and valiant personality.

The second phase began during these same discussions of

November 21. It might be called the resurgence of Monroe—the final, the almost tragic utterance of the Virginia Dynasty. Adams had always intended that his assertion of all the principles of foreign policy (including Non-Intervention) upon which the government of the United States was founded should be confined to a diplomatic correspondence only. Monroe was of a different opinion; and Monroe, once he had brought himself to decide upon a course of action, was by no means the sort of man whom one could brush aside. Now he quietly produced a sheaf of papers and remarked that he intended to assert these principles of foreign policy, not in a private and confidential correspondence, but in his annual Message to Congress on the state of the Union. In a tone of "deep solemnity and high alarm" he read his draft to the Cabinet. For a while, Secretary Adams listened to it with a certain degree of complacency; it was more or less the sketch of foreign affairs which he himself had submitted to Monroe a week before. Then, suddenly, the President departed from his Secretary's text. He reprobated France for her late invasion of Spain; he denigrated the principles upon which it was undertaken; he acknowledged the independence of the revolutionary Greeks; and called upon Congress for the appropriation necessary to send a Minister to Greece.

It was typical of Monroe, whose antique dignity and revolutionary courage made such a deep though intermittent impression upon his contemporaries, that, after days of alarm and indecision, he should have decided upon a course that was singularly bold. We must not suppose, however, that he intended to support the revolutionary Greeks—still less the Spanish Constitutionalists—with a show of force. His words were simply ethical. They were filled with the innocence of Old Republicanism, which believed that it was the mission of the United States to transform the Old World, not by fleets and subsidies but by the magic of example and the force of morality.

Mr. Adams knew very well that he could not divert the

President from his intention of committing his statement on foreign policy to the Annual Message. But he earnestly besought him not to take so strong a line. Like gouts of water falling upon a blaze, like an extinguisher descending upon a candle, his arguments quenched all that was visionary, and, indeed, Virginian in the President's statement. It would imply, he said, a grave departure from the principles of George Washington. It would be a call to arms and for what causes? For the cause of the Spanish Constitutionalists, whom even the British had abandoned; and for the cause of the Greeks, who were already supported by Russian autocracy. It would result in a diplomatic rupture with Spain, France, and even Russia.

On the next day, closeted alone with Monroe, he reiterated his case with even greater urgency. "The ground that I wish to take," he said, "is that of earnest remonstrance against the interference of the European powers by force with South America, but to disclaim all interference on our part with Europe; to make an American cause, and adhere inflexibly to that." This was practical statesmanship before which mere visions silently retire. Two days later, when Monroe showed Adams his revised paragraphs on the Greeks, Spain, and South America, the Secretary found them "quite unexceptionable, and drawn up altogether in the spirit that I had so urgently pressed." Adams's reasons, given to the President in secret, were charged with an irony as deep as it was unconscious. He said that Monroe's period of service could now be considered as a whole, as a system of administration. "It would hereafter, I believed, be looked back to as the golden age of this republic." Let the Holy Allies be the aggressors; let the Administration end as it had begun, in peace and amity with the whole world. Thus the Secretary of State, who had just extracted all traces of Old Republicanism from the doctrine that was to bear Monroe's name, pronounced a last epitaph upon the Era of Good Feelings, itself the graveyard of Old Republicanism.

The second phase in the discussions that preceded the writing of the Monroe Doctrine was now complete. Monroe had decided to give the Doctrine to the Congress, the people, and the world; but he had agreed to do so upon Adams's terms. In the end the advice of Jefferson and Madison, and Monroe's own predilections, had been discarded as impracticable; and the Monroe Doctrine, construed sentimentally rather than doctrinally, pronounces—as it were, between the lines—a grave farewell to the Virginia Dynasty.

The Monroe Doctrine, as given to the world on December 2, 1823, was not a formulation of new principles, but a summing up of old ones, re-edited to suit the times. Nor did it contain, in its written form, the whole of itself. It had one corollary and two pendents, all of which were committed to separate documents. The third phase in the pre-Doctrine discussions is taken up with the writing of these documents.

The draft of certain observations upon "the Communications recently received from the Minister of Russia," to be delivered to Tuyll, was read to the Cabinet by Adams on November 25. It was immediately attacked by Calhoun as being too ostentatious in its display of republican principles, and all too likely to offend, not only the emperor, but Great Britain as well. Would not the relevant paragraphs in the President's Message serve as an answer to Tuyll? Wirt and Southard disagreed: the stranger had come into our house, they said, to proclaim the principles of despotism. He must be answered explicitly. But Wirt objected to the aggressive hostility of Adams's language—one of the paragraphs, he said, was "a hornet." He did not believe that the country would support the government in a war for South America; and, in any case, he had scruples against the use of warlike language when the question of peace or war rested with Congress.

Adams admitted that this was indeed "a fearful question." Congress could not be expected to support the President in a warlike posture if it was not shown all the papers: and both Canning and Tuyll had communicated their views in the strictest confidence. But with his wonderful prescience Adams assumed—and historical scholars have since agreed with him—that the Holy Alliance did not seriously intend to attack Spanish America in 1823. With the utmost reluctance, he agreed to modify his language—"the cream of my paper"—so as to bring it within the pale of the severest Constitutional scruple; but it took several remonstrances from the President before it acquired this shape. As read to Tuyll on November 27, the Observations declared that the United States would remain neutral between Spain and her colonies, so long as the European Powers did so. They went on to say that the President took it for granted that the Russian emperor's remarks, about restoring tranquillity to all the states of which the civilized world was composed, were "not intended to embrace the United States of America, nor any portion of the American Hemisphere." They concluded with this resounding sentence:

> The United States of America, and their Government, could not see with indifference, the forcible interposition of any European Power, other than Spain, either to restore the dominion of Spain over her emancipated Colonies in America, or to establish Monarchical Governments in those Countries, or to transfer any of the possessions heretofore or yet subject to Spain in the American Hemisphere, to any other European power.

This was a grand reiteration of the No-Transfer Principle which, more than ten years before, Congress had applied to the Floridas.

Adams assumed that these Observations, and the instructions to be given to Rush in answer to Canning's overtures, were, with the President's paragraphs in the forthcoming Message, "the various parts of one system." The instructions, which were dated November 29, 1823, made only an oblique reference to a joint declaration, but said that if Great Britain acknowledged the independence of the Spanish-American states, then and only then would the United States move in concert with her. It is perhaps unnecessary to remark that a movement in concert is not a joint action. By the time these instructions were received in London, indeed not long after they were written, Canning had transmitted to Rush a copy of the Polignac Memorandum. He had then referred to his late courtship of the United States in terms of wistful regret. Rush duly communicated his instructions of November 29. All that Canning said in reply was that intervening events had put an end to the state of things on the basis of which he had made his first approaches.

It is necessary to the understanding of this third phase to examine one sentence in the supplementary instructions Adams sent to Rush on December 8, six days after the President's famous Message had been given to Congress. "The President is anxiously desirous, that the opening to a cordial harmony, in the policy of the United States and Great Britain, may be extended to the general relations between the two countries." Adams meant by these words, whose friendliness was only on the surface, that the British government should be asked to review its traditional policy on Maritime Rights, in order to bring it into line with the views of the United States. He had no reason for supposing, and probably did not suppose, that the British government would actually do so.

It is sometimes maintained that George Canning was willfully blind to this opportunity of making a new and progressive Anglo-American entente. But this is to misunderstand the nature and limitations of Liberal Toryism. Lord Liverpool's government, as an economic innovator, attempted to set certain practical Benthamite doctrines into the framework of the thinking of Burke. That is to say, it strove to release the energies of industry and commerce without departing from its fundamental belief that society was a compact between the living and the dead. It was not yet ready—nor would it have been permitted—to make the break with tradition which Adams demanded of it. In its American Trade Act of 1822 and in Canning's overtures to Rush in 1823 it had gone as far as—and indeed somewhat farther than—it could be expected to go. The response of the United States, whether we examine it in Rush's instructions or in the Monroe Doctrine itself, was an unequivocal rebuff.

It would be a poor tribute to James Monroe not to repeat in full the paragraphs in his Message which constitute the Monroe Doctrine. It would be wanting in respect to him not to mention that it was he who took the very bold step of rescuing this doctrine from the secrecy of diplomatic correspondence and giving it to the nation and to the world.

The first significant paragraph was as follows:

> At the proposal of the Russian Imperial Government, made through the Minister of the Emperor, residing here, a full power and instructions have been transmitted to the Minister of the United States at St. Petersburg, to arrange by amicable negotiation, the respective rights and interests of the two Nations on the North West Coast of this Continent. A similar proposal has been made by His Imperial Majesty, to the Government of Great Britain, which has likewise been acceded to. The Government of the United States has been desirous by this friendly proceeding, of manifesting the great value which they have invariably attached to the friendship of the Emperor, and their solicitude to cultivate the best understanding with his Government. In the discussions to which this interest has given rise, and in the arrangements by which they may terminate, the occasion has been judged proper, for asserting as a principle in which the rights and interests of the United States are involved, that the American Continents, by the free and independent condition which they have assumed and maintain, are henceforth not to be considered as subjects for future colonization by any European Power. . . .

The language of this paragraph and its doctrine of Non-Colonization were both the work of John Quincy Adams. The Message now dealt at length with a number of domestic issues before it returned to the subject of foreign affairs. It then spoke as follows, and the language was Monroe's:

> It was stated at the commencement of the last session, that a great effort was then making in Spain and Portugal, to improve the condition of the people of those countries; and that it appeared to be conducted with extraordinary moderation. It need scarcely be remarked, that the result has been, so far, very different from what was then anticipated. Of events in that quarter of the Globe, with which we have so much intercourse, and from which we derive our origin, we have always been anxious and interested spectators. The Citizens of the United States cherish sentiments the most friendly, in favor of the liberty and happiness of their fellow-men on that side of the Atlantic. In the wars of the European powers, in matters relating to themselves, we have never taken any part, nor does it comport with our policy, so to do. It is only when our rights are invaded, or seriously menaced, that we resent injuries, or make preparation for our defense. With the movements in this Hemisphere we are of necessity more immediately connected, and by causes which must be obvious to all enlightened and impartial observers. The political system of the allied powers, is essentially different in this respect from that of America. This difference proceeds from that, which exists in their respective Governments, and to the defence of our own, which has been achieved by the loss of so much blood and treasure, and matured by the wisdom of their most enlightened citizens, and under which we have enjoyed unexampled felicity, this whole nation is devoted. We owe it therefore to candor, and to the amicable relations existing between the United States and those powers, to declare that we should consider any attempt on their part to extend their system to any portions of this Hemisphere, as dangerous to our peace and safety. With the existing Colonies or dependencies of any European power, we have not interfered, and shall not interfere. But with the Governments who have declared their Independence, and maintained it, and whose Independence we have, on great consideration, and on just principles, acknowledged, we could not view any inter-

position for the purpose of oppressing them, or controling in any other manner, their destiny, by any European power, in any other light, than as the manifestation of an unfriendly disposition towards the United States. In the war between those new governments and Spain, we declared our neutrality, at the time of their recognition, and to this we have adhered, and shall continue to adhere, provided no change shall occur, which in the judgment of the competent authorities of this Government, shall make a corresponding change, on the part of the United States, indispensable to their security.

The late events in Spain and Portugal, show that Europe is still unsettled. Of this important fact, no stronger proof can be adduced, than that the allied powers should have thought it proper, on any principle satisfactory to themselves, to have interposed by force, in the internal concerns of Spain. To what extent, such interposition may be carried, on the same principle, is a question, in which all Independent powers, whose Governments differ from theirs, are interested; even those most remote, and surely none more so than the United States. Our policy in regard to Europe, which was adopted at an early stage of the wars which have so long agitated that quarter of the Globe, nevertheless remains the same, which is, not to interfere in the internal concerns of any of its powers; to consider the Government *de facto;* as the legitimate for us; to cultivate friendly relations with it, and to preserve those relations by a frank, firm and manly policy, meeting in all instances, the just claims of every power; submitting to injuries from none. But, in regard to those continents, circumstances are eminently and conspicuously different. It is impossible that the allied powers, should extend their political systems, to any portion of either continent, without endangering our peace and happiness, nor can anyone believe, that our Southern Brethren, if left to themselves, would adopt it of their own accord. It is equally impossible, therefore, that we should behold such interposition in any form with indifference. If we look to the comparative strength and resources of Spain and those new Governments, and their distance from each other, it must be obvious that she can never subdue them. It is still the true policy of the United

> States, to leave the parties to themselves, in the hope, that other powers will pursue the same course.

We can see, therefore, that the Monroe Doctrine was concerned with two principles:

I. Non-Colonization. No European power could, in future, form colonies either in North or South America.

II. Non-Intervention. The United States would abstain from the wars of European powers, since their political system was quite distinct from that of the American hemisphere. Conversely, the United States would regard as an unfriendly act any attempt on the part of a European power to oppress or to control the destiny of any of the independent states of the New World.

And to these two great principles should be added:

III. No-Transfer. The United States would not submit to the transfer, by one European power to another, of any possession in the New World.

These principles must be considered first as the best guardians of a nation with a great continental expansion still before it—as the natural foreign policy of what was afterwards to be called Manifest Destiny. Then, again, in their resolute challenge to the Holy Alliance and the champions of absolutism, they may properly be described as contributions to the cause of world progress. The Doctrine, it is true, had no force behind it. Even if he had been supported (and he was not) by a resolution of Congress, Monroe could not have made good his words without the support of the British fleet. He did not himself believe that he was addressing these words to anything but an immediate crisis; that they would one day be called the Monroe Doctrine would have filled him with at least as much surprise as gratification. This does not mean that he was deaf to the insinuations of fame. All Americans in those years had a touching belief in the force of language; and Monroe may well have hoped that his words would live after him. But he would hardly have expected them to play the part they did in American foreign policy; and, indeed, it is not until Polk's first Annual Message in 1845 that they were again made to play this part, and then only as regards the North American continent.

As part of the literature of republicanism and self-determination the Monroe Doctrine, none the less, and regardless of its future, would have commanded respect. As an example of Presidential courage—for it must be remembered that Monroe had no knowledge of the Polignac Memorandum—it would certainly have been applauded. Nor would the future have ignored John Quincy Adams, who stiffened and guided the resolution of his President. Whether the Message would or would not have had a nobler appearance with the addition of Monroe's original phrases in support of Spanish and Greek revolution—whether Non-Intervention is not really a form of intervention—these are questions that could be debated forever.

The continental European Powers did not take the President's Message very seriously as regards its physical force. Their statesmen uttered the expected epithets—"blustering," "monstrous," "arrogant," "haughty," and so forth. They still thought of the United States as a littoral republic, poor, disreputable, unprovided with a fleet or an army. No formal protests were made. The Baron de Tuyll was told by his government that "the document in question . . . merits only the most profound contempt. His Majesty therefore invites you to preserve the passive attitude which you have deemed proper to adopt." This Russian attitude was shared by the other Powers, every one of whom regarded the Polignac Memorandum as being the decisive document for the time being. As to the moral effect of the Message, however, they were of a different mind. Political morality to them was a question of Order and of suppression; and they paid the Message the unanimous and enduring compliment of assuming that it was highly immoral—that it would help to advance the cause of republicanism and of popular government. Since the European peoples most interested in these causes had at the time little or no access to recorded history, we are left guessing whether it did or whether it did not.

In Latin America, it was cordially received by liberal thinkers. The governments of Colombia and Brazil immediately endorsed it. But second thoughts, and particularly the second thoughts of conservative leaders, were not too favorable. The advances of five of the new states, either for actual alliance or for provisional assistance, were declined by the United States in language that must have seemed both chilling and evasive. The American delegates to the Panama Conference of 1826 never arrived there. "The declaration of the late President," said Secretary of State Henry Clay in 1828, ". . . must be regarded as having been voluntarily made, and not as conveying any pledge or obligation, the performance of which foreign nations have a right to demand. When the case shall arrive, if it should ever occur, of such an European interference as the message supposes, and it becomes consequently necessary to decide whether this country will or will not engage in war, Congress alone, you well know, is competent, by our Constitution, to decide that question. In the event of such an interference, there can be but little doubt that the sentiment contained in President Monroe's message, would still be that of the People and Government of the United States." Such were the small echoes of Monroe's words.

To the Latin American states, therefore, the Polignac Memorandum, duly and sedulously circularized, must also have seemed the decisive word. And did not England have more to offer—cheap manufactures, loans, a protecting fleet? It was by no means either cynical or ungrateful to prefer these to a trade that was still embryonic, and to promises that grew yearly more lukewarm.

The reaction of Great Britain to the Message was quite another story. At first, it seems, George Canning was very pleased with it. He assumed, quite rightly, that his overtures to Rush had been responsible for its appearance; and he was at first disposed to interpret it, quite wrongly, as the obedient reflection of his own diplomacy. "The Congress," he said, "was broken in all its limbs before, but the President's speech gives it the *coup de grâce*." What actually gave the projected Congress on Spanish-American affairs its *coup de grâce* was Canning's refusal, on January 30, to send a British representative to attend it. This refusal was a logical outcome of his foreign policy, and the President's Message had little if anything to do with it.

As he examined the Message more carefully, however, Canning was infuriated by the Non-Colonization portion of it. "It is Mr. Monroe's declaration in his famous message," Christopher Hughes wrote, three years later, "that it was time for the old world to be taught, that the new was no longer to be regarded as a region open to future colonization (or to that effect) that sticks in their [the British] throats. I know, to use the words of a great British employee, 'there was not a man in the British councils, whose blood did not tingle at his fingers' ends, on reading that proposition of President Monroe.' " Huskisson asserted that the unoccupied parts of America were "just as much open as heretofore to colonization by Great Britain as well as by other powers." Canning found himself unable to continue his plans for a joint representation with the United States at St. Petersburg regarding Russia's pretensions on the northwest coast. It is quite evident that, by the end of January 1824, British statesmen had reached the conclusion that the Message—however useful its Non-Intervention passages may have been—had not been written in a spirit friendly to Great Britain.

But the United States had set themselves forward as the protector of Spanish America; and it was urgently necessary for Canning to assert himself. He had first to overcome his own predilection for Spanish-American monarchies: this seems to have occurred about the middle of 1824. He was much assisted in this respect by a Memorial from Sir James Mackintosh in favor of recognizing the independence of the South American states. It presented on June 15, 1824, and it bore some of the great City names—Montefiore, Baring, Ricardo, Benjamin Shaw. He then had a more difficult task—he had to persuade the king and the Ultra Tories in the government to consent to this step. His great supporter, the Earl of Liverpool, was a very sick man, who now put both his legs upon his seat in the House of Lords; and never did Canning need support more desperately. If Liverpool failed him, he knew that he would succumb. Once again the hopes of Madame de Lieven and Metternich revived. Wellington would not speak to Liverpool except in the Cabinet, and George IV announced that Canning was a scoundrel. But their hopes were dashed by the resolution of Lord Liverpool. Towards the end of November 1824 he circulated a Memorandum to the Cabinet, advising the recognition of Colombia and Mexico; and, when Wellington threatened to leave the government, came back with yet another Memorandum to the effect that he and Canning would themselves resign if their wishes were not attended to. Wellington's great political virtue was always to realize when a successful counterattack had been delivered. He now came to the conclusion that his position was untenable and, calling for a retreat, carried with him the grumbling figures of Lords Eldon, Westmorland, and Bathurst, and of George IV.

Colombia, Mexico, and the United Provinces (Buenos Aires) were recognized by Great Britain on December 31, 1824. This was made known to Parliament in the King's Speech on February 7, 1825. Lord Eldon, as Lord Chancellor, was obliged to read this speech, which he did with a very bad grace; the king himself declined to have anything to do with it. His Majesty said that he had a bad attack of gout and that, in any case, he had mislaid his false teeth.

More than a year and a half later, Canning came down to the House of Commons to defend his continued toleration of the French occupation of Spain. He based his defense upon his new concept of the balance of power, and concluded with some words that seemed to annihilate history . . . the heroisms and agonies of Bolívar, San Martín, and Sucre, the recognition of Spanish America by the United States, the President's Message. "Contemplating Spain," he said, "such as our ancestors had known her, I resolved that if France had Spain, it should not be Spain 'with the Indies.' I called the New World into existence to redress the balance of the Old."

We are told that after he had pronounced these empty words there was a silence, a titter, and then a great cheer. Afterwards, however, there was not a little criticism of them. But it was not the singularity of Canning's boast which disturbed the House of Commons: it was his use of the first person singular.

The original overtures of Canning to Rush must be held responsible for the appearance of the Monroe Doctrine in the President's Annual Message of 1823. These overtures, as has been indicated, were more directed towards the safety of Cuba and the diplomatic rebuttal of the Holy Allies than concerned with the preservation of Spanish-American continental markets. It was easier for Great Britain to protect these markets on her own: more dramatic, more suited to the robust genius of Canning. As the Polignac Memorandum showed, they were never in much danger, so long as Great Britain was the commander of the seas. No doubt these markets entered into Canning's calculations when he first approached Rush, but it is difficult to believe that they held a leading place there, or even a very considerable one.

It is, of course, delusive to look beneath the surface of events into those depths where everything becomes dim, mysterious, and wavering. None the less, no one can study the Liverpool-Canning-Huskisson era in British Toryism without realizing that these statesmen were, in some degree, the instruments of early British industrialism. Their motives were complicated and various, but they had been deliberately seeking the friendship of the United States in the belief that its free market was necessary to the prosperity of Great Britain. In the same spirit they shrank away from antirevolutionary Europe—not because they were friendly to revolution, or because their institutions were founded upon the gentlemanly Revolution of 1688—but because the autocrats of Europe were in a sense the symbols of exclusive trade practices. Aside from their obvious reasons for a diplomatic understanding with the United States, they sought to transcribe into friendly language the dominant energies of British coal and British iron.

The reaction of the United States in this respect is suggestive. Jefferson, who was a convinced agarian, and who saw no reason to object to the free exchange of American cotton and British manufactures, was willing to go all the way with Canning. Madison, at best a moderate agrarian, was also willing, but far more mistrustful of the motives of Great Britain. Monroe originally agreed with his two predecessors, but subsequently allowed himself to be persuaded by Adams into taking an opposite course: and Monroe's whole Administration is marked by a gradual abandonment of agrarian principles. Calhoun, who was both a South Carolinian slave-holder and, at the time, a nationalist, oscillated between submission to Great Britain and a confused belligerence. Southard supported Adams, and Southard was to become a pillar of the Whig Party. Adams, who took Henry Clay for his Secretary of State, and whose Presidency was an honest but tragic commitment to economic nationalism, invariably opposed any joint declaration with Canning.

This strain of economic nationalism in the President's Message is worth isolating only because it provides a clue to the politics and tragedies of the next five years. The Message was followed, in 1824, by a protective tariff that seemed to complete the answer to the friendly gestures of Lord Liverpool and George Canning. At the same time the navigation controversy, which constellated around the word "elsewhere," increased in bitterness. This was the American response to the courtship of British industry.

The Message itself, becoming in the fullness of time the

Monroe Doctrine, passed beyond these considerations. Interpreted at times in accordance with its expressed aversion to European politics, it was never able to lose its original and valiant quality of committing the United States—prematurely, indeed, in 1823—to a leadership in world politics. This gives it its singular claim to the attention and indeed to the veneration of all those who ponder the American past.

For Further Reading

Dexter Perkins, *History of the Monroe Doctrine, 1823–1826* (1927) has long served as the standard work on its subject, though some of Perkins' emphases have been challenged by subsequent studies. Recently the event has been set into broader perspective in the diplomatic histories of Samuel Flagg Bemis, *John Quincy Adams and the Foundations of American Foreign Policy* (1949), and Bradford Perkins, *Castlereagh and Adams: England and the United States, 1812–1823* (1964).

Diplomatic negotiations with Spain, highlighted by the purchase of Florida, are analyzed in Philip C. Brooks, *Diplomacy and the Borderlands: The Adams-Onis Treaty of 1819* (1939), Charles C. Griffin, *The United States and the Disruption of the Spanish Empire, 1810–1822* (1937), and Arthur P. Whitaker, *The United States and the Independence of Latin America 1800–1830* (1941).

Other aspects of the period between Madison and Jackson have been lucidly covered in two works by George Dangerfield: *The Era of Good Feelings* (1952), from which the reading above was taken, and *The Awakening of American Nationalism, 1815–1828* (1965). Politics in the 1820's are discussed in Shaw Livermore, Jr., *The Twilight of Federalism: the Disintegration of the Federalist Party, 1815–1830* (1962), and in Robert V. Remini's two books, *Martin Van Buren and the Making of the Democratic Party* (1959) and *The Election of Andrew Jackson* (1964). On the Missouri Compromise, see Glover Moore, *The Missouri Compromise, 1819–1821* (1953); and on the emergence of Southern sectionalism, see Clement C. Eaton, *Growth of Southern Civilization, 1790–1860* (1961). Useful biographies that deal with this period include Marquis James, *Andrew Jackson: Border Captain* (1933), and Thomas Govan, *Nicholas Biddle* (1959).